Women, War and The Third Reich

Women, War and the Third Reich

Elizabeth Gordon-Werner

ISBN:978-0-9873122-6-6

Front Cover: The Hug by E Gordon-Wener

DEDICATION

To the women who entrusted me with their stories I say a heartfelt thank you.

TABLE OF CONTENTS

A NOTE FROM THE AUTHOR

Women are often blamed for the rise of Hitler and his fascist State. Stories about women finding Hitler fascinating and following him with stars in their eyes are common. But was this really true? How much did they know about his plans for the Jews or, later, the concentration camps? Were they interested in his plans for the German people?

When I moved to Wiesbaden in Germany in 1972 with my German husband and two babies, these questions were not uppermost in my mind. It took me some time to realise that I had been affected by the anti-German wartime rhetoric that was still prevalent in New Zealand when I was growing up in the 1950s/60s and that it was impacting on my life. I assumed once in Germany, that many of those around me had been complicit in the war and I wondered which of them had worked in the concentration camps. I felt very alienated.

I suffered an acute culture shock. On top of the German/English divide, there were cultural differences between the old world and new world to digest. Culture shock, language shock, two babies and a travelling (and often absent) husband were more than I could cope with and I became ill. My energies were completely depleted when I came home from hospital after a major operation and for a while I needed help in the household.

An elderly woman, Frau Schwensetski (Frau Schw. in this book) came to help with the housework. During the war Frau Schwensetski had lived in what is now Poland. We discussed the war and when she said, "Hitler came to my village once, but I didn't want to see him. I just kept digging potatoes!" I realised that my view of Germans might be significantly skewed. I decided to interview women about their war time experiences in an effort to adapt.

I made a list of questions to ask and set about finding women to interview. I started with my German teacher and her mother, then the women in the book club I had joined to help me learn the language. I interviewed my husband's female relations and women I met on a farm holiday. Then I advertised in the local paper for women who could tell me their stories and many women living in and around Wiesbaden replied. I was not selective but rather I interviewed everyone who offered, as my aim was to understand what these women had experienced.

Many refugees had settled in or near Wiesbaden and my respondents were from all over Germany and what is now Poland, Russia and Czechoslovakia. They were old and young and from all social strata. They were born between 1926 (my German teacher) and 1899 (my German teacher's mother). The interviews were in 1976-77, so the youngest of them would be over 90 today if they are living.

I also spent hours in the local library while a friend looked after my children. My grasp of the German language improved and I learned to read the Fraktur script used in Germany in the early twentieth century so I could understand 1930s newspapers and war reports. I felt my ideas about Germany change radically when I read Hitler's speech to the press from 10 November, 1938 (reproduced in Part 1.5) in which he discussed how he had had to manipulate the population into war.

Being a history novice was of benefit during the interviews because my interviewees quickly realised I knew very little, much less than they assumed, and they filled in the gaps. I went through my list of questions about their pre-war and war time experiences but typically I would get yes/no answers before one question would suddenly release a flood of reminiscences. At the beginning of the interview they often glossed over embarrassing information but when they realised they had a sympathetic ear, they added much more detail.

I asked whether they had special recipes due to food shortages, whether they had known about the concentration camps, whether they had admired Hitler, if the war had made them more independent. They volunteered a lot of information about things I would not have known to ask. So many of the women had had traumatic experiences and we wept together as they spoke. Several told me that they had suffered amnesia and had never told anyone else about their experiences, even family. Most had been apolitical but I was discovering the effect that politics had had on their lives.

I had to take a break from this interview process due to the emotional toll it was taking. I went on holiday to London with my family to visit friends. While I was there I advertised for respondents and interviewed a number of English women. I had grown up with their stories but now I found them different to those of their German counterparts. They had not had pleasant wartime experiences either but they had not been as traumatised as the German women I'd spoken to. English women had had their government on their side and that made a big difference. Their stories seemed trivial by comparison and I have not included them in this book.

When I listen to these interviews today I am stuck by how honest these women were. I still see them in my minds eye as I read their words and I humbly thank them for trusting a young New Zealander with their stories. In particular I am indebted to Frau Schwensetski who started me on this project. By the time I finished the collection I had recovered from culture shock and was starting to love my new home.

I sent a copy of their transcribed interviews to each women and many offered to help in publishing where they could. I found a publisher, but it went out of business before the book was in print. By that time we had moved and I was studying again. I showed the manuscript to an historian at the university where I was enrolled and she suggested I submit it for a PhD but I was studying biology and wanted to continue on that path. The tapes and documentation were put into the bottom drawer for the time being.

I have moved many times since then but always with the big plastic box of tapes and transcripts. I feel a great sense of indebtedness to the women whose stories I collected and I always hoped their words would see the light of day.

I thought these stories might help people understand how nations can fall into the hands of rulers with fascist ideologies but since then we have seen other examples of how easily that can happen. Still, there is much to be learned from the experiences of the women whose words grace these pages.

Part 1 is an overview of women's place in Germany in the 1930s and 1940s which gives context to the voices of the women interviewed. It is interspersed with quotes from the women. Documentation cited is from the public library in Wiesbaden. Recently I fact-checked my sources and discovered that many of the writers I cited at the time went on to have illustrious careers in historical documentation. The manuscript remains as it was written in the 1970s. I am not an historian and I have not attempted to add anything from today's perspective.

Part II is a transcription of the interviews with German women, starting with the youngest interviewee and progressing to the oldest. The interviews have been translated from German by the author and some interviews have been slightly re-ordered so they are sequential

Elizabeth Gordon-Werner

May, 2021

Marga S. When I told my husband you wanted to interview me he said, "Why does she want to talk to you? You weren't in the war."

Charlotte N: It was not the case that only the men were at the front. I think that what we women suffered on the home front was much much worse. Of course out there on the front it was awful, but what we had to go through with the children and the fear, when you continually thought that you might be killed leaving the children to fend for themselves. That was frightful too wasn't it?

Frau Schw: If there is ever another war I don't want to live.

PART 1:WOMEN IN GERMANY 1918 -1948

1. WOMEN AND POLITICS

In the years between the first and second world wars German women were in an invidious position. In the early 20th century neither progressive nor reactionary forces in Germany considered a political education appropriate for women yet they were expected to vote in elections which had major impacts on their lives.

Most women were uninformed about political ideas and regarded politics as a male domain. The exception were the feminists, mostly highly educated intellectuals, who had fought for female suffrage for years. They had been surprised when women were granted the vote in 1918[1].

> *Inge Z.: In our generation it was thought that women belonged at home with the family, that a woman should stay at home as soon as she married and had children. The woman was not to have a political opinion at all.*
>
> *Elisabeth B: I was interested in politics. I was in the Democratic Party, that was what it was called at the time, in a women's group and we had lectures. I myself had to give a lecture on peace and how we could avoid war.*

Women voted in the 1919 elections for the National Assembly that drafted the constitution of the Weimar Republic, then in the elections for the Weimar Government which replaced the Imperial Government in August 1919. During the elections for the Weimar legislature all parties vied for the female vote and all parties had several women on their

---

1 Katherine Thomas, *Women in Nazi Germany* Victor Gollanz 1943 p19

candidates list. All except the NSDAP (National Socialist Workers Party, called the Nazi Party from here) who thought political women were a danger to society and had no women on their lists.

The SPD (Social Democrats) had been the largest party in the Reichstag of 1912 and they remained the largest party in the Weimar Republic. As a result of the proportional representation electoral system women held approximately eight percent of the seats in the Weimar legislature but having the vote did not mean having political clout. The few highly educated women who had been politically active, often in feminist-related activities, took the first seats in Parliament but they had little support from mainstream politicians and the rights guaranteed to women under the new Constitution turned out to be empty promises which male biased Social Democrats refused to put into practise. The female parliamentarians discovered that they could do almost as little to better the lot of women within the system as they had been able to do from the outside.

Most women remained more concerned about their security than about political representation. During the 1914-18 war large numbers of women had been forced to replace men in industrial jobs but then in the chaotic conditions after the war they were the first to lose their jobs when the war industries closed down and men needed work.

Employers were obliged to dismiss anybody who was not unconditionally dependant on their wages. ... in the following order of priority: 1) Women whose husbands had a job 2) Single women and girls 3) Women and girls who had only 1-2 people to look after 4) All other women and girls. [2]

Since women had little say in trade union politics they could not stop the trend supported by both the trade unions and Social Democrats of sending women back to the kitchen. Women in Parliament were just as powerless as those in the unions to alter the traditional male prejudice against working women. Added to male indifference or outright opposition was the attitude of the women themselves. Most were pleased to take on the traditional role again as they were exhausted.

---

2   Werner Thönnesson, 1969. *The Emancipation of Women. The Rise and Decline of the Women's Movement in the German Social Democracy of 1863-1933.* Pluto Press, Frankfurt A.M.(1973) Translated by Joris de Bres. pp 90-91.

Katherine Thomas (respected journalist forced to flee Germany) wrote: *German women (were) worn out physically and morally ... and actually nature itself went on strike – the number of miscarriages reached monstrous proportions*[3].

Table 1 Numbers of German men and women in the professions (1925 data)[4]

Profession	Men	Women
Engineer/Architect	141,379	226
Chemist	9,653	921
Teacher	211,066	97,675
Lawyer	13,975	54
Doctor	45,332	2,572
Dentist	8,302	835
Dental technician	19,347	3,272
Veterinarian	6,240	10
Spiritual	40,746	610
Pharmacist	4,791	910
Editor	5,915	331

The female proportion of the unemployed in Germany fell from 39.2% in 1925 to 21.2% in 1931. (Similar falls were registered in England and Wales[5].) Most German women worked in unskilled jobs with few in professions other than teaching.

The early years of the Weimar Republic were made very difficult by the victors of the first world war. They divided German colonies between themselves, cut back German borders, effectively destroyed the German

---

3   Katherine Thomas 1943 *Women in Nazi Germany* Victor Gollanz, London p14

4   Gertrud Bäumer, 1931. *Die Frau,* Heft 3, 39 Jahrgang 1931-32 F A Herbig Verlagsbuchhandlung GmBH, Berlin p155

5   Manuel Saitsew, 1932. In: *Die Arbeitslosigkeit der Gegenwart (Erster Teil).* Ed: Manuel Saitsew Verlag v. Dunckler & Humblot, München u. Leipzig p145

army and navy, imposed huge war reparations, granted administration rights over German coal fields to France and administration of Germany's industrial heartland to the the League of Nations. In 1923 Germany defaulted on a payment and the French blockaded the Ruhr district causing financial collapse.

The hardship caused by these conditions engendered bitterness in Germany and a sense of guilt in England that had a significant effect on policies in the 1930s.

> **Herta S.**: *After the first war Germany had been occupied by the French. The contract they made with the Germans was not fair. We were left so poor after the first war that there were civil uprisings. They really made a mistake and pressure creates more pressure.*

Between 1923-1929, the Government became more stable. Germany's new Constitution created the conditions for intellectual freedom and Berlin became the hub of the literary and theatrical world. Educational reforms were much discussed, ties with other countries were cultivated, feelings of world co-operation grew and nationalism went into decline.

Then in October, 1929 the New York Stock Exchange collapsed and everything changed. Germany's prosperity had been dependent on foreign credit and the stock market crash plunged the country into the Depression which hit Germany harder than any other country. By1932, six million Germans were unemployed. (Table 2).

Neither the Social Democrats nor the unions had supported equal pay for equal work for women with the result that the lower paid women were now in demand by industry. Many women who would rather have stayed with their children were forced to work, while men remained unemployed[6].

Katherine Thomas: *The war had taken their sons, their breadwinners, now the inflation took their money and all their hopes. It was these "Kleinburger', the people of the lower middle class that suffered most and it was this class that would later on listen to Hitler as their saviour.* [7]

---

6   Max Koch, 1931. "Die Arbeitslosigkeit; Ihre Ursachen und Ihre Beseitigung". Staatspolitischer Verlag GmbH, Berlin p4.

Table 2. Unemployed per 1000 of population from 1927 to 1932 [8]

Country	1920	1927	1928	1929	1930	1931	1932
German Reich	6	21	22	30	48	71	88
Great Britain	41	29	32	32	48	66	64
France	9	27	9	3	4	20	33
Italy	16	10	12	11	15	26	39
Austria	2	30	28	29	36	45	59
Czechoslovakia	7	5	5	13	37	62	
Poland	5	8	6	6	10	13	13
Belgium	24	5	5	4	11	30	45
Netherlands	5	8	7	7	9	15	31
Denmark	45	50	41	35	30	39	67
Sweden	44	21	19	18	21	29	45
Norway	35	52	40	32	34	36	42
Switzerland	15	3	2	2	3	6	13
Russia		13	15	14	11	4	3
Ireland	25	26	23	22	23	26	32
Canada	31	11	10	13	24	35	41
U.S.A.	47	21	35	28	25	63	75
Australia	26	18	26	26	46	63	64
New Zealand	11	15	19	14	19	29	35
Japan	4	5	5	7	9	10	11

In addition, inflation decimated the savings of   large parts of the population and women who had never had to work before were forced into the workforce[9].

---

7   Katherine Thomas 1943 *Women in Nazi Germany* Victor Gollanz, London p21

8   Manuel Saitsew, 1932. In: *Die Arbeitslosigkeit der Gegenwart (Erster Teil)*. Ed: Manuel Saitsew Verlag v. Dunckler & Humblot, München u. Leipzig p148

> **Herta T**: *My generation is scared by the events of the twenties. I was young in 1922-23 when suddenly all our money was worth nothing. The older people who had saved all their lives and had money in the bank or shares, suddenly they had nothing and they had to queue up at charitable organisations and be looked down on by them. Then they were living as their cleaning ladies had once done.*

The German Women's movement had had an atmosphere of intellectual exclusiveness[10] which precluded the broad masses of women from joining it and during the depression the Social Democrats joined the Centralist and Liberal parties in supporting the traditional view of women. The Communists became the only remaining supporters of women's emancipation.

Gertrud Bäumer, one of Germany's leading feminists, wrote in 1931: *It is becoming ever clearer that a reaction is taking place against everything that has to do with the 'women's movement', a concept once again becoming increasingly misunderstood.*[11]

The Weimar Government seemed unable to do anything about the country's economic difficulties and most people saw a change as the only way out. Editor Katherine Thomas saw an increasing number of letters to the editor from both men and women advocating some sort of military training for boys[12].

---

9   Max Koch 1931 *Die Arbeitslosigkeit; Ihre Ursachen und Ihre Beseitigung.* Staatspolitischer Verlag GmbH, Berlin p4.

10   Katherine Thomas 1943 *Women in Nazi Germany* Victor Gollanz p20

11   Gertrud Bäumer, 1931. *Die Frau,* Heft 3, 39 Jahrgang 1931-32 F A Herbig Verlagsbuchhandlung GmBH, Berlin p175.

12   Katherine Thomas 1943 *Women in Nazi Germany* Victor Gollanz, London p11.

> *Herta T: We had this world financial crisis but no one understood that conditions were difficult everywhere because the papers didn't write about it. We had seven and a half million people without jobs and we have only sixty million people. I don't know what percentage of the working population that would be, but with seven and a half million unemployed and youths hanging around everywhere you can imagine what it was like; the insecurity, the burglaries.*

The Communists who saw complete economic reform as the way out of the country's woes had a significant following but the Nazi Party who called for the restoration of Germany's national pride and an end to the unemployment became the biggest party in Parliament, although without a majority.

They were also formulating their policies on women. Goebbels noted in his diary on March 29th, 1932: *The Führer developed quite new thoughts on our position concerning women. They are of imminent importance for the next election since we were weakened in exactly this area in the last election. The woman is the partner of the man both sexually and in the area of work. She always was and always will be. That must also remain so in today's economic circumstances. Earlier in the fields, today in the office. The man is the organiser of life, the woman his helper and implementer.*[13]

In the March 1932 election the Nazi Party got 13.7 million votes but there was an extensive shift in the sympathy of voters through 1932 and in the November 1932 election the Nazis Party won only 11.7 million votes, a loss of two million supporters. However, they remained the largest party in Parliament.

In January 1933 when Hitler was proclaimed Chancellor, Nazi Party members were heavily outnumbered in the coalition and the ruling forces thought this would tie Hitler's hands.

The British Ambassador in Berlin wrote: *On the whole the press has taken the appointment of Herr Hitler to the Chancellorship with almost philosophic calm. As the Deutscher Allgemeine Zeitung put it, it was just as*

---

13 Dr. Joseph Goebbels, 1932. In: "Von Kaiserhof zur Reichskanzlei."
    Zentralverlag der NSDAP Frz. Ehr Nachf. GmbH München (1934) p23.

well for Germany to take the plunge and get it over with [14]

Hitler persuaded the Cabinet to call another election for March 5th, 1933 and in the interim used his new-won power to clamp down on the opposition. The Nazi Party used every weapon, legal or illegal, to influence the election results, disrupting the meetings of other parties and suppressing their newspapers. In many places the police were forbidden to interfere with the Nazi sympathisers who resorted to thug tactics.

> *Gerda D: Before the war we lived in Berlin. We had an apartment on the ground floor and our balcony was on a busy street where protesters marched on their way with petitions. We were sicked once Hitler assumed power how the protesters were treated. Their hair was set alight with burning sticks carried by the police. It was dreadful. They all dashed past our balcony. By the time the war started there was of course no opposition left.*

The Nazi Party appealed to the emotions of the German people, making much of the unfairness of the Versailles Treaty and the need for Germany to regain its lost national pride. They blamed the signing of the Treaty on the democratic and republican forces and called for a strong man to lead Germany back onto the path of economic recovery. Finally on 27th February, 1933, the Reichstag was burnt down and, on the pretext that the communists were preparing a plot, the Government seized emergency powers.

The British Ambassador in Berlin wrote in March, 1933: *The political purge is proceeding and officials of so called Marxist sympathies are being dismissed throughout the country. Charges of corruption are raked up against prominent visitors of former governments. In fact political persecution on a considerable scale cannot be denied.* [15]

The Jewish population was particularly targeted by the Nazi Party.

---

14 Sir Harry Rumbolt to Sir J. Simon. No. 105 (C1046/319/18) Berlin, February 1, 1933. In: *Documents on British Foreign Policy 1919-1939. Second Series Vol 4.* Eds. E.L. Woodward and R. Butler. H.M. Stationery Office, London. p401.

15 ibid

> **Ruth L.:** *Berlin was such a big city and everyone lived for themselves. One day my music teacher said to me 'you shouldn't come back,. You might already be watched because I am Jewish you know." He left sometime later. The Kristalnacht was deplored, at least by people in my circle.*

The British Ambassador reported on 5 April, 1933: *"I find that all my diplomatic colleagues are as shocked as myself at the behaviour of the Nazis but it is only fair to record that, even in Nazi circles, the Jewish persecution is not universally approved, while in other circles it is severely condemned.'* [16]

On 7 April he wrote: *The supporters and advocates of the Hitler regime base their support on two main arguments. The first of these is that the regime has saved Germany and Europe generally from Bolshevism ... the second is that the Hitler experiment must be made a success, failing which Germany will be plunged into chaos* [17].

Alfred Milatz later remarked: *It is undoubtable that the electors on 5th March, 1933, could still vote freely and independently. But many of those opposing the national socialists were already under great psychological pressure because of the crippling effect of the arrest of numerous leading personalities of the left, especially after the Reichstags fire shortly before election day, and the restrictions on public gatherings and press freedom. On the other hand, the National Socialists (Nazis) who now had the state services under their command were able to carry out their campaign with undiminished energy.* [18]

Despite their heavy propaganda campaign and their wide use of subversion the Nazi Party won only 43.9% of the vote in the March, 1933 elections (Table 3).

---

16 Harry Rumbolt, Sir H.R to Sir J. S. Berlin April 5, 1933. In *Documents on British Foreign Policy 1919-1939, Series 2, Vol 5.*

17 ibid

18 Alfred Milatz 1965 *Wähler und Wahlen in der Weimarer Republic* Bundeszentrale für politische Bildung Bonn. p148.

> **Elsa W.:** *My father said to my mother, "Don't you dare vote for Hitler. He wants war, that's all." My mother would have voted for Hitler because everyone else was. She had no idea about politics. How could she? She was at home until she was sixteen, then married and behind the cooking pot with a room full of children. That's how it was for women in those days.*

They had not persuaded the citizenry of the need for a strong leader to follow.

Table 3. German Election Statistics for 1932-1933 (in thousands)[19]

Election date:	31.7.32	6.11.32	5.3.33
No. of authorised voters:*	44,211	44,374	44,665
Non-voters and invalid votes:	7,329	8,903	5,322
Parties			
NSDAP (National Socialists) *i.e. Nazi Party	13,769	11,737	17,277
DNVP	2,177	2,959	3,137
BVP	1,193	1,095	1,074
Centrum	4,589	4,230	4,425
SPD (Social Democratic Party)	7,960	7,248	7,181
KPD (Communist Party)	5,283	5,980	4,848
Other parties	1,911	2,222	1,401

* votes by gender are shown in Table 6.

Hitler was undeterred by his lack of a majority. By arresting members of the opposition and intimidating or placating his coalition partners he managed to pass the *Enabling Act* which gave the Government the right to issue decrees independent of the Parliament or President. The Communists had all been arrested or expelled from Parliament and the only opposition to Hitler was from those Social Democrats who remained in Parliament.

---

19 ibid p150

They voted as a block against Hitler, an act of courage in the face of Nazi terror (two parliamentarians were arrested on their way to vote[20]). This was the last public act of defiance. The enabling act gave Hitler absolute authority.

Hitler had many supporters who liked him as a 'man of action' but the reaction of the German people to their new Führer (= leader) was not always enthusiastic.

Vera Brittain writes of seeing the film 'Cavalcade' by Noel Coward in Berlin in 1933. ('Cavalcade' described a war in which Britain captured the German colonies and took the German fleet).

"As the film ended with its toast "Auf Wurde, Macht und Frieden" - to dignity, greatness and peace, - the packed Berlin audience which had remained silent when Hitler appeared on the newsreel, applauded again and again.[21]

Herta T:: *I was in high school when Hitler took over and I must say that at first people were disgusted. I remember a teacher who said we had our lives in front of us and we would have to adapt or we wouldn't survive, but that he was too old. He was probably about 35, that teacher. I am sure he would have adapted later too so he could keep teaching.*

The response in England to the growing brutality was equivocal as many preferred Hitler to the Communists.

The British Ambassador was frustrated by his inability to convince the UK Government of the threat and wrote increasingly desperate reports.

One of (Ambassador Rumbolt's) despatches gave so vivid a picture of how the parliamentary regime has been replaced by 'brute force' that it was ... circulated in cabinet.[22]

---

20 Erich Mattias 1968 *Der Untergang der alten Sozialdemocratie 1933*. In *Von Weimar zu Hitler 1930-1933* Ed.: Gotthard Jasper. Kippenheuer and Witsch, Berlin p296

21 Vera Brittain, 1957. *Testament of Experience*, Victor Gollanzc Ltd. p100

After a visit to Germany in 1934 Robert Boothby wrote:

Events have moved very rapidly in Germany since my last visit in April this year. The second revolution - or as many openly called it, the 'bloodbath' - of June, 30 was followed by a considerable diminution of public enthusiasm for the regime but also an enormous consolidation of its real power.

It is difficult to estimate the number of people assassinated. Official figures put the total at under 100, unofficial at between 600 and 700. ...

It is impossible to obtain an authoritative list of the members of the present Reichstag, even in diplomatic circles, and the most obvious explanation of this is the fact that so many have been bumped off. ...

One of the most curious and sinister features of the whole affair was a secrecy which enshrouded and still enshrouds it. Many families today remain in complete ignorance of the fate of one or more of their members.[23]

> ***Irma A.**: When Hitler came to power many of the people living in my area were taken away to concentration camps. We had a very good idea of what the concentration camps were. We believed that you had to work hard there, got bad food and were quite likely to die. We didn't know the extent of the atrocities though.*

---

22 Gilbert and Gott, *The Appeasers* Wiedenfeld and Nicholson, London, p29

23 Robert Boothby, 1947. *I fight to live*, Victor Gollanzc Ltd. p127.

2. WOMEN AND THE NAZI STATE

Once the opposition had been eliminated or silenced, the Nazi Party set about their campaign to create a pure Nazi state. They aimed to create a nation whose people were all devout Nazi Party supporters believing in the natural superiority of the Aryan race (non Aryans were seen as subhuman and destined to serve) and ready to fight any battle to regain the lost honour of Germany and place her in her rightful position as leader and director of Europe. Anyone disagreeing with these principals had either to be won over or eliminated.

Nazi youth organisations were created, for boys the *Hitler Jugend* (Hitler Youth) and for girls the BDM (German Maidens Association). Life was made unpleasant for families who didn't enrol their children and teachers were subject to particular scrutiny. The Nazi Party came into conflict with both Catholic and Protestant organisations, who wanted to propagate their own ideals.

> ***Marga S.****: I grew up in Hitler's Germany and I was a member of the BDM, although I joined very late. That shouldn't be seen as an excuse, I was Catholic. I was a member of the catholic youth and it took us a long time to become part of the BDM.*

The Jews were blamed for most of the nation's ills (including feminism) and by 1935 they had lost most of their civil rights. The persecution of the Jews, thought by some to be a means of diverting the people from aspects of the Nazi state they did not like[24], climaxed in 1938 with the pogrom of 9-10 November, during which most Jewish property was confiscated.

---

24 Marlis Steinart 1970 *Hitler's Krieg und die Deutschen* Econ Verlag, Duesseldorf p57

Fritz Lehmann: It is important to know that these actions (against the Jews) did not come from the people, as Goebbels maintained, from cowardice, not standing up for his own orders. I have been able to establish from reliable sources that the burning and plundering crowd was made up of Party-SS- and SA men, members of the National Socialist student organisation and other similar organisations who were there on order. These heroes appeared, again on order, in civil clothes, not in uniform.[25]

However, it is true that these hordes were joined later by local thugs. On one of the first nights of violence a woman living near the synagogue opened her window and shouted to the plundering crowd, "There is a Jew living in this house. Shall I come down and open the door?"

The factory-like murders were to be kept as secret as possible; whoever spoke of them was to be shot. All instructions were to be verbal or declared as secret government business which were to be destroyed in the event of an enemy approach.[26]

> *Anne Marie H.: Again and again it was said that the Jews were responsible for the first world war and and second world war, but that is not true. If Hitler had accepted them into the army instead of persecuting them, if he had taken German Jews as soldiers I am certainly they would have fought bravely for their nation and their country*
>
> *Luise G.: We heard for example that there were concentration camps. Not one of us knew about them and you didn't dare talk about it. One heard things, but nothing detailed.*
>
> *Anne Marie H.: Yes, one knew because I had Jewish friends who were sent to concentration camps. They didn't make any exceptions.*

The disappearance of Jews impacted on women in an unforeseen way. Before 1933 there had been one doctor for every 2,000 of the population.

---

25 Fritz Lehmann, 1946. "1939 - 1945, Beobachtung und Bekenntnisse." Hoffman u. Campe Verlag, Hamburg p9.

26 Marlies Steinert, 1970 *Hitler's Krieg u. die Deutschen* Econ Verlag: Düsseldorf. Vienna, p249

After the elimination of Jewish doctors who were the elite of the medical profession, there was a doctor for every 12-15,000. The anti-Semitic rabble-rousing might have been a strategy to divert the population from unpopularity of the Nazi Party themselves[27] but it had dire consequences.

When possible, Hitler worked within the law. His task of rooting out democracy and abolishing individual rights was made easier by the legal profession which was one of the reactionary elements that had resisted the Weimar democracy.

Ilse Staff remarked in 1964: Some people today who are concerning themselves with the Third Reich...think primarily of concentration camps, of the crimes of the SS, of unlawful acts that affected endless numbers of people within Germany and outside. Very often forgotten is the fact that most of these crimes were carried out within the regular legal framework[28].

The place of women in a Nazi State was clear from the beginning. According to Nazi doctrine, men were the rightful rulers, the purpose of women being to breed Aryan sons (future soldiers) and Aryan daughters (future mothers) for the fatherland. Politics and money earning were the business of men alone.

Although the Nazi Party was a 'purely man's party', women did their share to support it behind the scenes.

As Goebbels noted in his diary on 11th January, 1932: *"The women's organisation has taken the financing of our struggle into hand. It hopes in the nearest future to produce RM 50,000.- and with that we would again be solvent.[29]*

After their defeat in the elections of 1932, the Nazi leaders had developed a platform on women that looked back to the traditionalist idea of women still supported by many. They did not include any women in

---

27 ibid p. 57

28 Ilse Staff, 1964. *Justiz im Dritten Reich. Eine Documentation.* Fischer Bücherei pp 9 & 17.

29 Dr. Joseph Goebbels, 1932. In: "Von Kaiserhof zur Reichskanzlei." Zentralverlag der NSDAP Frz. Ehr Nachf. GmbH München (1934) p23.

their list of candidates but Hitler appealed to women as the queens of the home without whose support men could not stay afloat.

From the 1933 book 'This is National Socialism':

> *There is no place for the political woman in the ideological world of the National Socialists... The intellectual attitude of the movement on this score is opposed to the political woman. It refers the woman back to her nature given sphere of the family and to her tasks as wife and mother. The post-war phenomenon of the political woman who rarely cuts a good figure in Parliamentary debates, signifies robbing woman of her dignity. The German resurrection is a male event.*[30]

Interference by women in matters of State was seen by the Nazi Party as dangerous and likely to lead to disaster for the nation.

Reichsminister Dr. Frick: *The goal we are striving for must be seen as this: The mother should be able to devote herself entirely to her children and the family, the wife to her husband, and the unmarried girl should be referred only to such careers that fit the female essence. In other spheres, employment should be left to the man.*[31]

Hitler, at the 1933 women's Conference in Nurnberg: *That is indeed the wonder of nature and providence, that no conflict between the sexes in possible as long as each part fulfils its duty. The word 'women's emancipation' is a word invented by the Jewish intellect and its meaning is imprinted with the same spirit. The German woman has never needed to emancipate herself in the really good times of German life. She has possessed exactly what nature has invariably given her, as a blessing for preservation and administration; exactly as with the man who in his good times never needed to fear that he would be supplanted in his position opposite the woman. His place was least disputed by women themselves. Only when he himself wasn't certain in the acknowledgement of his duty, the eternal instinct of women for self and race preservation began to revolt.*

---

30 Englebert Hubner, 1933. *Das ist der National Socialismus* Stuttgart: Union Deutsche Verlagsgesellschaft pp121-122.

31 Reichsminister Dr. Frick, 1934. *Die deutsche Frau im Nationalsocialistischen Staate.* In: Fr. Mann Bäd. Magazine. Heft. 1400 Hermann Beyer u. Söhne (Meyer & Mann) p10.

Then out of this revolt began a change that was not natural and that continued until both sexes returned to the position that had been eternally allotted to them by fate. When one says that the world of men is the State, the world is his struggle, the readiness to act for the community, one could say that the world of women is smaller. Because her world is her husband, her family, her children and her home. But where would the bigger world be, when no one wanted to look after the smaller?[32]

In line with Nazi doctrine that women should concentrate on procreation and leave ruling the country to the rightful rulers, women were forced out of public office and women's organisations were disbanded one after another.

Frau v. Zahn-Harnack reported in 1933: *One step back followed the other. Now a single person was affected, now a whole group. Here it came to a special law against married women being hired as civil servants, there to impediments to education for careers. We tried to stop the developments in many various fields, but we had as good as no success.[33]*

Katherine Thomas remarked: *But why did women not stand up against these ruthless restrictions? I have only been able to give one reply 'Because it was then too late.'[34]*

Marriage loans were introduced whereby couples getting married could get a loan of RM 1000.- provided that the woman had been working before marriage and would give up working on being married. The loan was at an interest rate of 1% (one percent) a month, but with each child the amount would be reduced by 25% (twenty five percent) and payments would be suspended for one year.

Schemes were introduced by which families with many children could

---

32 Adolf Hitler, 1934. *Die Volkische Sendung der Frau* Rede des Führers auf dem Franerkongress in Nürnberg am 8 Sept. 1934. In: *Nationalsocialist Handbuch.* Eds. Ellen Semmelroth u. Renate v on Steida. J.S. Lehmenns Verlag. München (1934) pp9-10.

33 A. v Zahn-Harnack, 1933. Schlubbericht über die Arbeit des Bundes Deutscher Frauenverein". In: "Die Frau" 1933 Heft 9 p553.

34 Kathine Thomas 1943 *Women in Nazi Germany* Victor Gollanz p31

get household help regardless of their class. As early as 1934, girls leaving school were required to do six months service. Many of them did household service helping overburdened mothers. For the first time such mothers were officially recognised for the work they were doing and positive steps were made to take some of the burden off their shoulders. They were given the possibility of holidays as well as household help.

> **Herta T:** *A group of us volunteered to support the house-girl scheme. We went around to the women who lived locally and said to them "Things are going well for you. You are earning enough and you could make things simpler for yourselves by taking on a girl to help you in the house. They are unemployed and doing nothing and you could teach them how to run a household."*

German feminists had been very active and had produced literature of high academic standing but they also had traditional views about the nature of women's place in life. The Union of German Feminist Organisations (Bund Deutscher Frauenverein) which won many new members during the Weimar Republic, saw "motherhood" as the highest calling of women and although it worked to have the professions opened up to women and supported equal education for girls it did not support changing the anti abortion laws and refused to support the Society for Mother Protection (Mutterschutz) which was grounded with the aim of helping unwed mothers to financial viability.

In May 1933 the organisation dissolved itself in order to avoid being controlled and some of the leading members who were Jewish left the country in fear for their lives. Each individual member was left to decide for herself whether she would join the new women's organisation run by the Nazi Party and many did.

Hitler in 1934: 'Women's Emancipation' is an idea created by the Jewish intellect and has a Jewish spirit. The German woman living in really good German times never needs emancipation.[35']

The Nazi women's organisation offered the possibility of social work on

---

35 *Die volkische Sending der Frau.* Rede des Führers auf dem Frauenkongress in Nurnberg am 8 Sept., 1934. From the NS Hanbuch. Hrs. Ellen Semmelroth und Renate von Steida

an unparalleled scale and was well organised. Women who wanted to remain active often joined even if they didn't entirely agree with the Nazi philosophy as there was no alternative. Many of the women who joined were unaware that male members rejected in principal the idea of collaboration with women. Although the leaders of the women's organisations were themselves women, they were selected on all levels by political leaders who were men. This was a very effective way to ensure that women who wanted to change the status-quo never got the chance.

Steinert reported that women in general often irritated the government. Women of the upper and upper-middle classes attempted to escape the influence of the Nazi Party by forming their own groups to collect funds for the Red Cross, garnering the particular ire of the Nazi leadership[36]. Alternative organisations were increasingly targeted by the Nazi Party and although in the beginning joining the Nazi women's organisation was a matter of choice, it later became an obligation for many. Not joining was seen as a slight to the government with grave consequences.

The removal of women from political life did not worry the majority of German women. Politics had always been a dirty word and politically active women were a small minority. The majority of women voted the way their husbands or fathers told them to and many male Social Democrats saw nothing wrong with that.

The propaganda campaign encouraging women to remain home and have children was intensive and successful. The birthrate which had been declining since the 1870s changed course and by the end of the thirties, the birthrate was showing a marked increase.

On announcing the creation of the Medal of Honour for prolific German mothers, Reichs Physician Leader Dr. Wagner announced: *The prolific German mother is to be accorded the same honour in the German community, as the combat soldier, since she risks her body and her life for the people and the fatherland as much as the combat soldier does in the war and thunder of battle*[37]

---

36 Marlis G. Steinert, 1970. *Hitler's Krieg und die Deutschen* Econ Verlag: Düsseldorf. Vienna. p119

37 George L. Moss, 1966, *Nazi Culture* W.H. Allen, London.

> **Charlotte N.** (on Hitler's idea women should breed many children):
> Hitler, he had bats in the belfry. I actually had to hear the same thing
> from my husband too.

Intellectual women were shocked by this campaign but they were Nazi targets and particularly dis-empowered. Many others were unimpressed by Nazi methods but the great majority of women accepted the changes either neutrally or with enthusiasm. Many of these women did not want greater independence, the idea of being protected was appealing, and they saw the new regime mainly in terms of employment for their menfolk.[38]

The Nazis showed.... a certain instinct in the way it organised the women. It gave them duties - in the areas of welfare, mother-care, defence work, on the work front, etc. - that they grasped eagerly and carried out faithfully, developing their social energies and demonstrating their readiness to help.[39]

Despite Nazi rhetoric and women's willingness to stay home other influences were creating a social dichotomy. At the same time as women were being disenfranchised politically the trend towards an industrial state was forcing ever more women into the workforce. The number of women in the workforce increased from 4.24 million in 1933 to 4.52 million in 1936 and 5.2 million by 1938. Women's exclusion from the political arena, however, remained complete.

Gertrud Bäumer: The National Socialist State was basically a men's state built on the principal of 'hardiness', which was constantly hammered into the people ... If the question of state authority was decided purely to the disadvantage of women, not only was the subordination of a man under a woman rejected, but the un-wished influence of women, her interpretation, opinion and attitude towards the National Socialist state was also rejected.[40]

---

38 Marlis G. Steinert, 1970. *Hitler's Krieg und die Deutschen* Econ Verlag: Düsseldorf. Vienna. p56

39 Gertrud Bäumer, 1946. *Der neue Weg der deutschen Frau.* Stuttgart. Deutsche Verlags Anstalt p23.

40 ibid pp23-24

Women were in the position of having as much work and responsibility as formerly, but no say over their working conditions or the laws regulating their lives. They were a force to be manipulated rather than a force able to manipulate.

Herta T: Mostly we just didn't realise what was happening. We were so cut off and didn't realise our newspapers were restricted. You know there was burning of books, but somehow we were oblivious.

3. HITLER'S STRATEGIES

Hitler was a born popular speaker ... gifted with the great secret of being able to address each member of the audience separately.[41]

Luise G.: *Hitler was fascinating in a certain way. I had an aunt, an elderly very nice woman and she didn't like Hitler at all. Once Hitler came to Wiesbaden and he drove through the streets in an open car. Everyone went to see him and this aunt went too. When she came home she said to me "Luise you should have come too, he is wonderful man. I looked him in the eyes and at that moment I was exalted."*

Elisabeth B: *Hitler embodied the ideas of the NSDAP. So women were enthusiastic about him and then accepted his ideas and I was a real exception. I was always very quiet when people spoke about him.*

Luise G.: *My friend [who met Hitler in person] told me, 'you wont believe it but Hitler had no effect on me, he looked to me like any ordinary citizen. He didn't talk much and was certainly not fascinating. Goebbels was different, he spoke a lot, but Hitler looked like a tired and used-up man.' We thought about that a lot. I think Hitler must have taken some sort of drug or medicine because he did have a radiant look at times.*

In the 1930s both women and men were still active in the peace movement which had developed after the First World War. Women had realised that war was no longer a matter just for men. The *International*

---

41 Katherine Thomas 1943 *Women in Nazi Germany* Victor Gollanz p25

Women's Action for Peace and Disarmament was formed in September 1932 after the League of Nations decided to involve women more in peace making activities and in the same month the Peace and Disarmament Committee of the International Women's Organisation was established. A disarmament petition gathered the signatures of nine million men and women.

Hitler was a clever strategist and used the universal desire for peace to his own advantage. Hitler knew his goals for Germany were probably unattainable by peaceful means but because the desire for peace was so strong among the population he and his strategists could not overlook it. Instead they undertook to convince the German people that war was necessary to preserve peace and Nazi slogans were full of the word 'peace'. Hitler's manipulation of the people was skilful.

Vera Brittain (in 1936): Already Berlin had become a city of flying flags and election posters... The vast insistent propaganda terrified us by its incongruous emphasis upon peace and honour. Hardly a slogan that we read failed to mention one or the other: Work - Honour – Peace"(Arbeit-Ehre-Frieden); We are protecting the world from Bolschevism (Wir schutzen die Welt vor dem Bolschevismus); The spirit of the new Germany is the spirit of peace (Der Geist des neuen Deutchlands ist der Geist des Friedens).[42]

Hitler himself provides the most interesting lesson in his methods. Following is a quote from his speech to the German press on 10 November, 1938:

We have set ourselves several goals this year which we wanted to reach through our propaganda.... First the slow preparation of the German people themselves. Circumstances have for years forced me to speak almost only of peace. Only with the continuous stress on the German desire for peace and intention to keep the peace was it possible for me to win, piece by piece, freedom for the German people and to give them the preparation that was always necessary for the next step. It is to be taken for granted that such year-long peace propaganda would have its questionable aspects because it could too easily lead to a situation in which the idea that today's regime is identical with the resolve and

---

42 Vera Brittain, 1957. *Testament of Experience* Victor Gollancz Ltd., London.
    p149.

determination to preserve peace under all circumstances could become stuck in the minds of many people. That would not only lead to a false judgement of the aims of this system, but would also lead to a situation in which the German nation, instead of being armed against events, would be filled with a spirit which if continued would and must, as defeatism, lead to the loss of precisely the successes of today's regime.

I was coerced into talking about peace for years. It was at this time necessary to gradually rearrange the German people psychologically and slowly make clear to them that there are things which, if they cannot be obtained by peaceful means, must be accomplished by force. For this it was necessary... to illuminate certain foreign occurrences in such a manner that the inner voice of the people themselves began to cry for force...

This work took months... Many have not understood, Gentlemen, many thought it was all a bit exaggerated. Those were the over-cultivated intellectuals who have no conception how one can bring a people to the readiness, at last, to stand straight, even when it begins to flash and thunder..

(the German people) must learn to believe so fanatically on the end victory that even if we suffer defeat at times, the national will... look at it from a higher viewpoint: That is transitory; in the end victory will be ours...

For that it is necessary that precisely the press keep blindly to the basic axiom: The leadership is in the right.[43]

At the same time Hitler was re-arming Germany and introducing conscription to create an army of thirty six divisions, both acts in violation of the Versailles Treaty but neither provoking more than protests.

> **Herta T**: *There were jokes made at the time and I suppose a lot of people must have known what was going on but somehow we just didn't realise what was happening. I remember one joke that went through the newspapers – that there was a new milk bottle factory or baby-stroller*

---

43 Adolf Hitler, 1938. "Rede vor der deutschen Presse am 10.11.1938". In: "1939-1945. Der Zweite Weltkrieg in Chronik u. Dokumenten." Ed. H.A. Jacobsen. Wehr u. Wissen Verlagsgellschaft, Darmstadt (1959) P. 91/92.

> *factory but however you put the pieces together the product was a machine gun. But by that time Hitler was in power and there was no going back.*

On 12 March, 1938, Hitler's forces occupied Austria. Other powers protested but did nothing.

Hitler then demanded the cession to Germany of Sudetenland, a part of Czechoslovakia inhabited primarily by Sudeten Germans. Those who had read Hitler's book *Mein Kampf* were not surprised.

On 29 September, 1938, under tense conditions, Neville Chamberlain flew to confer with Hitler in Munich. He secured the cession of the Sudetenland to Germany and flew home again to applause, announcing that he had won 'peace in our time'. Sudeten Germans were euphoric about finally being 'brought home' to Germany.

> ***Hildegard D.:*** *My father was unemployed for six years until Hitler came and brought us home. He freed us from this yoke. My father had not had work because the Czechs had occupied all the work places. ... There were Communists and Social Democrats in Czechoslovakia and in Sudetenland and of course they thought differently but we were completely German nationalistic. For us the Führer was a saviour.*

The exploitative mentality of the victors of World War I which had caused so much suffering in Germany was playing into Hitler's hands. In March 1939, on the pretext of the bickering between several factions in what remained of Czechoslovakia, Hitler annexed the whole country. With these triumphs up his sleeve, he finalised his plans for German expansion to the east.

The securing of a greater "living area" for the Germans was one of the basic aims of the Nazi Party. The pretext for foreign expansion was the re-occupation German settled areas that had been cut off from Germany after World War I and Hitler seemed to be able to accomplish so much so quickly where his predecessors had seemed so powerless that he won local approval. Nevertheless the situation was tense.

There was a noticeable nervousness in the city, because the horror of

41

*war had not been forgotten by the present generation. The disquiet was
alleviated however by a trust in the authorities.*[44]

In the beginning the reaction of the British people to this aggressive
dictator was as varied as it was in Germany. People were initially unwilling
to believe that the reported brutality of the Nazi Party was true. The
disappearance and murder of opposition politicians was seen as a bi-
product of revolution and the persecution of the Jews was viewed with
mixed feelings as England was not free from anti-Semitism[45] The British
press reacted with tolerance.

*From 'The British Press and Germany 1933-1939' : None of the popular
papers except the daily mail actually supported ... Nazi Germany, but they
were ... reluctant to to adopt a hard line towards it. Readers did not want
to read it and the intellectuals did not want to write it. ... Besides there was
no lack of prospective enemies ... and ... Hitler's was a stable government
... and seemingly interested only in internal reform and equality of
international status for Germany.*[46]

The British Ambassador in Germany was one of the few who had read
Hitler's book *Mein Kampf* and understood the implications of Hitler's ideas.
He was witness to the events as they unfolded and sent increasingly
alarmed reports back to London which were not taken very seriously[47].

As historians Gilbert and Gott reported: *The Jews were an
unsympathetic,unloved people and their presence in the capitals of Europe
was frequently resented.... Not all Hitler's criticisms of Jews were
discounted as absurd. Rumbolt hated the anti-Semitism; other Englishmen
were less certain in their condemnation.*

---

44 Fritz Lehmann, 1946. *1939 - 1945, Beobachtung und Bekenntnisse.* Hoffman u.
Campe Verlag, Hamburg pp10-11

45 Martin Gilbert and Richard Gott 1963 *The Appeasers* Weidenfeld and
Nicholson, London

46 Franklin Reid Gannon 1971 *The British Press and Germany 1936-1939I*
Claredon Press, Oxford p2

47 Martin Gilbert and Richard Gott 1963 *The Appeasers* Weidenfeld and
Nicholson, London p28

On 1 September 1939 Hitler invaded Poland and on 3rd September Britain declared war on Germany.

Herta S.: That was logical, he had written a book and his whole program was there to read.

Charlotte N: There were some who said that the war was forced on us but there were others who said we had picked a quarrel.

Ruth L: In my circles people were not enthusiastic about the beginning of the war. They were sceptical if anything.

Marga S.: Most people were Hitler fans, even we late starters, so the beginning of the war didn't shock me. My mother was horrified. I remember so well how she said 'Good God, it is only twenty years since the last war!"

The German people already lived in a Nazi State and the declaration of war was another step in a series of events that began in 1933. The announcement of war meant call-up and the disappearance of husbands, sons and lovers. Ration cards were distributed immediately war was announced.

Herta S. In our area there was a Duchess whose husband was in the army. He was a Lieutenant Colonel or something like that. She came to me and hugged me and said 'What do you think of our Leader now? Not a single drop of blood!' She was very enthusiastic but I was frightened.

During the first two years of the war life for women in Germany continued, apart from the absence of men, much the same as it had been before the war. Hitler's military successes won him admirers, as had his political successes before the war. The Nazi continued to emphasise helping the needy at home and all Germans in foreign countries. A feeling of racial togetherness and shared fate was propagated.

After the occupation of Poland, Polish workers were sent to work in Germany. In the beginning they were not discriminated against in employment and were treated in a friendly manner by the women. Many were in agricultural work and farming families often took them into their homes almost as part of the family. They went dancing with daughters of the family as any German would have done. The Catholic clergy also treated the prisoners of war well.[48]

This was very much against the wishes of the Nazi leadership since on their racial hierarchy scale the Poles were near the bottom. Only the Jews were lower. The propaganda against the Poles was stepped up until it became incessant. Poles were represented, as were all easterners, as a lower form of life "especially born for low labour" as Hitler himself declared.[49] Poles were taxed higher than Germans in order to preserve a 'correct' social balance. Twenty percent of their wages was taken by the Government as a 'social equalisation fee'. In 1940, steps were taken to preserve the 'racial purity' of German blood. Poles who were known to be having affairs with German women were executed and their German partners sent to concentration camps. Germans who helped Poles were henceforth liable to prison sentences.[50]

At home in Poland, Polish women became active in the underground movement and were instrumental in thwarting the Nazi aim of destroying Polish culture.

A report from London in 1946 commented: *...where study was forbidden, as in Belgium, Norway and Poland, teaching was carried on underground and examinations were held in secret. In Poland in particular where the Germans, bent on wiping out national culture, destroyed libraries, museums, archives and priceless collections and closed all schools, women played an important part in organising an underground system of teaching by small groups that covered almost 100% of Polish youth.*[51]

---

48 Marlis G. Steinert, 1970, *Hitler's Krieg und die Deutschen,* Econ Verlag: Düsseldorf. Vienna. p103.

49 E.L. Homze, 1967. "Foreign Labour in Nazi Germany", Princton Univ. Press, N. Jersey. p41.

50 ibid p42

51 Bulletin of the International Federation of University Women. Nr. 25 Dec. 194 6Report of the 26th Council meeting, London 1946. p6.

4. THE SS IN CONTROL

Anna Maria H: I really resisted joining the party. It was my father-in-law who insisted I join, not so much my husband. My father-in-law really pressured me to join.

The SS was regarded as the cream of the population by the leadership and special efforts were made to ensure that they reproduced. In 1939, in an order to all police officers and members of the SS, Himmler stated that, unlike in the last war when men declined to have more children in order to spare their wives further trouble in case of their death, the SS should, at this time, feel it a duty to beget children. He said that he personally would appoint deputies to take over the guardianship of all children of good blood, legitimate or illegitimate, whose father had fallen in the war.

Women wanting to marry Party members had to produce proof of "pure" blood through the last three generations.

Liselotte S.: Girls married as soon as they could when they had a serious boyfriend, just as I did. We sort of stampeded into marriage because we weren't sure if he would come back or if he wouldn't come back. The proof of Aryan blood was very important. You had to be Aryan if you wanted to marry and if you wanted to marry a professional soldier or an officer or a civil servant then you had to present papers to show that three generations of your forefathers were Aryan.

In their effort to produce as many pure blooded babies as possible, there was even a scheme whereby any pure blooded girl could conceive by an SS man. Blood was important, legitimacy less so. Gertrud Bäumer tells of meeting one such girl on a train journey: *"She told me she was on her way to be 'mated' - she used this expression. "Three men will be introduced to me" she told me not without pride, "and I can choose between them." Then she said several times emphatically "I will be paid for everything."*[52] Bäumer goes on to say that the question was discussed by her students and she was often asked her advice as to whether it was a good idea.

The new hierarchy produced by the Nazi Party slowly became entrenched. Members of the SS and their wives, being at the top of the hierarchical structure, were the recipients of many benefits. They often acted as if they were above the law and in fact very often they were the law. They had power over the lives of their fellow citizens which they didn't hesitate to use. Many were corrupt or spiteful and they were fiercely resented by the rest of the population, especially the women, over whose lives they had so much control.

Ellen von A.: God how we hated the SS. The SS were pigs. Not the soldiers of course, the soldiers hated the SS too. One morning at the grocer's I said 'good morning' instead of giving the Hitler salute and I got hit on the head from behind.

Anne Marie H.: The SS man said, 'You are being impertinent" and gave her a push and she fell down. When she was lying there he said 'You old Jewish fetel, now you are making a theatre and he kicked her in the face with his heel so everything bled. I was so appalled and I wanted to scream at him that he was doing the whole German population a disservice, but I didn't dare. My sister was married to a Jew and my husband was a member of the party and ultimately I was as well.

Ruth L.:Women helped each other. We travelled for hours on the tram to pick cherries, but you had to be careful because if you were caught by the SS you would be punished.

The significance of living in a Nazi state became ever more apparent. In 1939, Hitler had started a Euthanasia program to eliminate all persons who were mentally sick, including those cared for by their families. No definite

---

52 Gertrud Bäumer, 1946. *Der neue Weg der deutschen Frau.* Stuttgart. Deutsche Verlags Anstalt p14-15.

announcements were made, but rumours grew and it became an open and uncomfortable secret. Families received notes saying that their relative had died of influenza or appendicitis (in some cases where the appendix had already been removed) and were told to collect the urn of ashes.[53] Some families hid their sick which was a difficult undertaking during a time of food rationing.

In March, 1940, special rules for the protection of German youth were publicised.[54]. Persons under eighteen were forbidden to be on the streets after dark. After nine o'clock in the evening, they had to be accompanied by an adult if they wanted to go to the movies or a dance hall. Smoking and drinking was forbidden. The rules did not apply to members of families of armed forces service workers.

Youth reacted variously to the new order, but girls in particular showed particular disinterest in the political situation. Many girls belonged to the BDM, the girls' organisation, but were seldom given permission by their mothers to attend meetings. Many mothers held the BDM in low esteem and felt that their daughters would just be spoilt there.

Only eight of the sixty girls working at the Junkerswerke belonged to the BDM (Bund Deutscher Maedel: League of German Girls) and when asked why, the parents of these girls said they thought their girls would just be corrupted if they belonged. .[55]

The Nazi Party were intolerant of any influence which could deflect the youth. Critical books were suspect and confidential lists were published naming books that were to disappear from the market and the libraries. Among them were the elites of German literature. Books by Thomas Mann, Carl Zuckmayer, Bertold Brecht, Ahre Gide and Franz Kafka were among the many forbidden.

---

53 Marlis G. Steinert, 1970. *Hitler's Krieg und die Deutschen* Econ Verlag: Düsseldorf. Vienna, p153.

54 *Maßnahmen zum Schutz der Jagend. 9 March, 1940.* In: Dokumentarische Zeitchronik 1940. Eds. E. Langenbucher u. H. Oehmen. Wilhelm Langewische-Brandt (1943).

55 Marlis G. Steinert, 1970. *Hitler's Krieg und die Deutschen* Econ Verlag: Düsseldorf. Vienna, p118

'Their work disappeared from the libraries and bookshops, they disappeared at the same time from the mental range of the people in Germany for whom at this time it was urgently necessary to hear critical voice."[56]

Parents were also seen as a possible danger. If a woman never attended a Party organisation herself, she was merely looked askance at. If, however, she seemed to be interfering in the political education of her children, it was not tolerated. In 1940, the parents of an eleven year old child who refused to salute the German salute in school, were taken to court. The child gave religious reasons for her refusal, quoting the biblical "Do nothing with a raised hand". The parents, who also had a six year old daughter, refused to interfere with the child's decision. It was reported that the parents didn't own a Hakenkreuz flag and that they didn't take part in any Party organisation, although they said they weren't against the Party. The courts decided that the right to care for both the children would be taken away from the parents. Since they stood in the way of the State's right to educate the children along Nazi lines they were "not to be recommended as parents."[57]

> **Elisabeth B.:** *In actual fact you could say every little, even within your own family. You see my son was born in 1929 and in 1933 Hitler came of power and at first that was all very seductive for a boy, dressing in uniforms, snappy, that was something kids loved. So we had to be very careful what we said, careful that we didn't say anything negative.*

Family tragedies were not uncommon: *Recently a solicitor was arrested in Berlin. He asked if it had been his son who had informed on him and was told, yes, it was his own son. During the search of his house he made use of an un-watched moment to slip into the adjoining room where his son was. He shot first the son then himself.*[58]

---

56 Ilse Staff (Ed), 1964 *Justiz im Dritten Reich Eine Documentation*, Fischer Bücherei, Frankfurt, p51

57 ibid pp72-73

58 Fritz Lehmann, 1946. "1939 - 1945, Beobachtung und Bekenntnisse." Hoffman u. Campe Verlag, Hamburg p85

Parents were in the position of being unable to educate their children to think critically and unable to express their doubts, if they had any, openly, in front of their own children.

Women who were not whole-heartedly behind the Party effort became ever more vulnerable. The wife of one Party member who refused to take part in Nazi organisations was divorced by her husband in 1942. The husband charged that his wife had not taken any active part in the Nazi organisations and that it had a deleterious effect on him in his position. The wife said that her pregnancy and the sickness of her child had prevented her from taking part. She also said that it was impossible for her to make any regular home life because her husband was away nearly every evening on Party business. In summing up the case in which divorce was granted to the husband, the following was said: '*The plaintiff can, as old political leader and Party comrade, demand that his wife take part in Party affairs as far as she is able; at least she should, by entering the National Socialist women's organisation, make apparent that she agrees with her husband and his interests.*[59]'

> **Ruth L.**:*We discussed the war situation and I asked her 'Frau X, do you really think we can win this war?" She went into a fury. If she had reported me I would have been taken away the next day. She was indignant that I could doubt that we would win the war. At the time I didn't realise the danger I was in. Only much later did I become aware that everyone was being spied on and that anyone could be sent to a concentration camp for saying something like this. That was the funny thing, that they kept it so secret. My second husband was in a concentration camp through the war. Our doctor, he was Jewish, and he was taken away and never returned.*

---

59 Ilse Staff (Ed), *Justiz im Dritten Reich Eine Documentation*, Fischer Bücherei, Frankfurt, p182-184.

5. GERMAN WOMEN IN WARTIME EMPLOYMENT

Women's position in wartime industry directly reflected Nazi ideals. In 1937, employment plans had to be worked out in Germany to be used in case of mobilisation.

A secret plan for the employment of women in case of war was prepared in 1938.[60] It stated that in order for men to be freed for the fighting forces women would be brought into industry on a larger scale, but that care must be taken to ensure that the reproduction capabilities of the women would in no way be affected by the work.

The report pointed out that because of their different mental and physical make-up, women could not be expected to take on all jobs formerly occupied by men:

1.4 Women should in general not be trusted with work that demands special technical understanding or knowledge

An example of jobs that were to be recommended for women:

2.7 Women are especially suited to the sorting, weighing, packing and labelling of tools as well as the cleaning of tools, to the giving out and receiving of work materials and tools and such like. For some of this work, however, long technical experience or special surveillance will be

---

60 Runderlaβ Nr. 426/38 Amt der Reichswirtschafts ministerium, Rechtlinien fuer die Beschäftigung von Frauen im Notfall, 19 Oct, 1938, Anlaβ. In: *Frauen im Kriegesdienst 1914 – 1945* by Ursula v. Gersdorff, Deutsche Verlags Anstalt, Stuttgart (1969) p286.

necessary.

How 'true' women should conduct themselves during times of war had been indicated in the 'German Women's Book' published in 1940.

Using the type of manipulative language that was Hitler's hallmark, women were told: "*A woman who wants war for it's own sake is either desperate or uneducated. Every true women defends herself against war. Every true woman however also disdains a peace which smacks of slavery. Every true woman abhors the wailing for peace during a war. War is a heavy burden that will not be made lighter by complaining. The demands of war are higher and more difficult than those of peace - the weak and the cowardly fail. Women who send complaining letters to the battle front help the enemy. Women who remain brave are good comrades.*" [61]

No general call-up for women was planned or prepared and the possibility of calling up women for the armed services was not even considered. When war did break out, industries not essential to the war effort were cut back resulting in the laying off of many women. War industries were able to cover their needs by employing volunteers, mostly women who had been laid off from other work so compulsory service was not necessary.

Between May, 1939, and May, 1941, the number of women in paid employment sank three hundred thousand[62] and industry was having difficulty in filling its personnel needs. After eight years of propaganda about women's place being in the home, women weren't willing to leave and appeals to women to take up paid employment fell on deaf ears. On 14 March, 1941, the 'German women help win' action was started, to encourage women to volunteer but the results were disappointing. Hardly a woman volunteered.[63]

---

61 Ilse Gromes-Bräuer, 1940. In: "*Das deutsche Frauenbuch Ein Buch für Werktag und Feierabend.*" Hrs. Oskar Lucas. Adam Kraft Verlag: Karlsbad-Drahowiz: Leipzig (1940) p28

62 Marlis G.Steinert, 1970 *Hitler's Krieg u. die Deutschen* Econ Verlag: Düsseldorf. Vienna. p196

63 ibid p179

Industry continued to cry for help but the Government continued to resist the idea of a general call up for women. Makeshift efforts to fill the growing need for workers were made at local level only and instead of using the full potential of women, more and more foreign workers were imported to work in German factories.

The absence of a general call-up caused resentment as women of the moneyed class were able to dodge work. Wives of military men were amply provided for so they didn't need the money. They had time to seek out food not on ration and were able to eat out at restaurants (for which one didn't need ration cards) and so get more than their fair share of available food.[64]

> *Liselotte S.: Whoever was married should have children and, for example, women who had children could leave work but those without had to keep working. You could only leave when you had children.*

In 1941, instead of assisting industry by enabling women to work, the household helper was given a new standing. After four years in service in a household with at least three children under fourteen years of age, the household helper was entitled to a payment of RM 600.- and RM 150.- for every further year up to a limit of RM 1500.-. This sum, however, was only payable to the girl on marriage or on her thirtieth birthday.[65] It was a measure designed to help mothers with many children and at the same time promote marriage.

> *Gisela P. : My school class had to do fatigue duty. For me personally, that was the most hideous part of my life.*
>
> *Hildegard D.: My mother was called up and worked for the postal service. The postman had been conscripted and my mother had to do his job. The women with very small children were allowed to stay at home but all others had to join the war effort. My aunt worked in a munitions factory and my mother worked for the postal service.*

64 ibid p119

65 Docky Hammer, 1944. *Das Weite Wirkungsfeld*, Hrs. von der Hauptabteilung Presse/Propaganda der Reichsfrauen Führung

> *Clara H.: I was working for the postal service. We were all mobilised. The Block Leader (member of the Nazi Party] had arranged all that, you didn't have any say yourself at all. If he said you had to do something, then you had to do it.*

In January, 1943, all women from seventeen to forty five were ordered to register for work in civil defence. However, the order was unclear and contained loopholes reflecting the hierarchy's lack of preparation for the mobilisation of women. Only women up to the age of forty five were required to register so many women above that age who had been working gave up their jobs.[66]

Having been so thoroughly indoctrinated that their place was in the home, women who could, stayed there.

> **Ruth L.**:The men had all been taken away and women had to take their place. On the trams and so forth. But the higher positions were always occupied by men.

Even as late as 1943, when the leadership was wanting women to work, Nazi literature included such comments as: *"The woman who forgets her origins and position, who becomes intellectual and erotic, shows the same type of racial degeneration as the man who denounced work and action and embraces a hazy type of humanism and pacifism .*[67]*"*

'During the war at the precise moment that they desperately needed adult labour, Germany experienced the converging of two birthrate trends. On one hand the size of the military age classes was smaller than usual - reflecting the sharp notch caused by the first world war's mobilisation and deaths - and on the other hand German women had more children than ever before."[68]

---

66 Marlis G.Steinert,1970 *Hitler's Krieg u. die Deutschen* Econ Verlag: Düsseldorf. Vienna   p356

67 August Reber-Gruber, 1943. "Von unsere inneren Kraft. Die Frau in Enropa und US-Amerika" Schulungsbrief der SDAP2 Heft. BAZSg 3/433. Steinert p359

As the need for army personnel became acute women were recruited into army jobs. This threatened to undermine Nazi propaganda about women's role so a special rule was made that forbade women to hold arms, even in the event of being taken prisoner. As the crisis deepened women worked not only in office and hospital jobs but were recruited in anti-aircraft units. One hundred thousand girls were allocated to join these units to free up men needed at the front[69].

> **Inge Z**: I had to join the *Flak*, the anti-aircraft unit. ...*There was absolutely no thought of progression in the army. It was simply a duty to serve because you could see that every soldier was away and every girl was necessary and that was an obligation. No one thought of taking on any special duties.*

When the idea of equal pay for equal work was presented to Hitler in 1944 he rejected it, stating that wages had a social function above mere payment for work and should be used to encourage men to marry and have families.[70] Paying women and single men at the same rates as married men would defeat this purpose.

Foreign workers continued to be imported to fill the gap.

---

68 E.L. Homze, 1967. *Foreign Labour in Nazi Germany,* Princton Univ. Press, N. Jersey. p9

69 Marlies Steinert , 1970. *Hitler's Krieg u. die Deutschen* Econ Verlag: Düsseldorf. Vienna. p505

70 E.L. Homze, 1967. *Foreign Labour in Nazi Germany,* Princton Univ. Press, N. Jersey. p428

6. THE INVASION OF RUSSIA AND THE LAST YEARS OF THE WAR

The reaction in Germany to the invasion of Russia was shock and dismay, regardless of party allegiances. The Women's Leadership Committee of the Nazi Party wrote in their April- June 1941 report : *The war with Russia was such a shock to our women because in previous meetings we had been told repeatedly that we had no quarrel with Russia. The news of our invasion of Russia hit us like a bombshell.*[71]

Not only was a war with Russia unexpected (the population had been told over and over that their leadership had no quarrel with the Russians) but it meant a lengthening of the fighting.

Poland had been the practicing ground for strategies later used in Russia. Following is an excerpt from a letter written by a German officer serving in Poland, on 31 October, 1939:

'... On top of that come all the unbelievable things that happened on the side, where we had to look on without lifting a finger. The most extravagant atrocity fantasy is poor compared to the things that this officially tolerated band of well organised murderers, thieves and plunderers did. One can no longer speak of the 'justified indignation about crimes against the German people'. This extermination of complete races with women and children included is only possible from a thug race that no longer deserves the name 'German'. I am ashamed to be a German!' [72]

---

71 Anon. Bericht der Reichsleitung der NSDAP, April-June, 1941- Gau Magdeburg-Anhalt BANS 22/vorl. 860. Cited by Marlies Steinert in *Hitler's Krieg u. die Deutschen* Econ Verlag: Düsseldorf. Vienna 1970. p 206

The soldiers were subject to constant propaganda about the populations to the east. All easterners were lesser beings who could only be controlled by elimination; they were dangerous Communists; they were beasts who were a threat to the lives of the women and children of Germany.

In Russia, hundreds and thousands of Jews, suspected Communists and others showing leadership traits were murdered, women and children included. Soldiers were often forced to take part in atrocities against their will and were forbidden to write anything about them in their letters home.

Word of the atrocities did trickle home, despite the precautions. Citizens were shocked by the stories and anti-Russian propaganda was stepped up in response to the increasing numbers of complaints by the citizenry.

> *Gisela P.: This Russian prisoner was really nice, but we didn't dare have any sort of relationship. I had to act as if he wasn't there. ... I remember him still because I was so surprised that he was nice.*

During the course of the war against Russia, nearly three million Russian men and women were deported to work in Germany. Most died on the way. Prisoners of war were left to starve in their camps. Alexander Dallin compiled figures for 1944 and registered 5,160,000 Russian prisoners of war (living or dead)[73]

In January, 1943, German troops suffered defeat at Stalingrad and in May they were defeated in North Africa. This proved to be the turning point in the fortunes of the German army. As they retreated in Russia, they carried out a burnt earth policy and the towns they left behind half demolished were only left that way because the army had not time to complete the work before retreating.[74]

---

72 Hans-Adolf Jacobsen, 1965 *Kriegstagebuch des Oberkommandos der Wehrmacht : Aus dem Brief eines deutschen Offiziers 31.10.39),* Frankfurt am Main, p437

73 Alexander Werth, 1965. *Russland im Kreig 1941 – 1945,* Droemer Knaur, Munich p447.

74 ibid p478.

At home, defeat merely made the leaders more fanatical..

On February 18, 1943, Goebbels appealed to his countrymen with these words: '...*the Führer awaits a performance from us that will throw everything that has gone before into the shadow. We don't want to fail his challenge. He should be able to be as proud of us as we are of him. In the great crises of national life real men defend themselves, but also real women. One no longer has the right to speak of the weaker sex because both sexes show the same will to fight and spiritual strength The nation is ready for anything.* [75]

By 1943, with bad news from the front, increasing bombing raids, often for nights on end, with unwanted war work forced upon them, many women were becoming disillusioned about the whole war effort. British bombing attacks became heavier and the Germans had little defence against the attacks so the civil population paid dearly. [76] Bombing news became more important to the women than the war-front news.

Each day people asked themselves "Will we be the ones bombed tonight?' ... The government reacted by repressing information with the result that the rumour-mill flourished and led to a radicalisation of the mood, seldom with anti-Jewish sentiment. Now the increase in carpet-bombing lead to a hate of the English, something the German propaganda machine had been unable to stimulate. [77]

> **Charlotte N.**: *I used to sit in the bunker with my children close beside me and say, 'Stay very close to Mummy so if a bomb hits us not a single one of us survives. Then we are all dead and none of you survives alone.'*

---

75 *Aus der Sportpalastrede Goebbels vom 18.2.1843.* In: H.A. Jacobsen, "1939 - 1945" p284.

76 Marlies Steinert, 1970 *Hitler's Krieg u. die Deutschen* Econ Verlag: Düsseldorf. Vienna. p363.

77 ibid p311

> *Ruth L.:* I was told that Oranienburg had been bombed and that was where my son was. I went part of the way back as far as we could, by tram and then ran along the tracks. I was not alone, there were lots of other people running back with me. We weren't just jogging, we were running.

Women and children had been advised to leave the big cities and those who could, did so but they often had difficulty settling into their new environments. The inhabitants of the small villages where they were sent were often withdrawn and unhelpful in their relationship to the evacuees. The fighting men had fewer holidays as the war progressed. When they came home expecting a holiday of honey and roses and were met instead by the thousand problems of the home front, they showed little understanding. Holidays often ended in arguments.

The sexual needs of the soldiers had been recognised by the regime which had established brothels on the front[78], but the women were meant to have no such needs.

In 1944 a report was prepared on the subject entitled "The Immoral Behaviour of German Women".[79]   It pointed out that an ever larger proportion of German women and girls were having relationships with men other than their husbands and in an effort to encourage women to tread the straight and narrow, a propaganda effort was launched emphasising the worth of German womanhood.

> *Charlotte N:* we lived as if there was no tomorrow, we didn't want to miss anything. We lived every day as if we would be dead the next because we thought, tomorrow you might not be here.
>
> *Anna Maria H. :* There was a lot of cheating during the war. The woman who lived upstairs cheated on her husband with other soldiers and the women who lived below had a child that people doubted was her husband's. It was not for money because no one was in financial difficulties. It was simply the sexual experience.

---

78 ibid p425

79 ibid p426

As defeat became more certain and morale fell, the authorities resorted to open threats and violence to keep the citizenry in line. On the first of August, 1944, it was announced that action could and would be taken against the families of any German soldier who turned traitor to the German cause.

Following is an extract of a letter written by a farmer's son to his parents on the third of February, 1944: *"Dear Parents, I have to inform you of very sad news, I have been condemned to death, me and Gustav G. We didn't sign up for the SS and they condemned us to death. You wrote to me that I shouldn't join the SS didn't you. My friend, Gustav G., wouldn't sign up either. We would both rather die than stain our consciences with atrocities. I know what the SS has to do. Oh, dear parents, as difficult as it is for me, and for you, forgive me for everything, if I have wronged you please forgive me and pray for me. If I died in war with a bad conscience, that would also be sad for you too. A lot of parents will lose their sons yet. A lot of SS men die too. I thank you for everything that you have done for me since my childhood, forgive me, pray for me."* [80]

Anyone, including women, who expressed doubt about the war effort was courting death. In November, 1944, Mrs. Frank-Schultz was taken to court and the following sentence passed: *"Mrs. Frank-Schultz said to a red cross sister that she regretted that the attempted assassination of our Führer had misfired and was cheeky enough to maintain that a few years under Anglo-saxon rule would be better than the present reign of force. She had, thus, conspired with the traitors of 20 July. Because of that she has forever lost her honour. She will be punished with death."* [81]

Elsa W: When Italy capitulated I said we should too. I was informed on by one of the women. But I was lucky because I sewed for the local policeman's wife and I knew the policeman. He found a paragraph in the rules that applied to me – my husband had died in the war. He called in the woman and told her what could have happened to me. Later she apologised She probably didn't mean it either.

---

80 In: Erick Kruby, 1956. "Das Ende des Schreckens". Süddeutschen Zeitung, Gesamtherstellung Süddeutschen Verlag. München. p35

81 Isle Staff, "Justiz im Dritten Reich". Fischer Bücherei, Frankfurt, p244.

In mid 1944, by which time one out of five workers in Germany was a foreigner, all women up to the age of fifty, with exceptions as previously, were required to register for work. Women in civil defence work were forbidden to leave their duties under threat of death.

Clara H.: *We had to stay and shovel graves, together with the foreigners. Four women had to do that and they said if we left our posts we would be shot, our own Germans said that. That was the Party; the soldiers had nothing to do with it.*

Frau Schw.: *We didn't want to leave [home], but we had to otherwise our own soldiers would have had to shoot us.*

A propaganda booklet put out in late 1944 encouraged women to take up a career.

Political activity, however, remained completely out of the question with the following argumentation: *"A female Member of Parliament would not be able to represent women's needs as she would be duty bound to represent the Party Program. Women would be represented in Parliament in such small numbers anyway that they would not be in a position to put their cause."* [82]

Even to the last the full work potential of women remained unused as the Nazi picture of the ideal woman never allowed for a general call-up of all women.[83]

By 1944, the civil population, indoctrinated as it had been with the supposed bestiality of the peoples to the East, were in a state of panic and those who could fled westwards. In July, 1944, the authorities forbade civilian movements out of East Prussia and the population had to stay put. Massive propaganda assured the citizens that there was no immediate danger and only the upper levels of society tried to leave.

---

82 Docky Hammer, 1944. *Das Weite Wirkungsfeld* Hrs. von der Hauptabteilung Presse/Propaganda der Reichsfrauen Führung

83 Ursula v. Gersdorff, 1969. *Frauen im Kriegesdienst.*Deutsche Verlags Anstalt, Stuttgart (1969), p75

> **Liselotte S.** *..From August 1944 until I fled in 1945 it was so dreadful that it doesn't bear thinking about. Everything became chaotic and there was no order at all.*

By December, 1944, the Russians were threatening Prussia and the western allies had already reached the Rhine but still Hitler refused to surrender.

At the last moment the civilian population was told to flee before the invading army. It was deep winter and the temperatures were well below zero. Those who had horse and wagon used it. Women without horses pulled sledges themselves, loaded with old people and children or they walked, children in their arms. Many of the children and old people on the wagons froze to death during the nights. Mothers discarded the dead in order to save the living. Some kept their dead children with them, unable to part with them even under such frightful conditions.

> **Clara H.**: *We were afraid of the Party, not the soldiers. The soldiers helped us leave.*
>
> **Liselotte S.**: *A lot of children didn't survive and died on the side of the road. Some of the mothers carried them even though they were dead because they couldn't bare to part with them. It was so cold and everything was frozen. The ground was frozen solid and you can't just leave your child lying there, so they were carried on.*

Refugee columns overtaken by the invading army were plundered. As the invading army overran Prussia, it murdered, raped and looted, behaving with the bestiality the population had been lead to fear. In those few weeks, one out of every five East Prussians, mainly women and children, lost their lives.

Towards the end of the war, the English devised bombing patterns which caused the resulting fires to use the complete oxygen supply and those not killed by the bombs themselves were asphyxiated. So many people were killed: neighbours, relatives, grannies, children and mothers. Many of those surviving had little interest in living further.

On the 13/14 February, 1945, the English-American bombing attack on

Dresden killed 135,000 (one hundred and thirty five thousand) people, mostly refugees, women and children.

> ***Herta T***: *The women had children; they had sat with those children under the bombs and they had either died or not – we didn't care either way. It was completely irrelevant to us if we survived. The only thing we cared about was getting the bed clean enough for the children to sleep in, that we got some sort of food and could cook it so the children had something to eat. We just wanted to be able to feed the children and do the washing, everything else was completely unimportant.*

7. WOMEN IN THE VANQUISHED GERMANY

> **Anne Marie H.:** *My father-in-law was convinced that Hitler would win the war until two weeks before the end.*

Germany capitulated in May, 1945. Women were regarded as fair game and Berlin became a scene of mass rapes. Women from eight to eighty were raped in what Professor Austin App called a planned attack[84] with soldiers queuing in front of their victims. Those who resisted were shot or degraded to such an extent they were forced to comply. Mothers hid their children and rubbed ash on the faces of their daughters. Later VD clinics were set up on street corners to deal with the rampant disease.

> **Herta T:** *I don't know if you know what happened in Berlin, but the Americans held back and regardless of your age, whether you were 16 or whatever your age, if you were a woman you were there for the Russians.*
>
> **Frau Schw:** *. My daughter came back once with her trousers all torn and streaming blood. She cried so much I wrapped her up in a blanket and took her on my knee. I had her on my knee for five minutes then 15 Russians burst in and grabbed my daughter and they all raped her. You can't punish a person worse than that.*
>
> **Charlotte N.** *They spat in their hands, put them into the ashes then they came and stroked it over my hair and they said, Mummy, no one will ever again see that you are have blond hair. That is what these small children said.*

---

84 Austin J. App 1950. *Der Erschreckendste Friede der Geschichte* Hellbrunn, p47

Food was very short, malnutrition rampant, and diseases like typhus the order of the day.

Eastern Prussia, food bowl of Germany, had been ceded to Poland. The main thought in the minds of the women in Germany for the next five years was "Where am I going to find the next meal for the children?" Those who could work did. The many for whom there was no work roamed the fields looking for edibles, stole when they could or sold themselves to the invaders. Many children died. The others had to fend for themselves while their mothers looked or worked for food. People in the farming areas were much better off then those in the cities. The displaced suffered most of all.

> **Gisela P.**: *If you had lived correctly in those days you would have died. You had to go out and get food somehow yourself.*

Capitulation marked the end of the fighting, but not the end of the war for the civil population in Germany, just as the declaration of war had not really marked the beginning. More than twenty percent of the population were now refugees in a land where much of the housing had been bombed flat. Nearly a million mothers had lost their children and were looking for them.[85] Surviving men were either in prisoner of war camps or had been transported to the east by the Russians to forced labour camps.

Table 4: Refugees in Germany in 19471	
American Zone:	0
British Zone:	3193000
Russian Zone:	3949000
French Zone:	50000

---

85 Anon 1954. *Flüchtlinge, Vertriebene, Kriegsgefangene.* Bundesministerium für Vertriebene, Bonn

Most women believed that their home was their castle which added to their suffering in their years in refugee camps or in the homes of other people.

> **Hildegard D:** *They used to call us potato grubs and say what a burden we were. The Germans didn't want us because they had nothing themselves.*

Refugee women also had particular problems getting work.

In general it has to be confirmed that the working refugee woman has sunk in social status. After the monetary reform there was even greater pressure on her to take up any work where she was not in competition with local people, no matter what her formal standard of education. If she was, until now an independent housewife, she is today a charwoman; if she was a secondary school teacher today she is a primary school teacher or clerk.[86]

In 1950 there were an estimated 938,000 war widows and 1,371,000 war orphans living in Germany[87]

> **Charlotte N:** *I stood at nights and washed shirts then ironed them dry so the children could be clean at least. Because I didn't want anyone to notice, even with the little money I earned.*
>
> **Herta T.:** *after the war we had so-called refugee-anaemia. Many of we women had no period for about nine months.*

Once again women were more oppressed by the economic difficulties than the men.

The results of an employment survey in 1946 showed that 37.6%, an unusually high percentage of the workforce, were women. Most were

---

86 Alice Scherer, 1951. "Die Frau, Wesen u. Aufgaben." Verlag Herder, Freiburg p265.

87 Anon 1954 Lexicon der Frau. Encyclios Verlag AG, Zürich p1646

employed on farms or in domestic service, work that required few qualifications and which gave little social protection. Many were forced by the economic circumstances to help in the small family businesses. Young women could not dream of marriage as their menfolk were dead or in camps.

Women earned much less than men just as they had before the war, whether or not they were supporting their families alone.

Elsbeth Weichman collated the numbers: (Table 5).

Table 5. Hourly rates of pay, in Pfennigs (pennies) in September, 1948 [88] .

	Men	Women
Skilled worker:	123.9	-
Trained worker:	115	74.4
Assistant:	100.9	67.3
Average:	115.8	72.1

The outlook for young women was grim. The market was not able to absorb the girls coming of working age.

From the apprentices in Hamburg 82.6% were male and 17.4% female. Among the students in the winter 1948/1950, 83.4% were male and 16.6% female. [89]

Women had anti-female prejudices to fight on every front. Nazi propaganda had segregated work into 'women's' and 'men's' work and this remained a barrier to women's progression. Many employers thought married women should not work and when women did work, they were

---

88 Dr. Elsbeth Weichmann, 1951. "Die Frau in der Wirtschaft: Entwicklung der deutschen Frauenarbeit von 1946-1951". Hrs. vom Buro für Frauenfragen in der Gesellschaft zu Gestaltung Öffentlichen Lebens (1951) p12.

89 ibid p35

offered only the lowest of positions[90].

Women were caught in a strangle hold whichever way they turned. They were even blamed in some quarters for the Nazi misadventure. The minister of work from Bavaria announced that he was 'very sceptical' about women's voting rights and said, 'A lot of the votes given to the Nazis in 1933 were doubtless those of women' [91].

In the face of these accusations, Gertrud Bäumer collated voting statistics for the 1933 Presidential elections which had been registered according to gender in some of the major cities and found no basis for the accusations. (Table 6) She did find definite regional variations: in catholic areas far fewer people voted for Hitler (16% female, 24% male).

Table 6: Percentage votes by gender for the 1933 Presidential elections[92]

	First round	Second round
Hindenburg	51.6% female 44.2% male	56% female 48.7% male
Hitler	26.5% female 28.3% male	33.6% female 35.9% male
Thälmann (Communist candidate)	14% female 19.7% male	10.4% female 15.4% male
Düsterberg	Not shown	

---

90 ibid p 30-31

91 Gertrud Bäumer, 1946. *Der neue Weg der deutschen Frau*. Stuttgart. Deutsche Verlags Anstalt , p29

92 ibid p30

Despite all the prejudice and suffering women did step up to the plate. They rebuilt whole cities with their bare hands. There was no alternative in a country full of ruined cities. It was this effort perhaps that finally put paid to the idea that women are incapable of 'men's work'. It is impossible to argue such a proposition in today's Germany, as women have shown what they are capable of.

> ***Ellen von A .:*** *The bodies were all thrown together onto special wagons. They were taken to the cemetery and were thrown into long trenches that had been dug there. And it was May and in the heat, how that stank. We all wore these masks, made of fabric and dunked in perfume or something so you could bear the smell and weren't infected. That carried on calmly and we were all given tea and a half pound of bread at the end of every day.*

The disillusionment of those who had trusted Hitler and the post war experience of women combined to alter ingrained attitudes.

> ***Gisela P.:*** *We were the generation that was betrayed, completely misled and betrayed. And maybe we were also proud and just didn't want to know that we had been so betrayed. I thought that such evil couldn't have happened.*
>
> ***Inge Z:*** *W felt betrayed, completely betrayed by having the whole national socialism forced down out throats, we were made stupid and kept stupid through the fine speeches. We had no way of seeing outside and that only became clear afterwards.*

If the German people, and particularly women, had been denied the opportunity to develop a political consciousness before the end of the war circumstances after the war were no less difficult. Most women had simply no time for thoughts beyond the basic essentials.

A study in 1952 indicated that 63% of the population in West Germany were either uninformed or deficiently informed. Twenty five percent of the women gave incorrect answers to every political question asked. The apolitical stance of women thus continued for long after the declaration of peace.

Elisabeth B.: I don't think people more politically aware now. I'm afraid political things just don't interest most people.

Gisela P. : if I was going to give advice to the next generation I would say "live consciously! Don't believe slogans but rather listen to what is being said and inform yourself from other sources; see if the words and actions are in accord.

Figure 1. Where the women lived during the War

PART 2: THE WOMEN SPEAK

GISELA P. 1926 : A MISLED GENERATION

Gisela P. born 1926. Lived in Halle during the war and is the daughter of Elisabeth B.

[Note from the author: Giesela P. was my German teacher at the school of adult education. She was a wonderfully warm person and full of good humour. I remember once she was explaining about old clothes collections in Germany and she told us how she had given away her Loden Coat, then later found she needed it and had to buy another. I thought most people in my class were probably British but discovered later that they were mostly Turkish.]

How old were you in 1939?

I was 13 years old.

Tell me, what was your reaction when war broke out?

Yes, it was critical somehow. We knew that something big was coming. My parents let me sleep and didn't wake me up punctually for school.

Then I got up and said, 'I have to go to school.'

'No, there is no school. War had been declared.'

I can still see the three of us upstairs in my room (we had a single family home) standing around, really agitated.

I remember thinking a really foolish thought. I thought to myself, 'Now I'll have a war too.' My mother had been about 15 when the first world war started and whenever I didn't want to eat or something and I was scolded she'd say, ' You know when I was as old as you we were fighting a war and we didn't have anything.' So now I thought we would be on equal grounds; silly just as thirteen year old girls sometime are.

What changes were there?

I can't really tell you, but I do remember that almost as soon as war was declared, in the first two or three days afterwards there was a bombing alarm and the sirens sounded. We went into the cellar and tried on our gas masks. I remember that the gas masks were in the cellar and this memory is a horrible memory for me; I thought oh my God, because you can't breath properly in those masks and I thought it was stupid to have them on. I was really reluctant to use it but my father was adamant and said 'you have to put it on'. There was never a gas war, thank heavens. But I remember that panic during the first alarm.

We didn't have mixed schools at the time, you went to a girls school or a boys school. I was 13 and didn't have any boyfriends and later, when I was 14 or 15 and went to the dancing school. Yes, they did exist during the war, the cadets dancing school. The boys there were young men who had been to war. So at fifteen I was in dance school with young men who had been to war. They came as officer cadets to Halle, where I'm from, and did their education there, and part of that were these dancing lessons. In wartime. That's when I first met these brave Fatherlands heroes.

Do you remember whether these young men were changed by the start of war. Were they more serious?

No, you couldn't say that, and anyway I had no way of comparing them with others. I had never had contact with young men at school except for this cadet school dancing class. Maybe they were more mature than today's youngsters, but I was not in a position to judge that at the time.

Was your time in school changed because of the war?

Yes of course because as time went on a lot of the teachers were called up and the school department cancelled a whole year of schooling. Normally we have thirteen years of school but we had only twelve. The 11th to 12th year was no longer taught so they didn't need teachers for that class.

We often missed school because of air-raid alarms. We were living in central Germany so we didn't get as many air-raid warnings as the areas to the west because of course the planes flew in from the west. When there was an alarm in the mornings we went into the school cellar and when there had been an alarm at night (and towards the end there were air raids almost every night) then school started one hour later than normal because the school was used as a hospital for the soldiers. Towards the end of the war, I don't remember exactly when, we had shifts at school because many of the rooms were used for other things.

You must have had aspirations as a young person. Did they change?

I aimed to do my school leaving exam (Abitur) and I did complete that, a year earlier than normal. That was late in 1943 and I was sick at the time. At the end of January we were suddenly told that the Abitur had to be finished by the 5th February. It all went so quickly that we were more or less excused from exams. We had to sit a couple of tests and have a small oral exam but it was nothing as serious as Abitur actually is.

After school did you want to study, and was that allowed?

No, I didn't consider anything more than Abitur and anyway most of the students in my class had to do fatigue duty. That included me.

What did that mean for you personally?

For me personally, that was the most hideous part of my life. I am a pronounced individualist and now suddenly I had to leave the security of my own home and go to a camp although I was only seventeen. That was in 1944. On 5 February we had Abitur and at the end of February we had to be at the camp. Each of my classmates was sent to a different camp, we were separated and scattered to the four winds. I was sent to the most awful camp, a barracks about an hour by car and two hours by train from my home in Halle, a terribly long way.

Did you feel responsible for your destiny in any way, or feel you were to blame in any way?

No, all school leavers had to do fatigue duty and we didn't think twice about it. Today's youth don't think twice about things that are taken for granted either. Of course we had heard reports from other school leavers that fatigue duty was great or that fatigue duty was awful, so were did go with certain expectations. For me fatigue duty was awful, not because it was arranged by the government but because the camp leader, our 'Fuhrerin', was so mean. I heard from other girls that the women who lead their camps were really nice and life was much more comfortable, even though they probably had the same duties. A great deal depends on how such a camp is managed.

How long did you stay in camp?

I was only there a short time thank God, because I got sick. We had had no proper heating in school Iand had become ill about three months before my Abitur. I remember our graduation celebration well, yes there were such things even then! We studied a theatre piece and it was put on in a hall that was ice cold. I caught cold in this ice cold room and then very sick. It developed into pyelitis (pelvic infection) then a gallbladder infection and uterine infection which eventually made me infertile. I was operated on later, but I can thank the war for these three infections. I can also thank these infections that I was released from fatigue duty so quickly. Actually they shouldn't have even accepted me for duty so soon after being so ill. While I was there they found protein in my urine and that saved me. I was released from duty. It was only eight or ten weeks but that was long enough for me. Normally I should have been there a year, although that was so uncertain as the war developed.

Because I had protein in my urine I was sent from the camp to a sick bay, a type of military hospital in Jena. It was specifically for girls during fatigue duty and I had to travel there.

While I was there I picked up scarlet fever, unbeknownst to me. There was a big outbreak of scarlet fever and I must have been infected without realising. Anyway, I was released from this sick bay to return to my camp, but I had permission to go via my home in Halle and that was really a piece of very good luck because while I was at home I came down with scarlet fever. I had a really bad case of scarlet fever and perhaps if I had been in camp I would have died from it, but at home under my mother's care I recovered. That was the end of my fatigue duty.

What sort of work did you have to do while you were on fatigue duty?

We lived in barracks as I said and for the first little while we were not allowed to leave its boundaries. There was a fence around it and we were not allowed to set a single step outside. It was like a large prison. It was here that I learned for he first time what it is like when you can't go where ever you want to. For the first week were had to clean rooms, endlessly clean windows, cook for the others then clean again. I can see myself now cleaning toilettes, these horrible dirty toilets, it was just awful. We were kept busy all the time.

After four or six weeks we sworn in. That meant we were 'mature' enough to leave the camp. Early in the morning we were allocated to farms that were in the neighbourhood. I was sent to a farmer's wife whose husband had been called up and who now managed the farm with the help of a Russian prisoner. We worked together but my output was meagre because I didn't have the strength.

Once I had to shovel out the dung heap. It is not only straw but cow-pats as well and that is really really heavy. You only realise that when you have had to do it yourself. I had to fork the dung onto the trailer and the trailer was then pulled to the fields where the dung was spread. The sweat ran off me, I shook and I just couldn't continue. I had so little strength after having been so ill but I did my best, just loading a little bit onto the fork and then onto the trailer. When the farmer's wife came out and looked she was horrified at how little I had done and gave me a dressing down. Then she and the Russian took the forks and it was done in a trice. I stood there and watched and found the whole thing just so depressing. Because I was incapable of doing that I had to go out onto the fields and clear stones away. Sometimes I had to clean in the kitchen and then at least I was alone. The others went to the fields and I was in the kitchen and although I couldn't cook I did the washing up and things like that. I remember that the floor was so filthy from the cats that I hated cleaning it. Today I would be able to cope with it, but as a young girl I couldn't.

What was the relationship to the Russians like?

This Russian prisoner was really nice, but we didn't dare have any sort of relationship. I had to act as if he wasn't there. Dimitri, I still remember his name, he noticed that I hadn't the strength for the physical work and was a gentleman and would say 'Come, sit down!' So I would sit down in the trailer when we were on the field and he would do my work as well as his own. I was really so very grateful to him and esteemed him highly, but there was never more than that. He was a prisoner and he was alone with a young and pretty girl in the fields. That could have been a temptation for him as a man, I don't know but it is possible. However if he had ever done anything to me he would have been sent to the war court and shot. They were very rigorous. Russians were just 'subhuman' and had to have nothing to do with German girls.

Did you ever notice he had any feelings for you.

Yes, I did notice that he noticed me and had tender feelings towards me, but I was a completely untouched girl, as one was in those days, and he must have noticed that was well. But sometimes, when I think back, I wonder if he had a relationship to the farmers wife. That was possible though I have no proof, but she was much nicer to him than to me.

Why did the Germans hate the Russians?

Propaganda! For years we had been bombarded with propaganda about the sub-humans from the east so that is what we believed, that the Russians would behave abominably. That was what coloured my own experience with the Russian on the farm, a man who was just a normal man, and even nice and sympathetic! I remember him still because I was so surprised that he was nice.

Did any of your classmates have more contact with the prisoners?

It was forbidden, but you know, even when things are forbidden they sometimes happen. I would like to think any such relationship was mutual.

I didn't really mean intimate relationships, but human ones.

You have to understand that I was so very immature at that time. The destiny of a prisoner of war was not a human destiny as far as I was concerned. I am ashamed to say it today, but that is how it was. We had been educated to think that they were not humans, neither men nor human, but of course they were both. For us they were cheap workers we were to have nothing to do with. Mostly we didn't come into contact with them at all so there was no relationship. I can't say what the relationship between others was like because at the time that was of no interest to me. I very seldom thought about things that I should have thought about.

You only saw things from one side I guess!

Today I think, 'How could you have been like that!'

Once you got home again, what did you do then?

I became a teacher because there was such a shortage. I knew almost nothing. I was just eighteen when I got home again and now I had to be slotted into this war effort. I wanted to study but that was not possible because everyone was needed. Whoever was healthy was not allowed to study. My husband for example, he was allowed to study because he had lost an arm in the war.

So the only people able to study were war wounded?

Almost the only people. They would have needed students so no doubt a few women who had their fatigue duty and war duties behind them also studied, but I was too young. I had to prove myself and then I might have a hope of studying later.

My father was a lecturer so he put me forward to the schools inspector and he said I could teach. I had a class of of sixty boys, a Grade two class so they weren't very big but there were a lot of them. Somehow I managed them, and to this day I have very good memories of that time. The children loved me and I loved them but I am not sure whether they learned very much. However they were taught by me and I used ounce of energy I had to teach them.

Did you get a proper professional training later?

The time I was talking about, with the teaching, was 1944. I started in autumn and I taught for half a year until the end of the war. After that there was no school for six months and in these six months I prepared myself to study. I taught a neighbour's children every day and for that I got a small sum. With this money I paid for private lessons in Latin. So for half a year I learned Latin. I was very diligent and learned hard every day. For the first time in my life I worked really hard and I learned Latin very quickly. Later I forgot everything equally quickly! So today I don't remember much Latin. But I wanted to study.

In autumn 1945 every thing started again very slowly. On 3rd October 1945 the Russians arrested my father and then I couldn't study. I had signed papers indicating I wanted to study but after they had looked at them I got a letter saying 'Thank you, but you have not been accepted as a student.' They didn't value me. So then I had to look around for something to do, something that would earn me some money because my mother didn't get any pension at all. Then funnily enough I was accepted as a 'new teacher', although today I would say how could they accept me as a teacher when they didn't think I was politically acceptable as a student? But they did accept me and then I was given a pressure-cooker course for teachers for three months. That was the beginning of 1946. For three months we were rigorously trained, on school benches! And then in later summer or early autumn I was already teaching in school, as a 'new teacher'.

And then you just continued?

Yes, as new-teachers we had to continue our education at the same time. That wasn't a University education but two or three times a week we had lessons in the afternoon. Later I took my exams and was qualified. Then I repeated the exams in West Germany later so I am qualified here as well.

All of the boys in your generation went to war didn't they and the girls were brought up to be housewives. So how did war affect you all?

Well I can talk about that from my personal point of view. I was thirteen when the war began and we began to notice that what we thought of as normal was not and that eventually conditions would be as they are elsewhere.

When I was very young, thirteen, I thought, its war and many men will die. Our generation knew we would not be able to have what we thought of an as ideal career, that of housewife with children simply because of the numbers, that is, there would not be a man for every woman. I didn't really want to marry so that didn't worry me. When I was a girl I wasn't that wild about marriage, but I did want to have children. I always said to myself, even when I was in school, that I didn't necessarily want to marry but I certainly wanted children, or at least one child. I didn't know at that time that I would become ill and have a pelvic and uterine infection that would make it impossible for me to have children. I did want a profession. I thought that I could have a career and then marry later perhaps. That was my end-goal. Most of us wanted to marry eventually.

That is quite normal!

You say that is normal but today it is not so normal for many young people. I don't know whether thy really don't want to marry or they just don't want to admit it.

So what happened then? You were new a teacher.

Yes, well I always had boyfriends. I never had a problem in that department because I was a nice girl and very open and communicative. Actually I can almost say that I had more friends that I could ever have wanted. In 1949 I married but I continued with my profession.

That was not a problem for you?

No that wasn't a problem for me but I saw that many others my age had a problem because they didn't have even one boyfriend.

Did these girls try to get a good education so they could stand on their own two feet?

Yes, they did attempt to build careers. We were all interested in careers because we had reached the stage when we said we didn't want to be bound completely to the kitchen and be 'just housewives'. We all wanted to succeed in our careers. My mother for example, was born in 1899 but she had a career. In my family it wasn't a point for discussion, you simply knew you were going to have a career.

But your ideal was to have a family later?

Yes and perhaps the thought of bringing new life into the world was unconsciously strengthened by the war because so many died. So many civilians died. A great many women and children were killed by bombs. But you know, perhaps I was protected by my parents from the worst because the propaganda that promoted the idea of German women being sort of birthing-machines passed me by. As a young girls I was in the BDM, that's clear, and in the organisation called 'Faith and Beauty'. Nowadays with books and television I am much better informed than I was then.. I had no idea at the time that there were quasi-breeding stations that were managed in horrible circumstances. I don't know if my parents knew because such themes were taboo in our house. I did know that the German race should be propagated and expanded and I knew that we Germans were infinitely superior to all the races to the East. I had learned that but I didn't make the connection or realised that a biological and sexual process was necessary to produce a new German super-race. I simply didn't think that far.

Was there a possibility for young people, in the SS perhaps, to have a

child if they wanted?

Yes that was true.

Did you know that?

No, I was a protected girl. We didn't hear about that, neither at school nor at the BDM nor at home. When I heard about these things after the war I simply didn't believe them at first. I thought, that can't be right, it is impossible!. I also didn't believe it when we heard about the concentration camps. I simply didn't want to believe it because it was so dreadful and one said to oneself that it couldn't be possible that one had been so stupid and not known these things. We were the generation that was betrayed, completely misled and betrayed. And maybe we were also proud and just didn't want to know that we had been so betrayed. I thought that such evil couldn't have happened, I simply did not want to believe it.

Did you hear about the Jews and the opposition? Did you know that many were in concentration camps?

I knew as good as nothing. Firstly I was too young and also none of our acquaintances were Jewish. We did have a Jewish paediatrician, a really nice man called Dr Weinberg. I knew that all at once he had left Halle. I remember that because I had really liked him, but somehow my parents protected me from the truth. He had simply left Halle. I knew he had left Germany, but I didn't know why. My parents had let me think the world was in order. It made my life easier to think we were living a idyllic world. Today parents don't do that, but I wonder if all the psychoses and neuroses and lack of energy amongst the youth today is because their illusions have been destroyed too early in life.

Were you anxious about anything at the time?

We were frightened of bombs and also we were anxious about our friends who were on the front.

I mean, for example, frightened of the SS.

My mother secretly listened to foreign radio, but she did it so secretly that we children never knew about it. My father believed more than my mother, he had so a naive belief in the Hitler propaganda, but my mother was much more discerning. But for me at the time the SS were not something to be afraid of, as curious as that sounds today.

Were women more critical of the Regime?

No I don't believe they were at all when I remember other women whose eyes shone when people talked about Hitler. My mother hated Hitler, but she couldn't tell us at the time because we loved him – we thought he was a god!

Near the end of the war when the Russians were already in Prussia and I was a bit older there was talk of Generals or members of the resistance they had not been able to capture so they arrested the families. Suddenly the penny dropped for me and I thought 'That goes too far, arresting families for something they didn't do. At the time I thought the resistance was unwarranted but when I heard that the families of people in the resistance had been arrested I became critical for the first time because they hadn't done anything wrong. From that moment, when families were affected, families like the ones I knew who were educated and had a certain position in society, then I understood that it could happen to me as well for all I knew. Suddenly it was clear to me what crazy times we were living in. Suddenly I remembered things I had heard about Jews being arrested and wondered if their arrests had been justified. Finally I started to have some doubts about the whole machine. But this awareness was only now just dawning and that was at the end of the war. The awareness only developed because people like those I knew had been adversely affected.

Did your experiences make you more independent?

No I didn't become more independent although we had to do a lot of the work that men would normally have done. I don't think we were aware at the time that this was a piece of emancipation. We weren't very reflective. We didn't think about that sort of thing because we had so much to do and so many other problems in our daily lives, like queueing for food, although that became very much worse after the war. We had school and air raid warnings, bombs falling and our own loss of a time to be young youth to worry about. As I have said, in spite of the war I did have a youth and I have my mother to thank for that. Somehow she managed to give me that.

When the refugees came, did they arrive in your area as well?

I worked at the station as red-cross helper. As the war ended I started to help and worked on duty roster at the station or in the refugee temporary accommodation. I can see myself still, making hundreds of dumplings. When I saw the refugee camps it became clear to me what war was, although I had no idea yet about the whole horror. I was a bit immature at the time; I don't know what it is like now for 18 year olds but I don't think they understand things the way I do. It is a question of maturity.

At the end of the war, for example, we took a refugee family into the family, my father's half sister. They came from Frankfurt on the Oder and when Frankfurt was evacuated suddenly this aunt appeared whom I had never seen in my life. We took them in for six or nine months. They were family even though we had never met them so of course they lived with us. Otherwise they would have been in a refugee camp or would have wandered around homeless.

If you had lived correctly in those days you would have died. You had to go out and get food somehow yourself. We cooked potato dumplings with onion and pretended they were herrings. We cooked potatoes in coffee and pretended they were fried. At least they were brown. Once someone asked us did we want a piece of meat or a bag of potatoes and we chose the potatoes of course.

You didn't see the Russians after the war.

We were lucky in that the American marched into our area and stayed for several months before handing it to the Russians, by which time the worst was over. I heard about the rapes with horror and great pity for the women involved. The Russian men took revenge on Germany by raping German women and I hated that and was very afraid. I heard from friends who lived in the Russian occupied area what had happened to them. It was dreadful.

What did the population think when the Russians behaved so badly?

When the Russian fighting men behaved as they did, it was a confirmation for us that Hitler had been right about them. We didn't think about the human causes and psychological stresses they were under. It happened was brutal and dreadful.

Did you experiences change your political understanding?

Yes. I look at things with a much more critical eye and don't believe the things our politicians say; but not only in the political world, but in day to day things. Recently an elderly person asked me about about my generation and why they are educating their own children in a very anti-authoritarian manner. I thought about it and said that it is because we don't want to have and don't dare have role models, idols or ideals after what happened to us and we are very careful not to indoctrinate our own children with such ideals. When children question our ideals we are willing to sit down and think about it and questions ourselves because our experience was that the ideals we were taught to honour were all rubbish. That made us deeply insecure. For me this time coincided with the time in my life when I was becoming more mature, starting to think about the world. Then came this rupture. For me and for my generation it was as if the rug had been pulled from under our feet and somehow we had to survive emotionally. That influenced us in ways we are unaware of.

What is your position to politics today. Do you take an interest?

I lived in East Germany until 1961 and for that reason I am more interested in politics than most women my age who have only ever lived in the west. Women became aware of what had really happened in 1945 but women in the west lived in a wave of comfort in a democracy and they relaxed and thought 'now everything will right itself'. So they are not as interested in politics as we who lived in the DDR are, because we lived in a Dictatorship, just like in 1945. The Nazi world and the DDR world were very similar.

What advice would you give the next generation, if they were in similar circumstances to the one you have been in?

I would say, "live consciously! Don't believe slogans but rather listen to what is being said and inform yourself from other sources; see if the words and actions are in accord. I would also advise taking a middle road instead of following any extremes.

Do you think other women of your generation feel the same?

It is difficult to tell. I have to be honest and say that most of the women I know here in Wiesbaden are much younger than me, I'm not sure why, perhaps just coincidence, but a few years makes a lot of difference, especially in these formative years. People who were small children during the war were not aware of what went on during the war as I was. I do meet my classmates occasionally but we don't talk about politics. There are four of us and I know two of them are very right wing and they both have very wealthy husbands. We meet very three to six months and we simply avoid talking about politics so we don't have arguments. Instead we talk about our problems and that is much better otherwise we would just argue. If we talked politics I think we would have heated arguments and that wouldn't solve anything or help Germany in any way, so I have just resigned myself to avoiding political discussions.

I am a person who lives by their feelings rather than by their intellect. At the time Hitler was the right man for me because he spoke to our feelings, our ability to become enthusiastic. I must say though that that works for me only up to a certain point. During Hitler's time for example, when soldiers or the Hitler Youth or some other group was marching with flags waving we were meant to stand on the side of the street with our right hands held up. I didn't like that and I went into the house so I didn't have to do it. I just found it stupid. I didn't resist for political reasons, it was not a demonstration against Hitler, I just found it idiotic. We had to raise our arms and say 'Heil Hitler' in the morning at school too and I didn't like that either and found it difficult to overcome my resistance. I find taking hats off to flags and anything like that ridiculous.

Were a lot of women persuaded by Hitler because of his habit of appealing to the emotions?

Yes, that is dreadful and upsetting. If you look at film newsreels from the Hitler time, then you will see all these women with enthusiasm shining from their eyes who were completely fascinated by him. If Hitler said 'Come' then everyone would have run.

One has to ask why?

He was a born folk leader, and then of course he had Goebbels his Propaganda Minister who only showed Hitler from the good side. Hitler was like a god for our generation and for a lot of adult women.

Did he influence men as much?

I think Hitler was more effective with women and softer people because he worked on the emotions. My father was an emotional man and my mother was more intellectual and my father was much more of a follower.

One shouldn't follow one's emotions perhaps!

People who were critical at the time, people who informed themselves, they didn't progress like the people who accepted everything uncritically.

What do you think about today's educational systems.

For hundreds of years we had an authoritarian system but now we think that children need to be freer. There were a lot of young left intellectuals think that everything before was wrong. They rebelled against the old ways and and who let their children run wild. That really upset me when people went completely in the other direction without thinking about it properly. Now the pendulum has swung back and we are about in the middle but a lot of harm was done in those early years when people gave their children no direction.

One has to be critical as well as tolerant, both at once.

Yes one without the other is a human mistake. You can be the most intellectual person but if you are intolerant of other ideas, you win nothing.

INGE Z. 1925: AN APPRENTICESHIP THEN ANTI-AIRCRAFT UNIT

Inge Z.: born 1925 lived in Wiesbaden during the war

"One grew up in the Hitler movement without question. I was 14 when the war started. All the girls in my age group were in the Hitler movement."

How old were you during the war, and did the war change your education?

I was fourteen years old when the war began and I stayed in school until I was sixteen. I was in middle school and did the middle school leaving certificate. Then you had to do a 'duties-year' and join a family to do housework/

Did you have to do household duties or was there some other work you could have done in that year?

No you had to work in a household, that was a requirement of the household duty-year. You were called a duty-year girl and you were sent to people who had two or three children and couldn't get household help because they were all away at war, so you had to help for one year.

Did you live with the family?

Most of us lived at home and went to help the family we were allocated to in the morning. The family where I worked were on the Sonnenburg so I took a bus there every morning and came back in the evening. I took my food with me. Sometimes I even had to go on Sundays but there were no buses on Sundays so I had to walk and it took me an hour to walk there. I had a seven day week. Once the year was complete I did a bookkeeping apprenticeship.

Was that a happy year with the family?

Yes, I got on very well with the family I was helping.

Was that true for most girls?

Others did not have the good luck that I had and were exploited and had to do horrible jobs. I was very lucky with the family I was allocated.

Would you have preferred to start your apprenticeship earlier?

No, but I knew that I wanted to do a business apprenticeship afterwards.

In that respect the war didn't change much!

No not really.

So what did you do next?

I did a two and a half year apprenticeship.

Was that just for girls or were there boys in your course as well?

No that was a very small business that made very elegant men's suits. It was known throughout Germany and served very rich customers. It served those from 'high society'. I managed business affairs and I also helped in reception and sales. That is where I learned everything. That was such a small business, three salaried employees and fifteen manual workers who did the cutting and so forth. I was the only female on the staff, the others were all men.

Was that during the war?

Yes, that was in the middle of the war which began in 1939.

Did you notice that the men were away, or what sort of changes were there?

There were very few men around, only the old men were left, all the young ones had been called up.

And after your apprenticeship?

In 1944 when my apprenticeship ended I was called up for war duties.

Did you have to go?

Yes, you had to go because each business was only allowed a certain number of salaried employees. That was worked out according to how many manual employees there were and if you were excess you had to do war duties.

Could you choose where you were sent?

No. First they wanted to send me to Kalle, a factory in Wiesbaden-Biebrich. I got my orders to go there but then there was an air-raid which destroyed a large part of Kalle and the production line where I would have been employed was no longer working. So then I had to join the Flak, the anti-aircraft unit.

Did the girls who had to do war duties had no choice.

Yes, you just had to do what you were told.

How did you feel as part of the armed services? Hitler had spoken so much about how women should and have lots of children. How did you feel being in the army?

Actually you felt displaced. You didn't feel as if you belonged there, didn't feel as if you could keep up with the men. You felt like a sort of sniper. That is probably the wrong work, but really you felt somewhat displaced.

What did you have to do?

We had these big searchlights and were trained to use them. When aircraft flew over German territory we had to train these lights on these planes so that the artillery could see them better and shoot them down. I was not responsible for the searchlights, I operated the telephones at this anti-aircraft unit. I was in communications but I had two hours 'watch duty' every night. I had to stand in the cold fields and watch for planes.

Were the searchlights operated by girls?

Yes there were only girls. We had fifteen girls in the searchlight unit and one man as our boss. That was an old man who couldn't go to the front but who had to do war service. He was responsible for we girls.

Did the girls progress to higher positions when they stayed a long time in the army?

No, there was absolutely no thought of that. It was simply a duty to serve because you could see that every soldier was away and every girl was necessary and that was an obligation. No one thought of taking on any special duties.

Did this experience during the war make you more independent?

Yes, it made me more independent.

How and why?

We were away from our families for the first time. Until then I had always lived with my family and at the time you did more or less exactly what your parents told you. And now we had to stand on our own two feet, we had to make our own decisions. In retrospect that was not at all bad. I found it really good.

It helped you?

Yes, I thought it was good experience for life.

Were the other girls happy about it too?

Yes, I think we all thought the same thing.

Do you think the girls who served were different from those who had not?

Yes, I think so.

And did you enjoy it?

There was nothing to enjoy!. We had absolutely no change or relief. We were in the field in barracks and from morning to evening we were completely dependent for conversation on these other girls. And the job was quite hard ad complicated. We did have some contact with local farmers who took us under their wings a bit and occasionally invited us to their place when we had a free afternoon or day. We were allowed to go there and drink coffee. That was our only outside contact. You can't talk of enjoyment.

How much free time did you have?

Very little. We had a half day off per week.

How long were you there?

Half a year, from May 1945 until the war ended.

How did the farmers treat you in general?

The farmers were really nice. Each girl knew a farmer and they would be invited there. If you had a Sunday free you could go there for your midday meal. That was really nice. Then when the English came they took us in completely otherwise we would have ended up in prison. Each girl went to their special farmer.

Did you know how Germany was doing actually and what did you feel about that?

I think we all knew that things had got out of hand and that we tried to do too much at once and that we couldn't achieve what we had set out to do, at least not the way Hitler was doing it. I think we were all relieved when it was over.

There were lots of difficulties after the war. How did you get home?

First I was with the farmers for six weeks. I helped them in the house and everything went well for me. We couldn't do much because you could not move about freely. The British troops were alright in the main but there were enough rape cases to make us afraid of them.

After six weeks six or seven girls banded together to go home. The farmers gave us some food and an old pram they had had in the attic and we set off from Bremen to Wiesbaden. We walked 25 km a day and sometimes we were lucky and got a lift with a truck. There were a lot of people on the roads and it was dangerous because the mental institutions and prisoner-of-war facilities had been disbanded and the guest workers or prisoners were all on the road too. The Jews had been released and of course they were against everything to do with the army and it was all very dangerous. We found farmers, thank goodness, who let us sleep in the hay in their barns. We barricaded ourselves inside with whatever we could find but we were always frightened. It was white-knuckle living but we had to get home. The trains were not running and cars were not allowed on the roads, only supply trucks with food, but we had to get home.

We had a man from Luxembourg with us for part of the way and he had a flag on his jacket. When drunken Poles wanted to get us he would say 'No, we are from Luxembourg" and they would leave us aloe. We spent eight nights in barns without lights so we didn't draw attention to ourselves.

What did you do once you arrived?

Here in Wiesbaden everything was destroyed. There was lots of rubble but my parents house was still standing.

My parents had a butchers shop. Of course during the war everyone asked for 'a little bit more' but we could not give it to them because we were only given as much meat as the cards from last week's sales. It was very strictly controlled and we were always frightened of doing something wrong, of giving something away.

Were they able to continue their business?

Yes they were able to continue but it was very difficult. They had to pay but they could continue.

It sounds as if you had little contact with the male army personal?

No, there were very few men there, we had women all around us.

You were so young before the war, I suppose you were not aware if the feminist movement was well known?

No, I was too young and can't judge.

From 1933 onward women were meant to be at home. That was your generation.

Yes, that was true. In our generation it was thought that women belonged at home with the family, that a woman should stay at home as soon as she married and had children.

Did you ever consider, for example, that a woman could have a different political opinion to her husband?

No, the woman was not to have a political opinion at all.

Did you ever know anyone where the man was in one political party and the woman in another?

No that was never the case.

Do you think the Germans were treated well or badly after the war?

The Americans were here first and, now I must think back, you couldn't move freely around but we were not treated badly, no I couldn't say that.

If there had been no war, would you have continued your work as a business woman?

Yes, I think I would have continued.

Did you continue working later?

Yes, I started work again once I was home, in the same business where I had been. I was there seventeen years. Today I look back and regret that I didn't go somewhere else and get more experience elsewhere even though I enjoyed working there and I could do everything. I worked there even after I married, but stopped when Bettina was born.

Was it normal at the time to work after you had married?

Yes it was normal because we had nothing after the currency reform. We had to build up a household and we needed money for that . Things had changed.

Was it difficult to change? Formerly women were not meant to work after marrying and now they had to. Were there difficulties?

No, things had changed and these different circumstances were simply accepted.

Were women worried they may not find a husband?

No somehow not. We had letter contact with a lot of men . Many friends were away but we wrote to them and we thought that we would see them again.

How did it turn out? A lot of men had died and even many married women lost their husbands.

I was never confronted with this problem. I think people think more about that nowadays!

The younger generation or your generation?

The younger generation too. The children suffered and the hardship and worry about getting something to eat every day was so big that we never had time for such worries.

And what was it like when you saw the other side?

Yes, we felt betrayed, completely betrayed by having the whole national socialism forced down out throats, we were made stupid and kept stupid through the fine speeches. We had no way of seeing outside and that only became clear afterwards.

Would you take a more critical stand nowadays?

Yes but more critical. Today we don't believe everything we are told and we listen to opposite opinions.

Do you think that your generation is all like this?

Yes I think so. My generation changed.

Did you worry that you would not survive the war?

No never!

Do you think the men changed more than the women during the war?

Yes I think so. The men on the front came into direct contact with the enemy but for us at home it was different.

Did the women change too during the war?

Yes I think women changed a bit too. They became more independent because they were alone, some were alone with children, and they had to make all the decisions themselves. When the men returned we often heard there was friction between couples. My own parents took their parents in.

Did they have especial difficulties?

Yes, they had been confronted by the Russians because they lived in the Russian zone. My husband's sister hid the girls from the Russians because they were frightened of being raped and such like.

Did you also experience such things?

No that was not as bad. People helped each other much more than they do today.

HILDEGARD D. 1923: THE SUDETENDEUTSCH

Hildegard D., born 9 November 1923, lived in Karlsbad CSSR (now Karlovy Vary, western Bohemia, Czech Republic)

What was the reaction of people when the war began?

Well, what did we feel? We were the people from the Sudetenland[93] and we had been 'brought home' into the Reich in 1938. Well, good, that freed us from the oppression of the Czechs. Then there was war, but we had no idea how deeply that would affect us. We had been freed but now we were confronted by a war.

We Germans in the Sudetenland had never been free, we had always been oppressed by the Czechs. Czech was the only spoken language – everything was in Czech. I had been to school in German but I had to learn Czech. We common folk had always worked well together.

My father was unemployed for six years until Hitler came and brought us home. He freed us from this yoke. My father had not had work because the Czechs had occupied all the work places. Germans had been shoved to the side and oppressed. Then that changed in 1938 when the Führer came and freed us and the Czech lands were divided off. The Czech lands were a protectorate but we in the Sudentenland became part of the German Empire in 1938, in October 1938. A year later war broke out. Poland was brought

---

93 The **Sudetenland** ... is the German name (used in English in the first half of the 20th century) to refer to those northern, southwest, and western areas of Czechoslovakia which were inhabited primarily by ethnic German speakers, specifically the border districts of Bohemia, Moravia, and those parts of Silesia located within Czechoslovakia. (Wikipedia, 20/6/16)

home and then Saarland[94].

The older people understood what that all meant but we children didn't. My father was called up into the German army. The Czechs were not called up, only the Germans. The Czechs were deployed in the interior in 1942 or 43. The whole of Czechoslovakia was occupied by the Germans.

Women worked in the munitions factories. We wished for others that they would be freed just as we had been, for example the Poles and the Ukrainians who suffered under the Russian yoke. Those people were also never free.

How did people react as the war became progressed?

We realised it was serious at Dunkirk[95] in France. The occupation of Poland had been quite fast, but when France was invaded we realised it was serious. All the men were called up, even youngsters, and the girls joined fatigue duty (*Reichsarbeitsdienst*). When the going got tough the women often didn't see their menfolk for a year at a time.

My siblings and I were still small but my mother was called up and worked for the postal service. The postman had been conscripted and my mother had to do his job. The women with very small children were allowed to stay at home but all others had to join the war effort. My aunt worked in a munitions factory and my mother worked for the postal service.

---

94 The **Saarland** located on the border between France and Germany was created as a state by the Treaty of Versailles after WWI. The inhabitants voted to rejoin Germany in a referendum held in 1935. From 1947 to 1956 the Saarland was a French-occupied territory separate from the rest of Germany. In 1955, in another referendum, the inhabitants were offered independence, but voted instead for the territory to become a state of West Germany. (Wikipedia, 20/6/16)

95 May 1940

Were the women happy at having to work?

You know there was a great variation in response. Some were really enthusiastic. We were very idealistic and believed in the Führer. We would have walked through fire for him. People here in Germany blamed us for calling to Hitler to bring us home and for wanting war but if they had suffered under that yoke as we had then they would have wanted to be freed. For us the Führer was a saviour.

There were Communists and Social Democrats in Czechoslovakia and in Sudetenland and of course they thought differently but we were completely German nationalistic. ('wir haben ganz Deutch gedacht'). We were different.

Those times were not so bad. We cooked in the evenings and sent packages for food to soldiers who didn't have relations. When the farmers killed an animal they always brought us something. We held very much together. Even today we have regular meetings with people from back home. We simply think differently from other Germans.

Did people help each other?

A lot of people worked in agriculture and many of the farmers were conscripted so other farmers helped out with their machinery. I worked in the agricultural industry monitoring milk. Actually I wanted to have a different career but that was made impossible by the war. I had to wait until after the war. A lot of young people were deprived of an apprenticeship by the war and even the schools didn't operate normally because teachers were conscripted. Classes were combined, and that never happened in peace time.

When did you start to think that this war would not be won?

At the retreat from Stalingard[96]. By that time we knew we had lost the war. Getting provisions had become more difficult. In the beginning we had

---

96 February 1943

reserves and food stores but then it got worse and worse. We had taken in a woman from Saarland who suffered from shell shock. She came to us to recover but we didn't have much ourselves.

Karlsbad was bombed for the first time in April 1945. I was at work and was entombed in a cellar. At the time there was a hospital in the railway station and that was bombed. Bombs were flying everywhere.

What happened after the war?

We were occupied by foreign troops. The Eger River was occupied on one side by the Russians and on the other by the Americans. We were in the Russian zone. We were not allowed to keep radio and there were no newspapers. It all became Czech. The overthrow was in 1945 and we all had to wear white armbands, just like the Jews. They also had to wear white armbands with a star. In 1946 we were evacuated. That was a hard time, much more difficult than previously.

We thought that this was not a proper peace, that peace could not be like this. We had Russian officers stationed in our house. A lot of them spoke very good German. One of them had a radio and one day he told us they would be leaving in September. Then the Czechs came and they were dreadful. We had thought ' they are people like us so nothing bad would happen, but we were mistaken. That time was very bitter. The Russians had occupied the country but they had not hated us. The Czechs hated us. In the beginning when the Russians came we were occupied by Mongols and they were also nasty. But we didn't know our luck because the Czechs were very much worse.

We asked the Russians why they were leaving and they said their time was up and they were withdrawing to Dresden. Later the Russians completely withdrew from all of Czechoslovakia and we were abandoned to the Czechs. They told us we all had to leave, but we thought why should we go? We just didn't believe it, but then we heard on the radio, that the whole area was to be evacuated and re-settled. The Czechs wanted the whole area for themselves. They didn't want us there. We thought, dear God, how will be manage. But then came the assault – evacuation.

Evacuation began in 1945. I was evacuated with my parents in September 1946. A Czech policeman came with a form to be filled in that asked how many people we were. We were allowed to take 50kg per person. We were told where to assemble for transport and we were moved to a camp. The door to our house was sealed off. We were taken to a camp near Karlsbad and checked again before we were put into livestock wagons and taken to Wedden on the border. Then we came here. We were in a camp in Bavaria first. We lived in a big school in Neuberg an der Donau. Then we had to work and look for accommodation. That was very difficult because before we could get work we had to show we had accommodation.

How many people were in these wagons?

There were about 30 people per wagon, about 30 people with children and luggage. It would be sealed as it sat at the station so we couldn't get out until we were in Germany. When they oped the doors, then we knew we were here in the Reich. That is what happened to us.

I have to say that here in the old-Reich, there were many more bombs, but we lost our home. I don't know which was worse. We suffered a lot from loosing our land and home. They at least kept their land and were able to rebuild. But we had no home, n o work, no apartment, nothing.

Do you feel like a foreigner in Germany?

No you couldn't say that. We are Germans like all the rest. But we are accused by some of wanting what happened. They say, 'You called for Hitler to bring you home into the Reich.' That really hurt.

That is no longer so today. They used to call us potato grubs and say what a burden we were. The Germans didn't want us because they had nothing themselves. They didn't have anything to eat, whole cities were bombed to the ground and on top of that they had to accommodate us, these thousands of refugees. But we had not fled, we had been evacuated. Some people came over the border without permission. I myself came over twice to see my husband. He was here in Mainz in an American prisoner of war camp. He couldn't come back home or the Czechs would have got him. They took every man who came back who had been German and they would have taken him even though he never belonged to any party. He was only a member of the gymnastics club but that would have been sufficient grounds to take him away and we would have never seen him again. None of the German men were able to come home. If they had fallen into the hands of the Czechs they would have had to work for them, deep in the coal mines and we wouldn't have seen them again. They took my uncle even though he had never been in the German army. He was too unfit for conscription and he stayed home and looked after those who had been left behind. He had no other function, but he was taken away to a camp that was like a concentrations camp where they had to do hard labour, loading rubble etc.

Do you think that war was different then?

Yes, maybe. Refugees always have a lot of difficulties. When you see the television reports of Vietnam you understand what the refugees are going through. We went through the same traumas.

Do you think that the women suffered as much as the men during the war?

Yes, the father was away. I would almost say that the women suffered more because they didn't know how they could carry on. The last attacks on us were in 1946. In Germany they had more problems during the war than we did and suffered more at that time, but we lost our homeland. The men had to go into the army at fifteen or sixteen. They were just children and had no idea why. We thought when we were brought home that everything would be good now, but the things that happened afterwards were not things we wished for. We thought that once we were free things would get better, but we were mistaken. Everything became more difficult than it had been before. We would not have been able to imagine that. There were more Germans in Czechoslovakia than Czechs. There were 30% Czechs and 70% Germans. The cities of Marienbad and Karlsbad were world renowned health resorts but no international guests go there now. . Everything is going to ruin, it is such a pity as they were such beautiful cities.

When we arrived here we had nothing but today almost all of us has a house or something. We worked ourselves up the ladder. Everyone says that, we helped the economy recover. There is no woman amongst us that doesn't work. We are used to working, we worked in our own homeland as well. When we came here we had to work to earn money and set ourselves up again.

Would you go back if you could?

If we could go back we would. If the Germans were there and we had a German government we would return immediately. My parents house still stands. We went back there four years ago and found everything as it had been. It was the first time my son had been there. He was born here and doesn't know his home. Every year at Pentecost a meeting of people from Sudetenland is held and thousands of people turn up. The feeling of belonging together is very strong because we all lost something. It was always very hard when we learned that a father had died or that a son would not come back. We all knew each other very well. It was tough.

Would you support setting up Government in Sudentenland again, possibly after war?

We would not want to have war again. We would only go with amicability. Certainly not with war. The area was German forever but we wouldn't want to take it back by force. I wouldn't have the nerve to go through that again. At the time it was all so different. There was no television, no newspapers apart from the small village papers. Today you can read and listen and be informed. We can't be misled as we were then. Today with the modern weapons everything would be even worse. If we lost everything all over again and had to start again, I don't think I could cope. That would be just dreadful.

GERDA D. 1922 : A CHEEKY BERLINER

Gerda D. : Born 1922, lived in Berlin during the war.

Handwritten

Before the war we lived in Berlin. We had an apartment on the ground floor and our balcony was on a busy street where protesters marched on their way with petitions. We were sicked once Hitler assumed power how the protesters were treated. Their hair was set alight with burning sticks carried by the police. It was dreadful. They all dashed past our balcony. By the time the war started there was of course no opposition left.

On tape:

It was high summer and I came back in August. They wanted to have me as hairdresser but I said no, I have already promised myself so I can't. Then they said to me, one path we cannot spare you is the one to Potsdamstrasse. They will ask you some questions there. On the way to the employment office was a telephone box. I rang my father quickly from there to tell him I had to go to the Potsdammerstrasse. I didn't know when Hitler was born, he had never interested me. My father knew all that sort of thing and he knew when the old Fritz was born. So I quickly wrote that down – he was born in Braunau in April 1923, or something like that. Afterwards I had to report there every week for a whole year. I was interrogated. I was so cheeky and naive.

Why did you have to report there every week?

I had to report because during Hitler's time I had been in a abroad for a year. The department I had to report to had all the singers and dancers and artists. All people, like dancers that had been in foreign countries. When they came back they had to report to this department and were sent through the political mills. So I had to go there too and was given a number and had to wait to be called. The people you reported to were all SS uniforms. You were given a four page questionnaire you had to fill in. You were asked when you had been abroad, why you had come back, if you had had contact with any Germans while you were away and who they were. Lots and lots of questions, but especially about which Germans you had had contact with while you were away. My friend said, when asked why she came back, that she'd been homesick. That is always true and it sounds good too. I wrote that as well. I also had to take passport photos.

My daddy had had made me a costume and dresses you could wear with lace blouses underneath, and a blouse which a prissy little good-girl collar. Then I was three years older than and had grown my hair long. Earlier the dresses had had flounces and were worn with organdie blouses. So now I had to get new passport photos so I had my hair cut and coloured a red colour in Berlin and had a completely different wardrobe. Then he said to me that I looked one way in one photo, a different way in another but in reality I looked completely different.

On the day I had to deliver my passport photo I noticed a young man with brown hair sitting waiting there. He had a civilian jacket on but SS boots and trousers. He was sitting there too but looked different to all the artists. After I was finished and had been booked in for the next Tuesday I went down the steps. He came after me and said he would like to meet me again and asked if we might make a date. I knew immediately that he was s spy. When you are young you have courage, particularly if you have a clear conscience. So I said, yes why not! I knew immediately he was a spy, a snitch. Then he asked if he could have a photo of me. Of course I had my photos with me but I immediately thought, there, that proves he is a spy. A photo so he could find me at our rendezvous. I told him it was a bit early for that. Maybe later if you are very good. I met him three or four times and he always conducted himself well. He never once asked any political questions.

One day there was a band playing beautiful romantic music and he came clean. His parents were Germans who lived in Czechoslovakia where his father had a factory and he was a student. His mother lived in a villa etc etc. Hitler had already been there with his hordes to soften up the masses. And just as their ideas were taken up by the youth here, so in Czechoslovakia the youth flocked to them, especially students such as this young man. He was convinced, he had let himself be persuaded and was now completely for Hitler. But the Czechs had got wind of what was happening and had not wanted a bar of it, which was their perfect right. They arrested these young men. But Hitler knew what had happened and which jail they had been sent to and his people attached the prison and freed these young men. They had been brought straight to Germany, first to Dresden and then further. And he had been recruited as a spy. He was not allowed any contact with his parents in Czechoslovakia. On that evening he was so sentimental and so 'had it'. He lamented his fate and said now he had to go to Dresden as he had a new case to follow up and spy on, someone he had had something to do with in Czechoslovakia.

As soon as I knew for certain that he was a spy I lost interest. I wasn't interested in him as a person. I had so many friends myself I didn't need to think about him.

And so it continued. The SS shouted at me, first one and then another and always in a different room. One of them shouted at me that now I was working and I was not allowed to and that by autumn I would be unemployed. I replied, well in autumn I can always hang myself. Then I was told to go back and bring my passport, but when I returned I only went with my passport number written down. I left my passport at home.

One day I had a free day and the bell rang at seven in the morning and it was the police who said they wanted to question me. The policeman said, listen to me, come to the station, room 28 to see Superintendent Schwetziner.

When I told him who I needed to see, the official downstairs said, 'What, you have to go to him?'

I said yes and he said, 'Then I'll come with you!'

So he came with me to a room somewhere on the second floor. In that room were three desks and three men.

Then the old man took me by the arm and said, 'Let me introduce you to my young friend, she is no Communist!'

Then they all asked questions. What newspaper did I subscribe to, which newspaper my parents subscribed to, where my nearest location group was and what they thought of me.

I asked, 'What is this whole theatre about, can you tell me?'

They said I had to accept the fate of an immigrant.

Then 18 months later I was called again, in the afternoon. The interviewer was in civilian clothes and I was given tea and cakes. I could see my file was very thick by that time, sitting on the desk. It had 'Gerda Meyer, Paris' written on the front cover. He asked me why I wouldn't say I had been in Paris. Finally he told me that they thought I was the Gerda Meyer who had lived in Paris with a Jew and had had a baby with him. Of course I had never had a baby, but he still didn't fully believe me.

Nine months later I met my husband and then I never heard another word. Then I was suddenly Frau T. and no longer Meyer with 'y'!

My husband was the only son of a father who had been killed in WWI. He had to do a short training, only 3 months and was due home on 1 September. His duty was extended by a month then he was sent to the front when the war began.

What happened when the war began?

We went to work as usual on 1st September. I wont forget that day at 11am. We had to fill out work operating sheets and such like. Then there was an announcement that we should all stop working. My boss had two doctorates, and an engineering degree. The technical drawing staff were behind a glass window. We turned on the radio.

"I have decided to take the Polish border!"

Hitler!

Now I must tell you something. My mother in law had a neighbour who always listened to the radio, enemy radio! She had called me to her and had said, 'Gerda, listen!' and that was the night when there was a Pole on the radio crying and lamenting. He implored God for help. This man said, and I will never forget it, 'Hitler stands at our gates. Our little Poland will be trodden on and destroyed. But you Germans, don't forget, that we have the whole world standing on our side. If Hitler invades there will be a world war.'

We in Germany had always wondered why the Americans had not reacted when Hitler marched into Czechoslovakia. They let it just happen. Why? I don't know the answer.

This Pole though, he said, 'We will be crushed but the world stands behind us!'

And now we are sitting at work and hearing 'I have decided to take Poland!'

Did women have to work?

My mother was an older woman but she had to work at the post office, sorting mail. She had compulsory service, I remember. I no longer lived at home as I was married. My husband was sent to France where he opened a Cafe in the Officers barracks.

What did you have to eat during the war?

We were frugal with food. When I remember back, these few grams. My father later rented half a farm. The other half was owned by the local farmers organisation.

Did people help each other?

No one helped me! Women became more independent, they had to. I was always self reliant. My husband's mother had bossed him around. In some marriages the man came back and found that their wives had taken in another man.

Was food short?

Yes, when I think about those few grams. Every ten days the butcher visited and each time he visited you had to give him a paper with your order for his next visit and you were only allowed the few grams that were recorded on your food ration card. You weren't allowed more. Today the war broke out and tomorrow the ration cards were there. Everything had been pre-prepared.

I married during the war. I got an allowance for one set of bed linen. I didn't even get one pair of shoes. I had to paint a pair of crocodile shoes I had black so they matched my black coat and black fur piece. That was at the end of October.

What did you do in your free time?

We had this small piece of land where we planted carrots and parsley and all sorts of herbs. Then they grabbed me. They said that in the fourth year of war you have no choice. They gave me along title, Clerical assistant to the Air raid subgroup leader! I had to do all the writing for the courses in air raids shelter and red cross. My mother did one of these red cross courses and in the fourth year I was ordered there They no longer requested, they ordered. I had to become a midwife. I had to carry a bag with all the things you need for a birth, ties for the umbilical cord, scissors etc that had been boiled. I took part in 40 births at the clinic, and then I was a midwife myself. I didn't want to do it, I wasn't made for that sort of work, I don't have the nerves for it. I had to do it once in an air raid shelter. I sent someone away for another midwife and she came.

Did you live in Berlin?

I did for the first part of the war but not later. I lived in the countryside just out of Berlin during the last part of the war.

Did you experience the bombing.

Yes, I was often in Berlin to do my shopping and sometimes there were two bombing raids in a night. My mother-in-law lived on the fourth floor and we had to go down with the baby to the air-raid shelter in the cellar. I was sometimes so exhausted I didn't even hear the sirens. Then I would wake and say 'Mummy, Mummy!'

But she just said 'Oh it's not so bad and I would put the baby on a pillow and take our small air-raid suitcase and down we would go . We had to go past the glass window on the landing and I was frightened to go past because of the flak splinters. The air raid shelter was in the courtyard immediately at the bottom of the stairs and the flak splinters rained down on the courtyard. Then I would sit down there and shake. Later the balcony was torn off the house and walls fell in. That's why I moved to the countryside, 128km from Berlin.

Did you know people there?

Yes my parents lived there. They had moved there in October 1940 when they had been bombed out. I took my furniture and was given a room with them. That was 1941. In 1942 my husband was killed. The baby was one and a half.

When Hitler was in Russia my father said 'now we have lost the war.'

My father always said that if we had won the war Hitler would have occupied Yugoslavia, Czechoslovakia,Sweden, Norway, Denmark – he would have occupied them all. And England and France. There would have been no one left in Germany. We would not have had enough people to occupy all these countries.

Were you informed of your husband's death by letter?

My husband had got a month's holiday after a year away and it was a wonderful holiday. From 1 May to 1 June, or something like that. We went to Kottbus and in the evening we went to the theatre. It was a wonderful holiday but then he was sent back to the front.

I put in a submission – I went to the police station and made such a theatre. Then I got a positive response and I could have hugged the whole world. Then I went back to my home. I had stayed 14 days in Berlin after he left and got letters while I was there and I read them and was so joyful and so happy. Well good, I went back to Berlin and I was there 5 days when the local administrator landlord came with landlord papers for party functionaries and also letters which he delivered. He delivered this letter. And I screamed 'It's not true, it's not true!'

My mother-in-law screamed, "My beautiful boy, my beautiful boy!"

It happened 14 days after his holiday. I got all the letters back that I had written him in the meantime. He had never got them. He died at 10:30 am.

They wanted to transfer me to a workplace in a factory that was miles from where I lived and I simply refused. I might have looked after the Kindergarten to help them, but I was not going to work for Hitler.

But now I was in a modern house where there was a wash-house with a lovely deep copper kettle. My mother liked to do her washing at my place because there was nothing like my copper at her old house. The village where I was living was Lug which was 15, 16 or 17 km from Senftenberg which is a coal area. The Leuna factory was a Benzine and Coal plant and interesting for the enemy. Many people where I lived and also many foreigners worked at the Leuna plant and now the English were bombing it. The bombers came now by daylight. They looked like silver fish in the sky. One at the front and the others all behind it.

Oh God, that didn't really worry us any more, we were so used to bombing raids by then. So they were flying over us as we were there washing in the old copper kettle. There were no washing machines. You put the clothes in the copper kettle and then boiled it. I ran into the house to get some more washing and my mother was standing in the wash-house stirring the clothes in the copper. The planes had just dropped their bombs over Leuna and I was standing on the doorstep of the wash-house when I heard a click of the bomb door opening. I was transfixed. I couldn't move a muscle. My nerves were completely shot. I just stood there. Later someone told me that if you hear the click you wont get hit by the bomb and in fact it landed 50 or 60 meters away. They had been aiming at a bridge on the autobahn, but the bomb landed beside it.

The husband of our neighbour who worked in Leuna told us that we shouldn't show our naked arms or hang out the washing because the enemy would see that. His wife sat with their two children in the garden. This man had made two small bunkers in the garden for them.

Some planes had been shot down near us. One Bronco and a Welzo. When the fighter planes climbed higher there was always a barrage but the farmers were so stubborn you know and didn't hear anything. But I dressed my child at night and waited downstairs. When Dresden was bombed then there was a big fuss, on the radio and everywhere.

As the war was ending did the Russians come?

First came the refugees. We had to accommodate refugees in our house. That was not my house but I was a good friend of the housewife. I had the attic apartment. A woman from Berlin and her daughter was placed beneath me in a single room. Then there were party people who worked in the electrical utility, with their son. The owner lived downstairs and in her living room there was a refugee family. I think they had five children. They had to sleep on the floor. My own daughter had a sweet little child's bed with a Raphael angel on it. My mother had given me material and I sewed a cover. It was such a sweet little bed. Ever since my husband had died my daughter said she dreamt about the big bad wolf and she wanted to sleep with me. Then my mother asked her if she could sleep in the sweet little bed and after that my daughter was happy to sleep there. That was her little heaven. My sister in Berlin had a daughter who was bigger and she had given me clothes

I gave these people so much. They said they had had to leave within two hours, take the things they needed for next day and go. She said, 'Oh I wish I had taken my best shoes.' Her husband has packed two sacks of flour onto the cart and when I brought all these things to her she gave me a pillow slip full of flour and one full of cornflour. Then an order came and they were swept away. I saw these people again in Magdeburg. Then it was January and it was ice cold with thick snow and suddenly there were refugees at the local farm-leaders. My mother was a red cross sister and she was ordered there. They arrived paralysed and frozen in their army vehicle. My mother helped get some children out. My papa and I went to our house next door and our mother came and said there is a pram, shouldn't we take that as well. And the grandmother said that was for the youngest child but he was frozen. They had had to flee Poland and the child died of cold. My mother was always so fond of small children and in the first world war a child had died on the way.

But now I have to tell you a sad story. The refugees had to go on to Senftenberg and the party member there was charged with looking after them. He asked them which of the sacks they had with them should be brought inside. They told him what was inside them, but said not to bring one sack because that was grandmother who had died on the way. He lifted the sack and said it doesn't feel like a person, so they opened the sack to see. They found a pig inside. Someone had robbed them on the way and had taken the grandmother in the sack. They would have much rather the pig had been stolen. They wanted to bury her. That actually happened, it is not a made up story. Someone took the dead grandmother. It is a tragicomedy isn't it? Now I didn't know the people personally, so I have a bit of a distance.

Then the Russians came?

Yes, five hours later. First the fleeing German soldiers came, came and came. Then there was five hours of shooting and then everything was quiet. Then a man arrived, the director of the electricity plant. He had his eye on me. He was a widower and he drove to our place. And everyone had to gather, me included. The groups leader, the air raid leader etc and we were told we had to defend to the last and if the only thing the women could do was throw boiling water out of the window, that is what we should do.

I said, I am very sorry but my husband is dead and I have to live for my daughter. One pot of boiling water is not going to win the war. If the German army can't stop them then my pot of water wont. He had no reply. I said that in front of everyone.

First we were told to flee, then we were told to stay and fight and not to flee. I had a lot of jewellery which I put in a box and buried. My sister-in-law did the same. If you have lived through so much terror you become incapable. First this shooting for five hours, then this conference where we were told to defend ourselves. I went from my apartment to the house of my parents and on the way I met a handsome man on a horse. He was Russian. The farmers told us there had been knocking on the window in the night – they had just wanted water, nothing else. They had heard bits of Russian and thought the Russians had arrived but it was not the Russians. It was the Flosek troops, the troops of General Flossek with Russian prisoners. He had put them to work but the Russians were not stupid. They had shown those on the other side vodka they had and had made them drunk on Vodka.

What was your experience with the Russians?

Okay well. Someone had hidden his motorcycle in the shed. Then someone from the army came and said we should open our windows and that he had been charged to detonate the autobahn bridge. My father told him that that was not going to change the war, whether or not he damaged the bridge.

Then my acquaintance said 'Come, lets drink a Schnapps beforehand, and we got him drunk and kept him busy so he didn't blow up the bridge. The Russians didn't use this bridge, it would have been blown up for nothing. They came through the woods or by road.

So now it was like this: now it was afternoon. My sister-in-law was gone with the refugees. The farmers had loaded up their wagons and had fled. We were from Berlin, we had no tractors or wagons. We couldn't run away. I had only a bicycle. Some people who had a bit of building expertise had built themselves bunkers but now they had all fled. I got the bicycle ready, with some biscuits, a bottle, my child and a pillow, if I remember rightly. In front I had a little saddle where the child sat, and I rode over to my parents. My younger brother was with them. He had bad asthma and they couldn't leave. My father said he would go in search of a bunker so we had somewhere to sit when they began shooting. I went over to my mother's who told me my father was out looking for a bunker. Then I realised my mother had no bread and that I had left the bread I had bought at home. So I told her I had bought a whole loaf of bread that morning. The road to the autobahn went directly past the house and I went out onto that street to ride to my house when a bullet whizzed past my head. A wounded German officer stood at the fence and behind him in the woods were the Russian reconnaissance troops. They had been shooting at him not at me, but I ran off. I was afraid to go back the same way so I ran through the fields.

I had heard from my husband that they were thieves. I was robbed. They could have shot me but they didn't. The English did shoot, at a wedding. The whole wedding party jumped into the ditch. Or if they saw a single person on the field, they immediately shot them, that is something I saw myself. But the Ruskies didn't.

Did you suffer at all under the Russians?

My mother had some flour in the cellar of the guest house, the sort of thing you have in storage. When the shooting started I ran with the child into the cellar. Mama, mama we are in the cellar. But my bike was left standing upstairs against the wall. I had our important papers with me and the bottle for the baby. I also took the cheap watch and put it on so I could give it to the first Russian I saw. There was a 16 year old Russian girl there. The farm was managed by a couple who lived in the town and they had brought the girl there. She cried the whole time for her mother.

At Pentecost we had to go through the kitchen to get to the toilet. All the foreigners went out walking along the village main street. We had our garden, our field and our chairs and it was good. Pentecost was hot and we went about without stockings. Maria had such lovely black plaits. The house had thick walls and had a small opening to the outside. When the

Russians came and were shooting Maria called out in Russian "Oh Russian brothers don't shoot, I am waiting for you." They stopped shooting. They were really upset.

Then they came back and ripped my bag from me and I helped them take off the watch. Everything was gone. They made us go upstairs, aiming their pistols at us. The General and his personnel and they were done up for sore eyes. Perfectly dressed with medals on their jackets. They went into the next room with us, my mother, me and my baby, my younger brother and Maria. Then suddenly they shouted at us that we were not to talk to each other. That was forbidden.

The General asked me something I didn't understand so Maria was asked to translate. He had asked why we were so pale. I answered that I was waiting to be shot. They all laughed and said 'Goebbels propaganda!' They wanted something to drink but we didn't have running water. Maria always had to drink first from anything they were given. They didn't trust us and they thought they might be poisoned. Then the asked about where our husbands were. We lied, and instead of saying they had died in Russia we said they died in France. At the time I was 33 but I looked younger and they didn't believe me and got angry. Otherwise they were like children, but if they thought they were being lied to they got really angry and became nasty.

Then it got dark. The neighbouring house was owned by a Swiss who looked after all the cows in summer. They were a married couple without children and the house was always an example of beauty and cleanliness. That house was next door with only a fence between us. The Russkies beat down that fence. They didn't know where the German home guard was which was why they shot the first house in the village into flames.

My child always had a good appetite. I was always reprimanded and told I should eat as well, but I couldn't, I always had a lump in my throat. But then I had a glass of champagne which tasted wonderful. Four weeks later my neighbour told me that it had been from France.

Three times it happened that he wanted to shoot me. He foamed at the mouth and, but Maria threw herself in front of me. But at the worst time I was strong, I pushed Maria out of the way and I took my baby and went with them. I thought I would be stood against the next wall and shot. We didn't have electricity, it had been cut off. The man who had told us to fight to the last had surrendered with a white flag. Now I was taken into a room that had been the bedroom of the couple. There was an empty bottle there with a candle, and he said 'woman and baby sleep there.' Actually, he protected me this night. There were two thousand Russian troops in our town. My child and I were so exhausted we fell asleep immediately.

In the meantime there were refugees who had arrived. They were from Breslau. We had chairs in the cellar. There was an old man and an old woman and they had a daughter with them of about 30. They had lots of jewellery and three fur coats with them in a pram. Ever since Breslau people had been telling them they should hide their jewellery. They asked me what they should do. I told them that there was a foresters house nearby and I knew the Forester. He said they could stay, the couple, a young woman. I never saw them again.

Where did I stop. Oh yes, my child lay down in her coat and slept. I sat on the edge of the bed next to the baby. I had never fainted in my life, but I fainted then. I thought to myself, now I am in the hands of the enemy in every sense of the word. The next morning they got an order to march on. Then they were out and I went looking for my mama. I found her and we went to our house with my brother. And the Russians were there, on the floor and everywhere. Our dog lay in the corner, he had been shot. It was awful. Then suddenly there were aeroplanes, and they were German planes. They knew where the Russian troops were.

Then the Russian girl Maria came and said she'd hide us. There were stalls at the group leaders place . The Russkies had let all the animals out because there was no one there to feed them. Now the bombs were falling and the Russians were running here and there. The conquerors had left and we had another group who wore leather jackets. Just as we were wanting to run off this chap came and grabbed us. The planes were overhead and there was chaos and shooting. The chap wanted to interrogate us but then he was ordered to move on. They were very jumpy. He left but he said we should stay where we were.

My mother said, 'Come, let's run, quick!'"I said " But we'll be shot if we run."

'Well if we are shot, then we're shot,' she said.

Then we ran to the stables. We crouched there as the war plans flew over, It was awful.

Then Maria brought us a pail of milk, an egg and food for the child. But we were discovered there as well and we ran again to a big shed. There was a huge pile of hay there, about two stories high. Really huge. We hid in the hay. I had a pillow over the head of my child and over mine. As if that would have helped! But anyway, we hid there until evening. We hadn't had anything to eat, but at least the children had had milk. That evening Papa came and the planes stopped, but the second wave of Russians also arrived. My parents couldn't go to their place any more so we ran to my place. My father said that a group of Polish men and women had met on the roads and were robbing places.

Now I must tell you, there came a great tall black officer, like a descendant of a dynasty of Princes. He grabbed me and took me with him upstairs to where there was a buffet of food. There was a bed and there I stood. I don't know why, it wasn't like that earlier. I had a costume on and over the top a coat and he shagged me like that.

There was another one there who said 'Now we should swap' and I thought that it could get interesting. But he said, no I wont swap! Man I was so relieved! That was great – I found that wonderful. In the morning they delivered food to us. More planes came in the night, German planes but he said not to to be frightened as they were the Amis and they knew where we were. I had not known the difference between German and American planes. Then they had to leave. Berlin had not yet been taken.

The commotion continued. Then one day there was a knock at the door and it was the officer who had not touched me earlier. It was the rule that a

Russian was not allowed to protect a German woman or treat her as his possession. She was the possession of all – that was the rule. The simple soldier was gone and my hero stayed – six or eight days, I am no longer sure. The others sat in front of the door. Then he did what he had previously not done.

Then the Tatars came. A handsome black fellow. He said 'I am Tartar, not a Russian. And some of them said "Stalin is shit!" and later they were sent to Siberia.

Then suddenly the daughter of Frau Meuer said "Mama I am hungry" and she replied "I have nothing here child."

The Russian came back and she asked but he said, 'Don't understand!"

She said "You say you don't understand. But you understand shit don't you?"

He laughed and tapped her on the shoulder.

 There were still some SS around and they were shooting at us. Then the Russians chased the SS like crazy. Then they sent us to the Foresters lodge. He had had the radio and he had been sent to prison in April. They came and took away the radio and we didn't know the war had ended. We had no electricity, nothing. The Russians who had occupied out area had an order to free the Autobahn. The prisoners of war came through there. Then they rounded up the cows again.

My landlord became the town mayor and I was his secretary. We made the inventory. The Russians took all the cows away.

MARGA S. 1919: WAR AS A YOUNG WOMEN

Marga S.: born 1919, spent the war in Frankfurt and München-Gladbach

[Marga S. typed some some additional notes to add to (or replace) the interview transcript when she reviewed it. These are in italics with the label 'Additional notes from Frau S'.]

"When I told my husband you wanted to interview me he said, "Why does she want to talk to you? You weren't in the war.""

When the war began. What did people think. Were they happy or surprised?

I was born in 1919 so I was twenty years old then. I grew up in Hitler's Germany and I was a member of the BDM, although I joined very late. That shouldn't be seen as an excuse, I was Catholic. I was a member of the catholic youth and it took us a long time to become part of the BDM. But we did become enthusiastic about Hitler and we thought, well now it begins. As 19 and 20 year-olds it was not shocking, but for my mother it was different.

I will never forget her saying, "For God's sake!"

At the time it was twenty or twenty five years since the last war, and I remember thinking as a young girl that that was a long time ago. Our parents were different, they said 'it is only just over' because 25 years is about a human life, more or less. So for me it was not frightening, but although we were not scared we were sad. In the first semester we had forty men, but in the second semester in autumn of 1939 the war had begun and there were only four men. And six girls.

Additional notes from Frau S.

When Hitler took power in 1933 I was 14 years old and when the war began I was not yet twenty. My youth was defined by his regime. I came from the catholic youth movement but by the time I was 17 I had been more or less pressured to join the BDM so I didn't offend more politically active people. My mother had been called to the school to explain why I had not joined. I came from a very strict catholic parental house.

Most people were Hitler fans, even if we late starters, so the beginning of the war didn't shock me. My mother was horrified. I remember so well how she said 'Good God, it is only twenty years since the last war!" For a young girl like me, twenty years seemed a long time.

In those months I was studying at the textile school in Moenchen-Gladbach-Rhydt in Rheinland. The war started during our semester holidays and from the 46 course participants in the first semester only nine were left in the second semester (40 men and 6 women/ four men and 5 women). We were not surprised but we were sad because firm friendships had been torn apart.

Was that at technical college?

Yes that was technical college and we were a bit biased because you couldn't be otherwise. After being shocked and sad, then we were 'Now we'll be bigger."

Did you have the feeling it was the only way out for Germany?

At that age I had no ideas, I didn't think about it. It is different today where 18 and 19 year-olds discuss politics but we grew up in a totalitarian state and there wasn't anything else. We had to believe what our German teachers told us. The religious instruction was evangelical.

Additional notes from Frau S.: At that age we had not through a lot about many things We accepted it because we were were made to believe that there was no alternative, that it had to be this way to make Germany larger and more powerful again. Today the youth ask questions in school and discuss political situations but in a totalitarian state we had to accept ideological theses that were taught to us in various subjects. Whether war was the only way out for Germany was never discussed.

Did the older generation understand what was happening?

I think so. I can only judge from my mother because my father died early, but my mother always said "Good that your father is dead, if he had had to live through this it would have been dreadful. As a catholic he could never have tolerated Hitler's ideas. He was a school teacher and he would have had to leave the school. Who knows what would have happened to him. That is what my mother always said. But today my husband blames that generation, also that of his elder brother, for not informing us or explaining what was happening.

Additional notes from Frau S.: yes I think so. I can only report about my mother. My father died early. He was a primary school teacher, an extremely religious man, strict but fair and with a very ethical character. According to my mother he would never have been able to adapt to during the Hitler regime and would have had to leave the school. We youngsters heard that but just shrugged our shoulders. We didn't take it nearly as seriously as if it had been told us directly by a family member, especially a male person of authority like a father. The forcefulness was missing and one was anxious about being denounced. My husband now blames his much older brothers and their generation, who were students at the end of the first world war, for not clarifying what was happening and informing us better.

The boys wouldn't have known anything either when they were sent to fight?

No. They just went. My husband says so as well. He was studied economics in Kiel and he acquired a different viewpoint and understood things better. He still talks about one man who came to give a lecture, I think he was in the navy. He was a high ranking official wand he gave a lecture to what I would call an illustrious group of professors and students.

He told them, "this is not going to end well. We will lose the war!" He illustrated his view from the economic perspective.

Additional notes from Frau S.: *I can't judge that, they simply went because they were ordered to. My husband was then my boyfriend and was studying economics in Kiel and had a wider perspective. A high officer who lectured to select circles showed them in 1940 that from the applied economics viewpoint the war could not be won by Germany. That was only in the second year of the war! My husband was called up shortly afterwards.*

Was that unusual?

That was very unusual.

Wasn't it dangerous?

I said later, "How could that man have said such a thing!" But as I said, that was said in a certain circle, the same sort of people who later formed the resistance. They were already there beforehand. So that was certainly dangerous, but …

Additional notes from Frau S.: *Yes it was very dangerous but as I said, this lecture took place with a select group of trusted students. The resistance was later formed from this and other such groups*

What did you first notice when the war started?

Nothing much changed in the beginning.

Just the boys were away?

Yes, that was the first thing. My husband was my boyfriend at the time, he was called up in 1940 straight after his exam. They went from the exam room to the barracks. For weeks, and then to foreign lands. My brother was also called up but came back from Poland badly injured after only six months. Later he was judged unfit for service because he had lost two fingers on his right hand. My husband served for four years on the Russian front with many spells in the field hospitals. He went right to east of Moscow and then was part of the retreating forces. His war was of opposing forces on the battlefield in all its real and gruesome horror.

It must have been difficult for your mother with your brother away?

Yes, yes certainly. My parents were married and they certainly felt everything more than my generation. We were so young and had not had personal experience and didn't understand the meaning or the consequences. But my mother said, 'Well now he is home, he lost two fingers but at least he is home.'

I married after the war. I was engaged during the war and my fiancée and I wanted to get married but my mother said 'Not with my permission', so we waited.

Additional notes from Frau S.: Yes indeed.! All women whose menfolk had to go to war felt the pain much more than we did. My mother was so happy to have my brother back home, despite his crippled hand.

Do you think, looking back, that she was right?

Yes. I think I came through the war with less scars than I would have had I been married or had children. I was free and independent.

So what did you do during this time. Were you studying or working?

Both! I finished my studies and then I started work as a fashion consultant in a textile factory and then after a year I was called up as well to do war duties. I had to work in a munitions factory. I was working in the office. The firm built mobile workshops for use in the field to repair all sorts of tanks and vehicles. So it was a type of armament factory.

Additional notes from Frau Scherer: *Both. After my second semester I stopped studying and worked then as fashion adviser and procurer in a textile factory. After a year I was obliged to join the war effort and I had to work in the office of a munitions factory. This factory produced workshops for the repair of military vehicles, tanks and armoured vehicles etc., for use in the field.*

Did you work on the factory floor as well?

No the women didn't work in the workshop but only in the office. The factory was counted as an armaments factory so the men working there were excused from military service, that is until later when every man was needed and they had to leave, But most of them did their military service in the factory.. But after two years there I was able to leave there. I had done a lot of work and running around to all sorts of government departments and people I knew and I was finally released and able to go back to my previous firm. I travelled around as a buying agent. But later they enlisted me again and sent me to work in a prisoner camp, actually a prisoner of war camp where English prisoners were kept after they had been shot down. They were sent to a camp near Frankfurt where they were kept for a couple of days and had their details taken and so forth. Then later I was sent to a real prison and worked in an office there. That was also counted as military service.

Additional notes from Frau S.: *No, only in the office. Men who had been released from military duty to work in armaments worked in the factory. Two years later, with the help of contacts who knew people in the bureaucracy I got my old job in the textile factory back. Men were missing from all industries and women had to fill the gaps everywhere, included responsible positions. I traveled by train to textile producers in all parts of Germany and also Poland and France to buy up for our wholesale firm, so we had products to supply to the small shops. I also had work for some time in a transit camp for English prisoners of war.*

Did you discover anything there?

That was in Frankfurt in the Pamengarten, the back part was separate and we didn't go there. Only our German officers had contact with the Prison officers, not we ourselves.

Additional notes from Frau S.: No. Only the offices had access to the camp. The office was outside the camp.

What were the first difficulties for you?

The fact that I had to leave my profession. That was when I first noticed the change, when I had to leave my job. But as I said, after some work on my part I was able to go back after two years. I traveled around the whole of Germany, despite the hail of bombs. I was in Leipzig, Chemnitz and Dresden. Later when the bombing became really bad I stayed home because it was too dangerous. The bombing of Dresden is well known. Thank goodness I only experienced that from afar, I was not there

My first really acute experience with the war was a bomb attack on Frankfurt.

Additional notes from Frau S.: That I was not able to do the job I had chosen My first acute experience of what ware means was living through the first bombing raid on Frankfurt.

Where you were working?

Yes I worked there and lived there too. My parents house was in Frankfurt and I lived with my mother.

Additional notes from Frau S.: Yes I lived with my mother in my parental home. The Textile wholesale firm was in Frankfurt am Main as well as the armaments factory and the transit camp.

Was the bombing in Frankfurt bad?

Yes, Frankfurt was destroyed. We lived just outside Frankfurt near the Stadium in Frankfurt-Niederrad, where the horse track in the state forest is, on the way to the airport. That was where my parents house was, it was all wooded at the time but now autobahns go through there. Two houses were hit there, so there was damage and also people died, but not to the extent that happened in Frankfurt where there was total destruction. We did have fire bombs on our house but my brother was there and put the fire out, but we didn't have the infernos of the inner city where everything just collapsed.

Additional notes from Frau S.: *Frankfurt inner city was completely destroyed. We lived in a suburb called Niederrad. There were houses near us that were damaged and some people died. My brother, with our help, saved our house from burning down after being hit by a fire bomb. The day after that my mother packed up and moved our household to her parents home in the Westerwald. We children went to Frankfurt every day by train because we had work and school there.*

Did people continue working after the bombing raid?

No. The day after the raid my mother packed her bags. My brother had got leave from the army and had applied to study so he was at home as a student. They left the same day for the Westerwald which is where my mother comes from. People tried to get trains, stood waiting at the stations. As much as they could they nailed everything shut.

My cousin who lived with us was employed by the post-office in Frankfurt and she had to stay. My humble self had to stay too because I was employed in a firm in Frankfurt.

The first thing I tried to do was to get to Frankfurt by bike to see if the building where my firm was had survived. That was in the Frankfurt area. The building was still standing but it was quite damaged. We started clearing it up. The firm moved to the Taunus mountains a couple of weeks later. They had established a warehouse there just in case. All the companies did the same. They moved to the city periphery as soon as they could. As soon as the rubble was cleared work started again. Everything that wasn't nailed down was transported to this very small village in the Taunus. That was what was done after the fist bombing raid on Frankfurt.

Additional notes from Frau S.: Not as much as previously. My firm moved to a small village in the Taunus Mountains where they had previously just had a warehouse. Those of us who worked there got rooms in the village so we avoided the bombing on Frankfurt.

You moved there too?

Yes, we moved too. We took rooms there with farmers. We took a few things that we needed from home and moved into rented accommodation. My mother and brother and my sister who was still studying moved to the Westerwald. When we could we went back home to Frankfurt. The house was still there but it was closed up. You had to just trust God that no one broke in. But actually that didn't worry us, the main thing was to escape with your life, like after the deluge, never mind what else happened. I can't tell you exactly when the first bombing raids in Frankfurt took place but my mother, who died recently at 92 years old, she could tell you the exact time and date and that would have been correct. So much happened at once, my parents had already lived one life, They were fifty years old at the time. That's what I am today. In younger years we only understood and registered half of what was happening, then the next thing would happen. After the war one married, had children, built a house. So that is all a bit blurry.

Perhaps it is better when one forgets?

Yes, it is also good.

Did people help each-other during this time?

Yes certainly. In the city there wasn't much available and people were evacuated by the bureaucracy. Whoever didn't have relations outside the city had difficulty and had to remain. But they closed the schools and families with children were sent away. The city authorities organised it. Many went to the Taunus or Westerwald or even further away. Many were evacuated to what is now the fruit area and people lived there and were accommodated. It is true that they were met with resistance at first from the local farmers who had not experienced bombing so they didn't understand

what it was like. They called them 'city-people, and said 'strangers had been
been moved into their hoses unasked'. Imagine that suddenly complete
strangers moved in and you had no idea with whom you are dealing or how
they might fit in. It was often very difficult to find a contact, where could
the evacuees go? The farmers had to share what they had and the evacuees
had nothing they could pay with. Money wasn't wanted. That is when the
goods-exchange started. The city people went back home and got clothes
or bedding or jewellery for the farmers. Or carpets. Later it was said that
the farmers carpeted their animal stalls with carpets.

Adversity made people want to what they could. One had to eat. Money
wasn't sought after, the main thing was to have food. You couldn't eat
money to get a full stomach. Butter, milk, grain and potatoes. The farmers
had those but they were not available in the city. What could farmers do
with money, they were the ones who had things. I can report what
happened in Westerwald because my mother was there. She had grown up
in the village but had spent 30 years in Frankfurt. My father worked in the
school there and he went to the farmers and advocated for the evacuees.
'You must be sensible. Go have a look at Frankfurt etc.' So whoever came
into the village as a stranger had problems. There was resistance at first.
The farmers only experienced the war when the Americans marched in
because they hadn't been bombed. You lay in bed with a heavenly calm and
said, you can live here. So the farmers had never lived the through the
shock and horror hours as the city people had who had lived in their cellars,
and they couldn't empathise with them.

Additional notes from Frau S.: *Yes of course! You helped your neighbours
immediately, cleared up, helped them with repairs, and sometimes cooked
on the same stove, if it was still functional. In general the state helped
families and school classes move to areas where there was less bombing.
Friends and acquaintances offered accommodation in the countryside
although there were initial problems to deal with there because the country
people had not suffered bombing and were reserved and distrustful towards
the refugees.*

**Were there any men there? I imagine thee must have been some
farmers?**

Farmers and many prisoners.

To assist?

Yes. For example we had a lot of Frenchmen in Westerwald. When Germany invades Poland and France they transported prisoners back to Germany to replace the Germans who were sent to fight on the front.

Was there a good understanding between the peoples?

Yes but secretly. My uncle had a young Frenchman, the French were also in his area, and that was a very nice young man. We youngsters had French people in the school and of course we were anxious to speak French with them. But that was not allowed by the mayor. That was forbidden. It came from the highest level. To talk to the prisoners, or to be a bit friendly to them. The Frenchman who was at our farm didn't sleep there. In the evening they were all collected and slept elsewhere, I think in the school where they had put up camp-beds. If a girl had anything to do with a French prisoner that would be severely punished. Those were dreadful times. Their hair was cut off after they had been beaten. I didn't experience that myself but I heard about it later. Those girls had a dreadful time.

Additional notes from Frau S.: Yes and no. My uncle had a young Frenchman to help on the farm. He was capable and open minded and there was a good understanding on the farm. We could understand him well with our school French but we had to keep to strict limits in our communication with him otherwise there would have been problems with the administration..

Was life without the men very different? Most of the men were away, how did you manage everything alone?

Yes, of course, those who were married or had families or ran a company or a farm. It was difficult. My uncle was over 50 so her didn't have to leave but all his sons were gone and there was no one to work on the farm.

Additional notes from Frau S.: In the beginning perhaps but when you have to, you can develop unknown strengths.

You weren't married so perhaps you didn't notice it as much?

No I was not married, but what I heard from others who had to manage their businesses alone. They had to do everything alone and they had no alternative. Either they managed it or they lost everything.

I imagine when the men came back the women had changed.

I can't really say for myself. I just had my work. Most of my colleagues were men in the armaments factory and when I traveled for my business I didn't notice that there were fewer men. I only really registered it because my boyfriend was away and wrote to me through the army postal services.. I sent parcels. Sometimes there was no mail and we didn't know what had happened. But for we young people, that was,... they returned home or others came home. That was not really noticeable for me.

Did women become more independent?

My generation had to become independent, Previously they had not been independent. That was the generation who thought that everything should be decided by the men, we would be housewives and make ourselves pretty. That's how we had been brought up. In my career I stood by my husband.

But in the family I was travelling a lot. I bought for the firm. I had to buy what we needed and had to do that according to what I thought. That was not normal. I was only 21 and was travelling all over Germany. For those times it was very unusual. But in wartime the farmers wives had to drive the tractors.

Additional notes from Frau S.: Because we were given no option, my generation became very independent. Women and girls who had been brought up to do housework were now doing work that had been typical men's work. The farmer's wife sat behind teams of horses pulling a plough, there were women working as train conductors and postmen. It became normal that men worked under the direction of women.

And previously?

That didn't happen before the war. Most women didn't know how. That was astonishing.

'Now look at that, so and so is sitting on the Tractor.'

Suddenly they could drive tractors. The men were away and they had to do that. Actually there were few tractors. At the time ploughs were pulled by horses or cows, but the women sat on them and pulled the reins. That was on the bigger farms.

And suddenly conscripted labourers were announced. Well, the others were at the external warehouse for four years or however long it was. I don't know if it failed or not but the women were all tired and overburdened. Most of them. I [saw that] with my uncle. In the last war years it was no longer possible to Frankfurt and you were a year with strangers and just waited to see what would happen. Every thing stopped in the countryside.

Was that a big adjustment afterwards?

I know that it was a very big adjustment for my cousin, for example. Her husband was away for a long time. After four years of doing everything herself,she and her husband had to start again from the beginning.

When the Americans came marching in I was at my uncles working in the fields. I helped with the harvest and everything, like a boy. You had to. You got up at four in the morning and went to work until the grain was in and the cows had been milked. That is the sort of work that you hope will end soon. We were overburdened. So when the men came back the women handed over automatically to the partner. How it was in business and the economy, not the farm economy,. when the men came back. But it was different when the men didn't come home. When the women were alone. Then the really hard years started for the women. When the women had children and had to manage alone. That generation became exhausted and didn't take part in anything, neither politics nor anything.

Additional notes from Frau S.: Certainly after six years of war a lot had changed. Women had been alone with their children and had to carry the upbringing and the worries alone. Where families found each other again, or built new ones, there were difficulties because people had changed, but these were mostly overcome through the effort to end hardship. Rebuilding required patience and good will. That was the only way to deal with the excessive physical and mental demands that were placed on everyone

My generation, things don't interest me now. But now the next generation is there. There was a decade or so in this post war period when people worked hard to rebuild and then they celebrated what they had achieved but lots of things happened that were not so good. Was it the children's education that we didn't have time for? One fell into a time of plenty and forgot a lot of what had been known previously. There were excesses which we have suffered from. The young people who rebel on the street lived in a time of plenty. Their parents are my generation and they had to work like the devil to survive, they had time for nothing else. Now that is passed but I think human values have become lost. That is just my opinion, I am not sure it is true but as far as family values are concerned, children are no longer cared for as before. We saw a lot of 'key children' whose parents didn't have time for them because they both had to work. You understand that!

Previously our parents were more modest, they could afford to be. They didn't have to fight for their existence in order to enjoy it later. They had a more normal life, even despite the first world war, but that was not comparable.

What sort of experience did you have of the Americans when they marched in?

My first experience of he Americans was in Limburg. I had taken my bike and pedalled from Westerwald to Taunus to collect my things from the apartment where I had been shifted to by my firm. I had collected the last of my clothes to take back to Westerwald. We knew how close the Americans were because we heard on the radio where they were. I didn't quite make it home to here my mother and grandparents lived but got stuck in a neighbouring village where I stayed the night with friends. The Americans came through that night.

Additional notes from Frau S.: *We heard the progress of the enemy troops on our radios. I rode my bicycle to Taunus to collect my clothes before we were occupied, a round trip of 60 km. In my way home I passed disintegrating German troop formations who were fleeing so they wouldn't be taken prisoner. Two kilometres from my grandparents house I sought refuge with friends in a neighbouring village because I could hear the American troops ahead of me and see the accompanying aircraft. That village was occupied that evening and there was a curfew, so I only got home two days later.*

Were the people afraid of the Americans?

Yes. But what is fear? People were happy, they had very mixed feelings. On the one hand they were happy that now its over, as soon as they get here the stuff from above will stop. We wont get bombed any more and the alarms wont ring. That was what we yearned for, but on the other hand we didn't know what would come next and what would happen to us. I think that the relief that the end was coming was the most important. There had been so much horror. The endless fear if you lived in the city, when are the alarms going off again, when do we have to go into the cellar not knowing if we will survive to come out again. The constant fear of death.

I cannot report that I had bad experiences with the Americans myself. Of course here and in Frankfurt they occupied all the houses they found that were empty. They broke down the doors to our house and occupied it and turned everything inside out. That is known. They looked for weapons and pictures of Hitler. So you'd find your dining room table in the attic and all the preserving glasses strewn everywhere, that sort of thing. Yes, my God, that is normal. When we marched in to other countries we did the same.

Additional notes from Frau S.: *At first people heaved a sigh of relief. Even the thought that no more bombs would be falling and that the war was ended so our soldiers would come home was uplifting. Happily there was*

no fighting between the population and the invading troops in our area.
Life with the American troops was a mixture of anxiety and curiosity in the
beginning. After a couple of days they lifted curfew and we could we could
ride further afield with our bikes, into Frankfurt. Everything looked
different. What we found was gripping.

What could they do if they found something. The men were all gone?

Yes that's right but I knew one family who had a picture of Hitler, or a
swastika, and they were registered and treated as Nazis.

I thought everyone had something like that at home?

No that was not always the case. There was nothing like that at our place.
My mother would never have hung that up. She never said 'Heil Hitler'. But
we did of course. But mama couldn't do it because of her education and
religion. But I know the soldiers made a lot of mess in houses where they
found such things. Nothing survived. The Americans had no understanding
for anyone who was a Nazi and for the Americans every soldier was a Nazi.

Additional notes from Frau S.: *Oh no! In my parents house there was*
nothing of the kind. There we had a Christian cross hanging on the wall
over the door and that was what determined the soul of the house. My
mother would never have suffered a picture of Hitler to hang in her
presence.

Do you have a different understanding of war now?

Yes certainly, even although I was never on the front and never had to face
the enemy with a gun like my husband who spent four years getting to near
Moscow then back again but we see it with very different eyes. As I said,
we were scared to death, not in the beginning but later very intensively.

Do alarms take you back there?

No, but if planes fly by very low my legs turn to jelly. Sometimes the
military practice flying low and fast. We have a small house in the Spessart

and it is on the flight path for the military air field. The jets go directly over the village. They travel faster than the speed of sound and you hear the bang after they have gone. If I am walking in the woods with my husband I grip his arm really hard without intending to because I am thinking the bombs are coming. That's how they flew then too. The dive-fighters. In the Taunus where our firm moved there was a warehouse in a neighbouring village and we had to walk from one village to the next. I had to take the girls who were working for me there and one day, in bright light, when we were walking along the road we were attacked by dive-fighters. We lay in the ditch on the side of the road and then they came, a whole bunch of them. A couple of them branched off and flew low, shooting as they went. We lay on our stomachs and thought 'thank God we are all still here.'.Some of the planes were shot down and the pilots came down with parachutes, but some of them were dead. That's what it was like, and through these experiences I can say I was half way on the battlefield. You don't forget something like that.

Additional notes from Frau S.: No, not that, but every test alarm brings it all back. The unpleasant noise exposure we are exposed to through practising air force planes still makes me shaky in the knees and I seek cover today just as I did in those days.

When you see TV about Vietnam or other wars, do you suffer with them?

Yes. My husband finds it impossible to watch and has to turn off the television. For me it is interesting to see films about the Nazi time because I am an adult now and can understand. I couldn't do that at the time. My husband says he has heard enough and doesn't want to know any more. He can't cope with it, nor with these Vietnam stories or other places in the world, Ireland or so forth where peoples houses burn. We feel with them.

If something similar would happen now, would you feel like your mother felt at the time.

Most likely yes. I often say nowadays how well I now understand my mother. If it was 30 years ago I would be saying, 'Good lord, it feels like yesterday'.' That was reckoned as a lifetime once, thirty years. A very dear friend of mine, a sort of competitor for my husband, he died in the first days of the war. I remember how much that affected me, I was very distressed at the thought that he would never come home, that he no longer existed, would never come back. A few days later we had evening mass, we are Catholics, and I remember sitting there and crying and crying, so much that people wondered what was wrong with me, what has happened. I remember how I felt to this day. I didn't intend to make a fuss, it wasn't my brother and my now-husband had not been called up yet.

You still feel it deeply.

Yes, that Edmund would never come home, that he was prisoner, that was something I couldn't imagine, that was the first emotional pain one felt. He was a student friend of my brother and I had always liked him a lot and fancied him, though he treated me as a little girl. But then he didn't come back and that was dreadful. Later many of my family died, cousins for example. One of my cousins was in Stalingrad and we didn't know what had become of him for weeks and months and two years. He was one who came back because of Adenauer.

There was great opposition to the refugees from the East. Suddenly there were 15 million more people in a land that was bombed out. They were put up by other families, had no habits, no money, were called dirty and lazy because they couldn't get work or anything to wash with and had different habits.

LISELOTTE S. 1919: A POLICEWOMAN IN EAST PRUSSIA

Liselotte S. born 1919. Lived in Koenigsberg during the war.

What was your reaction to the events of 1939?

We expected something. We are more or less prepared for something to happen after the events in Sudetenland (Czechoslovakia) in 1938. We were expecting something and somehow they indicated it would be a good thing. You had to very very skeptical about things in those days.

Did you have the feeling that this was the only way out for Germany?

Yes, that we had to protect ourselves against Poland and the whole world. That was what was implied.

What was the reaction of others. Did they feel that same way?

Well in my age group, the youth were practically born into the National Socialism. I was a child when Hitler came to power and it was somehow implied that you had to defend yourself, the Fatherland had to protect itself, that it wasn't an attack but a defense against enemies.

Did people have an opinion about what caused the war, economic matters for example, or did people just believe what Hitler said?

Actually yes, at least the young people with whom I was friendly. We just believed it.

Was there a difference between men and women in this regard?

No, everyone was just as enthusiastic. The reaction was elation, because we had to fight back against the enemy, that's how it was.

What did you notice first once the war began?

Well, there were ration cards, so that everyone got the same amount of butter and meat. That must have been pre-prepared or they would not have been able to distribute them so quickly. That was what we noticed. We didn't have bombs or attacks, nothing of that sort.

As the years passed, the men had to leave?

Yes the men were away and then there were other restrictions. You couldn't get textiles. Textiles were allocated and you had to work more. It was said that because the men were away, we had to do the decent thing and work extra without pay. I was with the civil service and when there was extra wok we were told that we had to work longer hours for the same pay because the men were away and we women had to contribute as well.

Were the women happy to do that?

Yes. Most women did it automatically and without thinking much about it. It was an emergency situation.

What sort of work were you doing and how old were you?

I was nineteen year old and I had left school and joined the workforce.

Did the war change your work?

No nothing much changed, just that we had extra hours, without pay or without regard to whether you wanted to or not. But we did that willingly and enthusiastically.

Did you have younger brothers or sisters?

I had a sister who was still in school.

Were the schools limited by the war?

No I don't think so but I can't really comment because I didn't live at home any more and my sister was nine years younger than me and that was a big difference. I don't know if they had less hours but I don't think she finished her schooling.

The men of your age were away. How did that affect you?

They were called up and left immediately. 1939 was the war in Poland and then France came in 1940 and the men came back only a couple of time for holidays. So it was a man-less time and of course there were no dances or things like that for girls to go to. All that sort of thing decreased then later such events were canceled completely because it was said that we couldn't celebrate when men were dying in war and anyway there were no men to take part. Of course you could meet up unofficially and do things, but not officially.

Did the women complain or did they just think it would get better eventually?

I would say they thought it would pass. The women hoped it would be over quickly because it was difficult to make your way alone.

I read that the National Socialists restricted the type of work women could do and that they wanted women to have as many children as possible. What did the women think about that?

Yes, whoever was married should have children and, for example, women who had children could leave work but those without had to keep working. You could only leave when you had children. I got married when I was 21 but I had to keep working. Men were away and women had to keep working. Only when you were due to have a baby, then you could stop working.

I suppose a lot of women had babies so they could leave work?

Yes, I tried to do that too but I was unsuccessful. I was six months pregnant but then I had an accident and lost the baby, so I had to keep working. I wanted to have a child and perhaps it would have worked because it would have been small when we had to flee. But later when we fled I saw so much hardship, particularly women with children who had no food or milk for them.

What did other women of your age think about marriage?

Girls married as soon as they could when they had a serious boyfriend, just as I did. We sort of stampeded into marriage because we weren't sure if he would come back or if he wouldn't come back. Those were war marriages and everything happened very quickly. Previously you'd had to wait for two weeks from the date you registered to marry, but now it took a coupe of days if the man had a certificate of non-objection.

Also the proof of Aryan blood was very important. You had to be Aryan if you wanted to marry and if you wanted to marry a professional soldier or an officer or a civil servant then you had to present papers to show that three generations of your forefathers were Aryan. I had to present certificates for my parents and my grandparents. My father for example was from Bremen and I had to write several times to get papers so I could marry, until the State gave me permission to marry. I had to prove that I was Aryan to the third generation, up to my grandparents.

What happened if you couldn't produce certificates?

I wouldn't have been able to marry a man who was in the employment of the State, that means a civil servant or professional soldier. My husband was a professional soldier, so I wouldn't have been able to marry him without the required papers. No one would think of such things now, but at the time it was necessary.

I've read that a woman who was not married could conceive a baby with an SS officer. What was that about?

Yes you see, at the time no one knew about that, honestly. That was the so-called 'Lebensborn'. That meant that the men and women both had Aryan characteristics, blond hair and blue eyes, well built, the men broad shouldered and narrow hipped. The children were not registered in the mother's home. Today you have to register a child born out of wedlock but at that time everything was kept secret. They had homes for single mothers and the child was not registered in her papers if she didn't wish it. If she preferred she would have not had a child officially and the child would be raised by the state. It was all kept so secret that no one knew.

Did you know?

No, I first heard about it a long time later. Probably very few people knew about it. The National Socialist leadership would have known but not the population in general. After the war it became known and we heard about it on television, but not during the war.

The men were away so were there jobs available to women that they had not had the chance to do before?

Yes, but only later, not at the beginning of the war I don't think. Perhaps in private firms but I was not affected because I worked for the police service. But women working in private firms were commandeered and told to go to work in the munitions factories, whether they wanted to or not. That was mobilised labour and you couldn't fight it. I had some girlfriends who had to give up good positions and go and work in the munitions factories.

With the men away were women promoted to more senior positions?

No, you had to be qualified. You had to present qualifications so it was not possible.

Were there any advantages associated with the absence of men?

No, I don't think you could name any advantages, there were only disadvantages to having the men away.

Lots of things were forbidden like listening to foreign radio. Did you do that anyway?

You had to make sure you weren't caught because you could be sentenced to death. Just as in the DDR, you never knew who you could trust and eventually you would be denounced. So if you wanted to listen you had to be completely alone in your apartment and you had to have the radio on very low so it wouldn't be heard by neighbours or even good friends because you didn't know who you could trust. No one could trust anyone. That began in 1943 actually and it was really bad.

There was an assassination attempt on Hitler's life on 20 July 1944 and because I worked at the police station where the information was processed we had to work the whole night. The National Socialist leader in Koenigsberg was the first person informed and we were the information service who had first access to the information. I was working and heard it on the radio so I rang my boss. Then all the superintendents and so forth were drummed up and the armed forces was dis-empowered and the Gestapo took over. They had the say about everything.

You knew and understood what was happening?

Yes, in my position I was at the source. The Wehrmacht (German army) had to eat humble pie. The SS or the State police had the say. The attempt was in August and after that it was dreadful, especially for all the important people. There were a lot of people in the resistance at the time and mostly the people who resisted Hitler were the more prominent and wealthy people. There were dukes and nobles and there was the so called 'Sippenhaft' – that means that families of people who were accused of being involved were also imprisoned. The men were shot and the women and children were sent to prison. Many in the East were involved and in Koenigsberg, which was the capital of East Prussia, all the threads converged. From August 1944 until I fled in 1945 it was so dreadful that it doesn't bear thinking about. Everything became chaotic and there was no order at all.

No one worked any more?

Oh yes we did. We had to work until we fainted. We worked until 10 or 11 at night. Then we were bombed and there were no trains or trams. Today you can can't imagine what it was like. I had to get home but the whole of the inner city was gone. You had to walk home or find someone to take you. There were no taxis and petrol was rationed. Many private cars had been confiscated by the army for the army officers and you could only get petrol if you could show it was for some public purpose. There was just chaos after the assassination attempt in August 1944 and it continued until I left in January 1945.

Were you forbidden to leave?

You could flee, but there was no organised help. It was everyone for themselves.

Did you try?

Yes. You could leave but in the end there were no trains and no connections and we wanted to go to Bremen because that is where my father was from. We went on foot and were on the rural roads for two weeks, in January with 20 degrees of frost and cold, with just a bag and later we lost our bags because it was 1945 and there were bombing raids and then the Russians came.

The Russians had been three kilometres from Koenigberg; we were surrounded and we were still there. I was one of the last women out. My father was not allowed to leave and they said he died of typhus because of the unsanitary conditions. That was the most dreadful time, fleeing along those roads, my mother, my sister and I. My father was not allowed to come because he was still young enough to hold a gun. All the men had to stay behind. After a few kilometres we were separated My mother and my sister stayed together and thought I had died. I thought my mother and sister had died. We had said we would all meet at my fathers house in Bremen and I eventually go there on 12 February. I wept the whole time because I thought my mother and sister had died.

You know the ship the Gustloff, the ship that sank with so many people on board? Well it had sailed just before us. There were so many people on the quay in Pilau which was where people were transported from; hundreds of people pushing and shoving. They pushed from the back and at the front some people fell into the water. They were unimaginable circumstances.

You were there?

Yes we wanted to go by ship but we weren't able to because women with children had precedence. I didn't have a child and I didn't have the courage either because I thought my mother had gone and I was completely alone. But I hung around and eventually I did get on a boat and we got to Hela, with was a peninsula. They stopped there and chased all the civilians off the boat. We were taken to a barracks and were each given a bucket of soup. We had spent five days on the boat without any food because everything was so chaotic. The crew had food, but how were they to feed hundreds of refugees? It took three of four days to get across because we had to stop at night because of Russian torpedos and bombs. So we sailed only intermittently and it took a long time. We got there but a lot of ships sank and I thought my mother and sister had died. But two days after I reached Bremen, there they were standing at the door. We wept of course and hugged each other and were pleased we'd all survived. That was the most dreadful time in 1945.

If you didn't have anything to eat, what happened to the children?

A lot didn't survive and died on the side of the road. Some of the mothers carried them evn though they were dead because they couldn't bare to part with them. It was so cold and everything was frozen. East Prussia is much colder than here. The ground was frozen solid and you can't just leave your child lying there, so they were carried on. We got to Gotenhafen near Danzig and from there a few trains were still leaving so you had to see that you got on them. There were no tickets. Whoever got on, through the windows or through doors on or the roof, those people went with the train. And the women with children, crying with hunger, or babies, some were dead. The staff on the train were soldiers as far as I can remember and they gave some of their rations so at least the children had something to eat. Dried milk powder mixed with a bit of water.

Did people help each other?

In the worst time, my experience was that everyone helped everyone else. There were no distinctions because everyone feared for their lives and everyone helped each other.

Was it the same during the war when there was hardship?

That was the same. When the Russians got close our army kept one road free so we could escape to Pillau, then the road closed again. It was really really bad. When we still worked there, day and night in the executive committee all we could hear were canons shot by the Russians three kilometres away, or bombs. In the beginning you flinched because you were so frightened but after a while you got used to it and became apathetic. Even when the bombs landed nearby we didn't react. We didn't really work any more. We just made food for the men. The storehouses were blown up and we got the stores and made meals for the men. But a lot of my colleagues were shot by the Russians.

Did women in these situations help each other more than formerly?

Yes, I have to say there was a wonderful camaraderie. There was no difference between people and even those people who hadn't liked each other previously, because you know there is always some jealousy between the women vying for men's attention. But at that moment there were no differences.

Did that carry on into the post war period, that women helped each other?

No that dissipated after the war because there were so many refugees from the east. They hoped we would go back again because we were seen as a burden. What are you doing here, they'd say, you just take our food away from us. Some people said straight out to us 'Go back where you came from!" But we couldn't go back to our home because now that is Poland or Russia. Koenigsberg is Russian and South East Prussia is Polish, so we couldn't go back even if we had wanted to. The people who had always lived there really let us have it; there was no understanding between people any more. They accused us of having had it easy because we had not had the bombing raid that they had. Hamburg and Bremen and the larger cities had all been bombed flat by the English and they said 'you didn't live through that!' We had our first bombing attacks in 1941, two years after the war began in 1939. We heard about the attacks on the radio because they would report that Hamburg had been hit or Bremen or another large industrial city, because of course they wanted to disrupt the economy. We didn't have any bombs until 1941 when the Russians bombed us, but it wasn't nearly as bad. We had a few bombs then it stopped. But when the American's came in 1944, in two nights it was all over.

Did you live with other refugees when you arrived?

No we lived in the house of my father's parents. They were dead but my aunt still lived there. She was very nice in the beginning when she thought we would leave again, but when her brother, my father, didn't turn up and she realised we would have to stay, then she was not so nice. So there we were, my mother, my sister, and me and we were just tolerated. They let us know in no uncertain terms that there were too many of us. It was so bad that we rented a room elsewhere, with complete strangers. I worked there in Bremen too. I had to register there and report for work.

What did you do there?

You had to go to the employment bureau and register. I said where I had worked and I was sent ot work in the Police headquarters again as secretary. I was there until the Americans came. It was not my choice, but that was where I was sent. Before we fled we had been told that whereever we landed up, in south or west, or where ever, we should immediately register again or otherwise there would be consequences. That's why I had to work there until the Americans arrived. The Americans came in April or May and occupied everything. Then in December 1945 I began work again but it was very difficult in my profession and I got a job with a private firm.

Were you frightened at the time, for example frightened of your own SS people?

No I was not frightened of them. We were frightened, really frightened, of the Russians because the Russians behaved appallingly, especially to women, raping them and so forth. That didn't happen to me but dreadful things happened to my friends and relations. I was very frightened in Koenigsberg because I had worked for the police. I tore up my identification card because we had heard that if they catch you and find your identification card you'd be shot, regardless of whether you had committed any crimes. I was also very careful in Bremen after the overthrow because I thought, well they had taken a lot of women, including my workmates and had shorn off their hair. The hair was shorn off then you had to work like peasant and the overseers were the Poles who had had to work in Germany as foreign workers. They were the overseers and they beat the workers, not only the men but the girls as well although they had only done what they were told. But a friend of mine from Hamburg had worked there as secretary and she registered, so then I registered too.

With the Americans?

I think so yes, the Americans or the English were in Hamburg.

The didn't put me in a work gang but I had to register every eight days with with people who were responsible for looking into the spy rings. They wanted to know they names of anyone I had worked with in Koenigsberg that I had seen in the west because they wanted to arrest all those people, but I hadn't seen anyone so I couldn't name anyone. I didn't know many names any more as I had been buried in 1944 during a bombing raid and they only got us out from under the rubble the next day. We were down in a cellar and we thought we would never get out of there and it caused some memory loss and couldn't remember everything although some things came back later. So they wanted the names but that was only six months after the bombing when I had been buried and I couldn't remember the names any more. There was a lot I forgot and only remembered later.

That must have been some sort of shock reaction?

Yes, it was awful.

The women were alone now and I wondered if they became more independent?

Yes, you had to be independent. There was no alternative.

The women had been raised to be married and suddenly they had to be independent. Was that difficult?

It was not difficult for me because I am a very active type of person but some women really suffered.

What happened then? I can imagine that when the men came back they would have wanted their higher positions again but women were probably a bit more equal?

I can't really comment from my own experience because my husband didn't come back. I imagine that would have been true because women had become much more independent and there must have been friction, but I don't know from my own experience because my husband never came back.

I wonder what effect that had on marriages after the war. You had a younger sister. Did the lack of men after the war affect her?

My sister was 9 years younger and was only 15 when the war ended so she was not affected as much because the men of her age had not had to go to war. The generation without men was my generation because so many men of our generation had died. My current husband was a friend of my father's from Koenigsberg. We met through the red cross. He had been in a prisoner of war camp in France. We found each other through the red cross. We shared many memories so we married.

Did this independence women now had continue or was it lost?

No, I think that they remained independent, that didn't change.

And did that have an effect on the next generation do you think?

Yes, I think it did because I told my daughters that my experience had shown me that you didn't have to marry and that I had been stupid to marry. Because only washing nappies and doing housework ... once the girls were bigger I worked again. I told my girls they should not necessarily marry because my experience had shown you don't need a man to protect you. I am proof that you can manage by yourself because I had to. One of my daughters is now married and now she is rattled, the other tells me she doesn't want to marry. She is only eighteen so whether she sticks to that is another question. I wonder whether she would do it, I don't think so because that would be stupid, to have to work for two or even more. A bit of emancipation.

You were in the west when the war actually ended. What was your reaction?

When we realised it was really over we just said 'thank God!' We couldn't have endured any more. That was not only the reaction of the people who had fled the east, but also of the people who were at home in the west. We had prayed to God that the war should end soon because we couldn't bear any more. No food, no men, bombing raids in Bremen. Yes, after we fled we were bombed in Bremen.

Were you frightened to ask if the war would soon end?

Yes, because officially you couldn't say anything. You couldn't say 'If only it was over' to a stranger, only to your closest family and those you knew really well. People were just exhausted.

What was your experience with the Americans?

Well, they were good. The Americans were alright.

I heard that some Americans didn't want to give the Germans food if they had excess?

Well my experience was that the Americans sometimes shared their ration packets. Then we were were really happy because we had nothing to eat. If you had any contact with them they were very good natured. The black Americans were especially good to the children. We had been frightened of the blacks because we had no experience with them but the Blacks were very good to the children.

They probably knew what it was like from home.

Yes because they were downtrodden at home by the white population. They were really nice to the children, gave them chocolate. It was amazing.

Did you have particular recipes you used during the war?

Yes we did because we had to try to make something from nothing. We has so little. When we were in Bremen, I remember once there was suddenly talk of horse meat being available. We had never ever eaten horse meat, but we walked three quarters of an hour, my sister and I to stand in a queue for horse meat. There was curfew at the time and Germans were not allowed on the streets before six in the morning but we went very early in the morning, always watching out to avoid the military police. We walked for 45 minutes to the butcher then we stood in the queue for horse meat from 7am until noon. There was a very long queue and they ran out of meat shortly before it was our turn, but there were still bones so that is what we bought. My mother cooked up a vegetable soup with the bones and we ate it with great enthusiasm, ate something we never would have touched previously. Those were different times.

Dried vegetables, for example cabbage was also popular. It had been cut up and dried but there was always sand in it so it can't have been very well washed. We cooked it up and it tasted like fresh cabbage but when you got to the bottom of the pot it was gritty. Those were awful times. There was nothing to spread on bread so we ate it dry. We women had to be creative. If we had a little fat, even a tiny bit, we would cut it very small and heat it so the fat ran out. Then we would cook semolina with water and perhaps an onion, then add the fat and mix it. That would be what we spread on bread. It tasted a bit like dripping so when you spread it on bread you had the feeling you were eating bread and dripping. We made cakes from potatoes because there was nothing else. We had to be inventive because there was so little. You had to have food stamps if you wanted to eat at a tavern or restaurant. There were stamps for 5 grams and 10 grams of white fat and, for example, if you wanted to eat soup you had to give them a 5 or 10 gram stamp. If you wanted to eat meat you had to give fifty or a hundred gram stamps. Then you couldn't buy any rations of your own. Those fat stamps were used for quite a long time. My oldest daughter was born in 1948 and I think there were still fat stamps in 1949. It wasn't as restricted as it had been in the war, but there were still limits.

Did you have food reserves?

There were people who had supplies because there was a lot of swapping. City peple would go to the country and swap carpets or other things for food maybe for half a pound of butter or a coule of eggs. We used to joke that the farmers would be able to carpet their cow stalls because people would give a lot for a little food. There was no relationship to the actual value of the goods swapped.

Did you have any experience with the black market?

Yes, you just had to make sure you weren't caught. Everyone knew which street corners were used to swap goods so you went there and swapped things from pocket to pocket. People would slide passed each other and stick their hands in the pockets and say 'I have cigarettes, what do you have?"You weren't allowed to trade like that and if the police came people pulled away.

Were there trading or pawn shops?

There was an official trading centre. An organisation , a room, where you could go and say I have a watch and I'll give it up for this or that. That was quite official, but you couldn't trade for food. It was more for textiles and second hand things.

Did people use that centre?

Yes, it was used. For example for children's clothing. Or you could ask for a set of cups or plates. Not food, that had to be traded on the black market.

Were there black market traders?

Yes some people did it professionally which added another layer. It was punished so when the police were nearby the traders disappeared. Or you could go to the countryside with your goods. The trains were sometimes so full you had to sit on the running board. It was bad for a long time.

If you see war scenes on TV, do you think of your own experience?

Yes always. I don't like watching reports about Vietnam. It reminds me of my own experience and I get too upset. I can't sleep because I can't stop thinking of what happened to me.

Do you think your experience has influenced how you think about war?

Do you mean for me or for the general population?

Maybe both?

I would think it terrible if we had another war, but I don't think the general population has learned much. If you take an interest in politics, you have to say we haven't learned much. It is only 30 years since the war ended but most of the population didn't experience it. My own children say to me that they just can't imagine it. The youth think differently now. You can tell them, but unless you lived through something like that you just can't imagine it. I get so upset. I had to live through such horrors. For men it might be different.

If you have a gun in your hand and can fight, then it is different to a woman with children and no gun.

I think the male and female psychology is different. Women are affected more because they don't want to take part. The men seem to have forgotten it sooner. I don't look at war films from principal and nor do I look at horror movies. I find them dreadful. My husband has to go by himself but he doesn't take it amiss because he knows they upset me too much.

LUISE G, 1918: THE FASCINATION OF HITLER

Luise G, born 1918. Lived in a village near Breslau, Oberschliesien (now Wroclaw, Poland) during the war.

What was the atmosphere when war was declared?

I worked at the time and was secretary in a factory that made compression rings for the aircraft industry and at the same time, there were two firms in the same factory and a book store. When the war began, I remember exactly the work in the whole factory stopped and we were all told we had to listen to the radio because a speech by Hitler would be broadcast. And Hitler screamed and yelled, 'they are all against us and we have to defend ourselves'. He had marched into Sudentenland [Poland?] and he made it sound as if we had been attacked. The Germans marched in and everyone was enthusiastic. It was awful. They yelled and danced and were glad about the war. It was dreadful. No one thought about what it meant.

What was your reaction?

We had seen it coming. It had been planned for a long time. And one was frightened, wondering what would become of the family and my parents.

My father had been a bit disadvantaged by the Nazis. He was a good catholic and the Nazis didn't like Catholics and there were always difficulties. We weren't in the party, we didn't belong to any party. My father was not careful enough. One couldn't say anything but my father said openly what he though and they threatened that if he didn't keep quiet he would be locked up. We were really frightened and the thought that there was a war coming made us even more anxious. You know when I listened to that speech I was as if paralysed, thinking that now it had happened. We had always hoped there would be no war, but now it had happened. It was a real shock.

Did people understand the causes?

You know that had a lot to do with the attitude to Hitler. Hitler was loved by the people. You can't imagine the awful time before Hitler, the unemployment and the misery and then Hitler came and suddenly all the problems were solved. People had work and things were good. Once again it was lovely in Germany. People could see that he was building Autobahns, but what they didn't realise was they he was building them for his troops. We didn't want to believe or perhaps we just didn't see was that he was arming his troops. If you were a bit watchful, then you knew a war was coming, but a lot of people didn't want to believe it.

Hitler's speeches were a fascinating example of how he persuaded the masses to follow him. He inspired such enthusiasm. People would clap and scream and jump for joy. The effect that this man had was quite extraordinary, but not only Hitler, Goebbels as well. Goebbels could talk like that too and he was really dangerous because he could say things that were just not true with such confidence that everyone believed him. Because people were so enthusiastic they thought that what they were told must be true, because when this person is so happy and that person is so happy, then I should be happy too. That was a real mass hysteria.

You yourself were anxious though?

Yes but you couldn't say anything, that would have been dangerous. If you said anything and were reported you were sent straight to prison or to a concentrations camp.

So they had control. And what were the first things that people noticed that there was a war?

In the beginning you didn't notice much but gradually there were shortages of everything. Food was in short supply and you couldn't buy textiles any more because there were no coupons. There were very few shoes. Everything was very restricted and you could no longer leave your workplace. I wanted to leave this factory and work in another one but I couldn't because this was an armament factory. You couldn't leave. There were a lot of restrictions, that was the main thing.

Were people upset about these restrictions or did they understand about the war effort?

People understood.

Which men were sent to fight?

My father was not called up because he was already too old. I had a brother who was younger than me and still in school when the war was declared. Later they even took boys from the schools. They were just boys but they were removed from school given a short course then sent to war.

How old were they?

Certainly not older than sixteen.

But that was later?

Yes, that was later, perhaps 1943 or 44, I am not exactly sure because I was no longer living at home.

What sort of work did the women do during the war?

Women all had to work during the war. Only those with children were allowed to stay home.

Older or younger children?

Young children. All other women had to work in factories and arms factories.

Did you have problems getting food or finding a living space during the war?

I had married in 1940 and we moved to Breslau where it was very difficult to find an apartment. First we lived in a furnished place in a room with no kitchen or anything. We looked for a long time but there were no apartments. I had an uncle with connections and he know as landlord who found us an apartment on the sly. We couldn't get one through normal channels. It was dreadfully difficult to get a place to live.

And was getting food difficult?

Well there was so little. You had ration cards for so much butter, 100g meat per week. That is not much, a hundred grams of meat for a whole week.

Did you have special recipes?

Yes of course! You couldn't cook as you once had. It was also difficult to get vegetables and such like. You had to queue for a long time at the shops.

Did you eat less?

Yes, we ate less. You had to because there was there was less food. And we ate much more simply. A few vegetables, potatoes and very little meat.

And bread?

There was not much bread either.

Were there enough potatoes?

Yes there were enough potatoes. At first there were plenty of vegetables too, but later they became scarce.

Were the teachers called up?

I am not sure, my children were too small. But let me think, I had a sister who was in school. But I can't remember if the teachers were conscripted.

Was your husband called up.

Yes, he was conscripted just as the war broke out. He was an eye surgeon and had just finished his specialist education when he was called up but he was in Breslau in an animal investigation unit where he did eye examinations. He was there until 1943 when he was transferred to a lazrett in Berlin, in the eye department.

What is a Lazarett?

That's a hospital for wounded soldiers. What is the word in English?

I don't know if there is a word. Hospital?

A Lazarett is not a hospital, a Lazarett, is for wounded soldiers, specifically for people who had been wounded in war.

Were there any rumours or speeches against the war?

In Breslau we had a circle that a Professor from the University belonged to. Once a month he had a meeting with his former students and at those meetings all the problems were discussed. They were psychological themes, religious themes – we were all Catholics, but also political themes.

Wasn't that a bit dangerous?

Yes but we all knew each other well. And we heard what was planned, but never exactly, no one knew that. We heard for example that there were concentration camps. Not one of us knew more about them and you didn't dare talk about it. You couldn't talk about them in public. I thought that cant be true, that could not be possible, but they did say that and we just couldn't imagine that something like that could be possible. One heard things, but nothing detailed.

Did you understand what you were threatened with if you were

overheard discussing the war?

Yes, one knew. If someone informed on us then there would be a court case and we'd have gone to prison. And then I realised that if we went to prison that meant the concentration camp. But no one knew exactly what that was and I never spoke to anyone who had been in a concentration camp. They seldom came back. We knew that dreadful things happened there but no one knew exactly what. You heard things and that was all said very quietly.

But you couldn't say anything out loud?

No you couldn't say anything out loud.

Did the Germans help each other.

Yes, everyone helped each other. When there were alarms at night you had to go into the cellar. That was the rule, everyone had to go into the cellar. The cellars were supported with beams and any windows were blacked out. I had small children and I was always helped. There were lots of steps and with children – people always helped me.

Also when you were shopping and had to stand in a long queue?

That was more difficult. There were possibilities if you were pregnant and expecting a child, then women didn't need to queue. One had to show cause and then you could go to the front. But I didn't dare to do that because there were always people who got really upset. Sometimes I went to the front when it became impossible. When women have to queue so long they become unbearable.

Did you have two children at the time?

No I had three children. The last was born shortly after the end of the war.

Were there changes because the men were away and the women were alone? Were the women stronger or more self confident?

Yes, the women had to work. They had to do all the jobs that the men had once done.

And were there problems when the men came back?

Yes. In our marriage it was very very difficult. My husband was in Breslau until 1943 and then we next saw each other when he came back in 1947. He had been in a prisoner of war camp. He had fallen into the hands of the British. He was with a Lazarett from Berlin and they had fought their way through to Holstein which was where the University Clinic from Breslau was transferred. The British put him in a camp and he worked there as eye doctor. He had to stay there. In 1946 he was released but he couldn't work in Wiesbaden. Up north he got a license to work so he opened up a Practise in Holstein near Kiel. My parents were here in Wiesbaden so I wanted to stay here.

While he was working up in Holstein I was trying to get him a license so he could work here. And I did finally succeed and then he came back here. We had grown very much apart. We had left everything in Schiesien. We had no money, we only had children and nothing else. My husband started his Practice again, very modest. In Holstein he had been able to take instruments from the Lazarett. So he had those. But nothing else. We lived in an apartment where there was just not enough room for children as well as his practice. It was dreadful. It was really extremely difficult.

How long was it so difficult?

It changed quite quickly. My husband quickly had a lot to do and made good money so at least we had money and could buy things we needed. Then we started to save for a house and things got easier.

While your husband was away those four years you had to make all the decisions for the children by yourself. Did you continue to do that once your husband was back?

I changed back. We had to come back to a common denominator. He developed a very busy practice so he didn't have time for the children. So then I made the decisions for the children again, but I always discussed things with my husband. At least we tried to find common ground. Otherwise it would have been unbearable. We had so looked forward to being together again and were so happy to see each other, but despite that it was awfully difficult. Sometimes I wondered if we might split up. You know perhaps it was just as well we had children. I think if the children had not been there we might have decided it was all too difficult and decided to divorce. When you have children it is more difficult to split up. You just grit your teeth and bare it. I think the children saved our relationship. My husband was a bit of a difficult character, you had to cater to him and I had forgotten how to do that.

Did you know of other women with the same difficulties?

A lot of couples split up. A lot of marriages had difficulties because the men were away so long and when they came back they found their wives had taken new partners. Their own husbands were away so long in prisoner of war camps. There were real tragedies. The men came back, so happy to be back

Was that before the end of the war?

The end of the war was in May. The Russians advanced so quickly and I was not at home. My husband had his birthday on 20 January and I took my oldest son Michael with me to Berlin. He was just three years old. I left the other two children with an acquaintances in the village. Every day the Russians advanced but we were not told the truth on the news. One morning they announced on the radio that the Russians were in Tschenztochau and that was only 100 km from the village where I lived. My husband got holiday leave and we left immediately because of the other children but the trains no longer went to Breslau, so we had to go by foot. Sometime we got rides in cars. When we got there the whole village was decamping

It was dreadful what I experienced there. It was deep mid winter, minus 16 degrees, insanely cold with lots of snow and everyone was trying to leave. But the trains were no longer running and it was so cold. And there were no cars. They had all run off the road and were partly frozen. The mothers had their children in prams but could go no further. I saw two young mothers who had made a sleigh out of bed boards and they were pulling their children with bedding through the snow. There were just dreadful scenes. There was an old woman who had tied her husband to a board, probably because he could no longer walk, and she was pulling him through the snow. There were just streams of people on the roads.

Because they were afraid of the Russians?

Yes the people were insanely frightened of the Russians.

Was that the propaganda?

Yes that was propaganda but people had heard heard that the Russians were very close. Villages were burning all of the place and those who tried to flee often died in the snow.

Did you find your children?

We found out children and then we had to think how we could get out of there. We had two children because I had taken the eldest in Berlin and we had left him there with our acquaintances. In those times we had large deep prams and I put the children's bedding in there and then the children, so they didn't freeze, and then we left on foot. I pushed the pram and my husband had two suitcases on a sledge. The farmers traveled with tractors. They had horses with wagons and they put everything in the wagons. They offered us a lift but we declined because it was so very cold and people were freezing to death on the wagons because they were sitting still and it was too cold. So we thought it was better to walk. It was too dangerous because it was so cold. We walked to the station and there was a branch line that was running. But it only went a couple of stations and then stopped and we could get no further. We had got as far as Neustadt in Schliesien and there we found a long lazarett-train. The Lazarett-train did not take civilians. My husband was in uniform and he found the officer in charge who said that he could travel with the train but his wife and children could not. My husband said 'but I can't leave them here'. Then a nurse said to him, "I have a little cabin on the train and you should put your wife and children in there. I am running to the operations hall for a moment so I don't want to see anything. I haven't seen anything."

That is how we got out of there. My husband left the train on the way but we stayed on board until it got to Nuremberg where the lazarett train stopped. My husband had had to leave the train because he had to make his way back to Berlin. He only had three days holiday. If he had traveled further with me he would have been court marshaled as a deserter. He was not allowed to stay with us. So I was alone with the luggage and the children. The train kept stopping so the trip took days.

Did you get anything to eat?

No nothing. In Nuremberg I had to leave the train and then it was really difficult. I had the pram and two suitcases and the trains went very irregularly. Everything was is dissolution. Trains traveled a couple of stations then stopped. I had the goal of getting to Wiesbaden to join my parents.

Where was your eldest son?

He was still in Berlin but my husband had told me not to worry, that he would find someone who would bring him to me.

And then I traveled for days and days, each day getting a little bit further. That was so difficult. The children needed food. Christine was three and a half and the youngest was eight months old and needed a bottle and nappies. But the stations were always very well organised and there was always help there. There were helpers who had organised themselves, what did they call themselves, Nurses for Hitler or some such. But it was dreadful when you were stuck and couldn't go further. There were always alarms and you had to go to the air raid shelter. But I was helped again and again. There was one time that I just didn't know how to carry on. I could not travel on and I was there with the children and I felt so abandoned I despaired and I couldn't go on. I stood in the station and cried and cried. A woman came to me and stood near me.

She said, 'Oh can I help you, come home with me and we'll bathe the children and I'll make you something to eat.' In that instant a train pulled in. I would have so liked to go home with that woman. She helped me get the pram on the train. There were so many people who wanted to get on so I needed someone to help me.

It took a whole week and then I arrived in Wiesbaden.

Did you have enough money to buy all the things the children needed?

No you didn't need money, it was all free. In the beginning it was a bit difficult to find things but I was lucky.

Then I was in Wiesbaden. My parents had been scared stiff when they heard the Russians were coming. They had collected all their things but they didn't know where to go. Then I was home and they were happy and I was happy. That lasted two days. Then in the second of February there was a big air raid on Wiesbaden. Wiesbaden was severely damaged.

We were in the cellar of our single-family house and a bomb came down in the back garden. The whole back of the house was destroyed. It was dreadful. Everything was rubble, only the cellar survived. It was awful being in the cellar when the bomb exploded. You could see the ceiling rise then fall again. Everything fell down but the cellar had been strengthened with beams and it held up.

So there we stood. The house was destroyed and everything broken. We had nothing. It was so difficult. We had no water. No electricity, nothing to eat. Wiesbaden looked dreadful. There was hardly anyone with an unaffected apartment. Even the houses that remained standing had had their doors and windows blown out. And it was cold. Not as cold as it had been in Schliessen, but still very cold. And everywhere with children. There were a lot of problems with children, especially washing them. And there was no food, no more milk. It was hard to find accommodation. A girlfriend took me in. She lived outside of Wiesbaden behind the pheasant enclosure. She had rented the club house behind the enclosure and managed it for the club. The tavern had been closed and her husband had been conscripted, but she still lived there and she had an extra room so she could take me in.

And your parents?

The house was destroyed so they had no where to go. They came out to us and we all lived there. We sat most of the time in the cellar because there were continuous alarms. We hardly ever went upstairs. They had a big cellar so we sat downstairs most of the time and we also slept there.

That was in February. What happened then?

That was March and April. Then the Americans arrived.

Were you frightened through all these raids?

Yes, the raid in February was so awful that we developed a real fear of bombs. I lived through a few air raids in Berlin when I visited my husband but nothing ever happened to me so I thought if nothing happens you don't have to be afraid. But if you are involved in a near miss, and many were killed in Wiesbaden, even people in their cellars, then you become afraid. But outside there were no more bombs when the Americans came, but there was a lot of shooting. There were a lot of German soldiers in the woods around us and they came with tanks and there were a lot of explosions. The club house got a lot of damage. But the shooting was not nearly as dangerous as the bombing. Upstairs was damaged but not the cellar.

Were you frightened of the Americans?

No definitely not. I remember when the Americans came. We went upstairs and looked out the windows and saw them. This clubhouse had a large stockroom with food and clothing. The Germans had help-trains. If a city was hit then a train was sent there with lots of wagons carrying the supplies they needed. One warehouse for these trains was in the club house and the American knew that. They came straight there and cleaned the place out, especially alcohol and such like.

So we stood there and looked down and saw the Americans, and we thought they all looked so nice, so likable. And they were very nice.

Did you have any difficulties at all with the Americans?

No, none at all.

What was the reaction of the people once the war was over? Were they sad at all?

No they were terribly happy. Mainz had the French and also the Americans before we did and people were saying that they could see people going for walks with their prams in the lovely weather we were having, and they are lucky while we were still sitting there in the cellar.

Oh the Americans were not in your area yet.

No but we thought they would be there soon and then there would be peace. We were very happy to see them.

What did the soldiers think, that people would be against them?

That was no longer the Germans but we had little to do with them. But they must have been happy when the war ended as I doubt they wanted to fight. Those were difficult times because all the bridges over the Rhine had been detonated and you couldn't cross the Rhine.

Oh that's why the Americans couldn't come immediately. And the population welcomed them with open arms?

Yes, the population welcomed them and was happy.

Yet five years before they had been enthusiastic about the war. Was the change because of difficulties in the war?

Yes I think so. Slowly things became very difficult and then there was the bombing and so many men died and there was a lot of hunger and need.

Slowly people realised what Hitler was on about. They didn't say anything yet but they thought it to themselves. I think the longer the war dragged on the more difficulty Hitler had convincing people.

Did Hitler clarify why the Germans were fighting the French and the English?

Well, it started in Poland and then with the Russians Hitler always said that they wanted to invade us. And then when the other nations joined the fight he probably said the same thing, that others wanted to get rich at our expense, that everyone else was against us and wanted to poke us in the eye.

And people believed that?

Yes, that is how he always talked, that we were in the right and he did it very cleverly, he was very clever psychologically. He was fascinating in a certain way. I had an aunt, an elderly very nice woman, and she didn't like Hitler at all. Once Hitler came to Wiesbaden and he drove through the streets in an open car. Everyone went to see him and this aunt went too.

When she came home she said to me "Luise you should have come too, he is wonderful man. I looked him in the eyes and at that moment I was exalted." I often heard people say such things, something in his look that fascinated people. I have no idea what it was.

I also had a friend who knew the wife of Hess who was one of Hitler's deputies and now sits in prison in Spandau. Because of her friendship with Hess's wife, my friend was invited to Hitler's place in Obersalzberg. He had a house in the mountains there. Hitler was there and also Goebbels.

My friend told me, 'you wont believe it but Hitler had no effect on me, he looked to me like any ordinary citizen. He didn't talk much and was certainly not fascinating. Goebbels was different, he spoke a lot, but Hitler looked like a tired and used-up man.' We thought about that a lot. I think Hitler must have taken some sort of drug or medicine because he did have a radiant look at times. That is what I heard from others too who had seen him when he was very down. That's why I think he pepped himself up with something so that he was completely there again.

That would have been during the war?

It was a mystery to me, after all the things I heard, how he managed to get people to follow him. No one had managed to do that before. People were ardent supporters and you didn't dare say anything against him.

What did people do in their free time, or didn't you have any when the men were away?

Well in Breslau I do remember that we had time at first. We went along to the Uni and sat in on lectures. My husband didn't have a great deal to do so he came as well. But then it became more difficult and he didn't have so much free time because he took over the practice of a sick colleague. Then later I was busy with the children and had little free time. When I went to live in the countryside with the children it was lovely. The children loved being in the countryside. We lived on a farm which they loved and I helped a bit. In return they gave us some food so we weren't hungry. We were all happy there. After the war that all changed. There was so much work, we had to do everything ourselves. I knitted whole nights through because there was nothing to buy but we needed clothes so I undid old things and re-knitted them. Jumpers for the children. You had to sew everything you needed and mend things that were damaged. There was nothing at all to buy and you were busy just surviving. There was nothing to eat so we roamed the fields after harvest to pick up whatever was left, even wheat grains which we ground up and cooked into a soup. Here in the area there were a lot of fruit trees and you were allowed to collect the fruit that had fallen to the ground so that is what we did.

Did you become exhausted, or how was it for you?

I was not very healthy at the time, not that I was sick but I wasn't capable of much. We were not well fed and we were all extremely thin and we had to work so hard. We had to do everything for ourselves. My parents house was damaged but you couldn't get a building firm to repair it because there were no bricks or cement, nothing available to buy. We had nothing. We went into the city and where the houses were rubble you could take bricks. We took hammers and chipped the cement off the bricks. Then a truck came and we had to load it full. I worked very hard at the time to get enough bricks to rebuild the house.

You did that all yourselves?

Yes, we all had to help rebuild the house.

And other people too, the women?

Yes there were no men there, almost no men at all. It was very difficult. The men dribbled back after some time. Women worked hard to clear up. That was how the heaps of rubble in the city were dealt with, the women cleared them up.

We had no heating either. My brother arrived back and went to work in the forest because in return you got wood for yourself. But you had to chop it up yourself, so we all had to help and that was really hard work.

When you look back, is there a particular point you always remember, a good or a bad point?

The bomb that came down in the garden and also the flight from Schliesien, when I was alone with the children. When my husband was with me it was not so bad but when I was alone with the children I often felt so abandoned and helpless. Though it was not as bad for me as it was for other women who had much greater difficulties. I had an aim at least, I wanted to get to my parents in Wiesbaden. But many people had nowhere to go and had to go to camps. I was very lucky in that respect.

Has your experience changed your position to war. I mean, do you think you think differently about war compared to the young people today?

I think that if you have not lived through a war you don't know how awful it is. Once you have lived through a war you realise that on no account should there be a war, no price is high enough. You must to do absolutely everything you can to prevent war because war is the worst thing you can live through. It destroys everything.

Is it the same for men, or different for women because they had children to protect?

For example, that bombing raid, I realised only afterwards that if you hear the hit then it is too late, it has already happened. You hear it all tiny bit later than it happens. I found after the hit that I was no longer sitting on the chair, I was lying over the children's pram. I threw myself over the pram without being conscious of it, to protect the children because stones were falling down. So somehow as a mother you always feel you must protect the children and rescue them. A lot of children died.

Do you think men are just as anti war? Men often think of wars as heroic.

But not if you are right in the middle of war. In the beginning perhaps when you march to music in beautiful uniforms. But if you have been stuck in Russia or experienced the misery of Stalingrad, then I don't think anyone is keen any more. They had had a belly full of it.

What do you think when you see other wars in television?

When you see how the civilians suffer you remember exact how it was for you yourself. When I see women standing in front of burning houses I remember what it was like for us standing in front of our pile of rubble. It is a dreadful moment, to stand there and realise everything is gone.

Our generation has not lived through war but I am starting to see how dreadful it is. I am starting to dream about bombing raids.

A bombing raid is horrifying. You are so defenseless, you can only wait until you hear the kaboom, and when you hear that you are happy because you have heard it and it is over. It is when you don't hear anything that it is dangerous. It all happens so quickly. That bombing raid on Wiesbaden was not very long, but it felt to me as if it had never ended.

How long was it then?

I don't know but probably ten minutes or quarter of an hour. People thought it was a very long time although it was quite short. It was dreadful.

Do you think women became more emancipated because of their experience?

Yes I do think so, I am sure of it. My husband tried afterwards, we tried to work together, married women, but somehow it was not the same. Women had become more independent during the war and that sits within. Later one tried, at opportune moments, to teach the men. I don't think you forget something like that.

I don't think so either. I can imagine that a man came back and was used to the wife doing what he told her but suddenly that was no longer the case. I am sure it was difficult, especially when they were away four or five years.

We were together three years, then apart for four years, and to come together again was very difficult, but we managed. My husband is no longer alive. He died three years ago. So once again I am alone and have to be independent. It is not so easy.

ANNELISE K. 1916: COPING WITH WAR AND FAMINE

Annelise K. born 1916, lived in Rosswein (East Germany) during the war.

What did the people feel about the war beginning?

The older people who had lived through the first world war were appalled. Younger people hoped that the war would end well. Their view of the world was a a bit perverse, influenced by the Nazis. The Nazis wanted to make everyone believe that Poland was about to attack Germany.

How did you notice that there was a war?

That was long before the actual war. There was no longer as much to eat as one wanted. Butter was rationed. You only got as much as there were members of your family. And it was weird, different recipes were propagated years before the war, for example how to cook rhubarb without sugar. They wanted you to use less sugar. People were already used to rationing their sugar.

Did the men have to leave a soon as war was announced?

Yes, they were called up shortly afterwards. My husband went of his own free will. At the time you were no longer allowed to shop at Jewish shops. That was forbidden. There were people who disagreed with that, but others thought it was right. People who disagreed were in danger because you could be punished if you were against the government. You heard on the radio that the only possible action was for Germany to declare war. Most people were for it. Almost everyone wanted it. You couldn't do anything

175

about it anyway.

Women who didn't have small children were mobilised. Women had to work in munitions factories.. Shopping was really difficult because not everything was available but women helped each other Sometimes you had to queue from eight in the morning.

In the building I was living in there were three young women with small children, all about the same age and we organised between ourselves that one of us would look after the children while the other went shopping. We alternated who went shopping. We also helped each other in the air raid shelters.

Were there women who were quite happy that their menfolk were away?

Yes I can imagine there were! Personally I was not one of them, but I am sure there were such women. But I knew one women who didn't cope with her husband leaving at all. She became mentally ill when she had no husband there. She was such a charming woman and she had a very normal husband who was a waiter in a hotel. She was delightful, I knew her well. When her husband was called up she changed completely. She went with other men, she got drunk, she took off all her clothes on the street when she was drunk. Such things.

Did friendships develop between women?

Yes, I think that is probably true. I always had good contacts but deep friendships didn't develop. I had my family nearby so I was not completely alone. My sister lived with me.

Were there problems for children.

Schools were open right through the war. With regard to food, only the real necessities were available. We lived in a city. It only became really dreadful after the war.

What did you do in the evenings during the war?

My sister lived with me and we read a great deal and we listened to the radio a lot. Always encouraging talks. There was always a spokesman, he was the spokesman for the nation. He was called Fritsch. They way he used words was unforgettable. He was very good. But of course what he said was not true, although of course we didn't know that at the time. We had a really small radio and we could only receive one station. We could only hear what this spokesman said.

Were you frightened of your own soldiers.

We were frightened of the Party people. If you listened to a foreign radio station you would be sent to a concentration camp. Once, when I was visiting a woman with a large Blaupunkt radio, I tried to listen to a London station. But then someone else arrived and I turned it off immediately. Occasionally you heard whispered rumours. You couldn't trust anyone.

People were pleased when the men came back on holidays?

Yes, that was wonderful of course.

How often did they return?

That was very varied. When the war was going well for Germany then they came home more often. My husband came home from Russia once. He had discovered what was really happening and he was no longer a Nazi. I had three small children and had not seen him for two years. You had to look after yourself and you had to be able to do everything yourself. There were no men to relieve you. The way things were, you were completely alone, but life had to go on. You also had to bring up your children by yourself. No one helped. But after the war it was much worse than during the war. There was nothing to eat, no electricity, nothing to heat with in winter. It was really bad. My husband died in the war.

What did you think happened in the concentration camps?

One thing I would like to say is that I really had no idea what happened in the concentration camps. Most people had no idea. I had a sister-in-law in America and she came home for a holiday. She told us what happened in the concentration camps. I didn't believe her and told her she was crazy. But she knew what was happening and I didn't.

I thought they were for political re-education. I thought you would have to work and that you would be re-educated so you were politically acceptable.

One day my neighbour said to me 'Look out the window!' and there was a whole line of prisoners in stripped smocks. It was terrible to see. Beside them was a line of SS officers with whips and big dogs. . It was awful. Everything was gray, the clothes were gray, the faces were gray. No one dared to say anything, no one dared to give them a piece of bread because everyone was frightened of those beast that were the SS officers. The prisoners were as thin as skeletons. The German officers killed the German soldiers so no one could tell anybody anything.

There were a lot of concentration camps in Poland and the Poles were happy to have them. They were happy that the Jews were taken away. They didn't help them. Before Hitler implemented his final solution he asked all the other countries if they would take in the Jews but they declined. After the war then the Jews wanted to leave. They all wanted to go to Jerusalem. The English promised the Jews they could go there but the Arabs had said they wouldn't let them in and at this time a lot of ships with Jewish people aboard sank . Or in Ceylon for example that was another thing, the world powers were happy to have the Jews off their backs. My stepfather was an instrument technician and he hated the Jews even though he had never met one.

At the time we didn't dare go to bed because the sirens would start. At eleven o'clock the sirens would start. Thank God we were not bombed, but Leipzig and Dresden were. We were always between them. At the beginning of the war my daughter got pneumonia in an air raid shelter. When I see fireworks today I always think of the war.

When did people grow weary with the war?

That was only much later, only really when we declared war on Russia. Everyone felt that that was the beginning of the end. That was on a wonderful spring morning. You could see people on balconies and in the street standing together.

And when the war ended?

Everyone was frightened. The men were all in prisoner-of-war camps. Everyone had camps, the Americans, the French. Many Germans were transported to camps in Canada. They were kept in England, sent to Russia. Here in Germany there was nobody at home.

What do you remember most about the post war period?

If there was any food available you had to stand in long queues to get some. We also swapped between ourselves, we stole from the fields. We swapped silver cutlery or good porcelain for eggs and fat. The farmers collected expensive carpets and fur coats and jewelry. The farmers swapped food for anything that had value.

The children were sick a lot because they didn't have enough to eat. We were always hungry. If my father had not been the local vicar we would have all starved. My father was cared for by the community.

There was a lot of theft during this time. People stole potatoes from the fields, they plucked the heads of wheat so they could grind the grains for bread. Those times were dreadful. There was simply nothing to eat. We fried potatoes using candle wax! We didn't have any oil so we used candles. We made potato dumplings out of rotten potatoes. They didn't taste good but there was nothing else so we had to eat it. We were happy to have rotten potatoes, that was better than nothing. Today you wouldn't even feed them to animals. You just wouldn't do it. But at the time we were happy to have them.

There were always shortages but the first years after the war were by far the worst. There was no gas, no electricity, no firewood. It was often cold and there were no shoes. We made shoes from old tires. I had a birthday and my father walked 10 kilometers with a suitcase for me with ten bricketts inside. It was the most wonderful present. The children were educated in the communist system.

My brother worked in a rapeseed mill. He brought us this crushed stuff made not from rapeseed but from poppy seed. It tasted revolting but we ate it because there was poppy seed in it. Maybe we had a deficiency and needed to eat it. My uncle said that he could swap this oil for anything. For that you could cook potatoes or cake.

Did the farmers help you?

No, very seldom. They watched over their fields. I personally saw how farmers defended their fields with firearms when they were harvesting. I remember collecting wheat heads after harvesting. We sewed ourselves big round aprons that were good for collecting wheat heads but it was difficult to walk with bare feet on the harvested fields. But even at these times we had fun on the fields!

What did you cook at the time?

We didn't have much choice. If you had potatoes, carrots and an onion that was a real delicacy at the time. But we didn't always have that. There was no meat at all. Sometimes we had beetroot. My sister was married to a chemist and sometimes he had a bit of oil. We used that for cooking and then the apartment wold stink of this fat for a whole week afterwards. You couldn't get that smell out of the place. The area where we lived was a sugar-beet area. There was a lot of sugar beet grown there. That was wonderful. We women formed a group and went collecting sugar beets. It took a long time together a hundredweight of beets and then it was a dreadful job washing them. You had to scrub them with a stiff brush and ice cold water. But once they were clean they were cut up in very small pieces and cooked in a big copper. That was not so simple either because first we had to collect enough firewood to heat the copper. That took a long time and when we had the wood we had to chop it up into small pieces. Once the beet was cooked the red juice was collected and cooked up again. I still like to eat that today. It is called sugar beet syrup.

Were the schools still open after the war?

After the war the schools started again bit by bit. It wasn't so simple as there were no teachers. Either they had been called up and they were in prisoner of war camps, or they had stayed home and had been rounded up because they were Nazis. Then substitute teachers replaced them and they came from all walks of life. They had been butchers or bakers – they came from all occupations. Even housewives. They were stood behind the lectern and had to teach the children.

During the war it was not as difficult as after the war. In particular people were very frightened of the occupying soldiers. Many people were so frightened that they took their own lives. They committed suicide. The worst were the Russians, there was a lot of defilement. We were pleased when the Americans came. It was better with them. We didn't have to be frightened of them

I had a girl who helped me with the housework and with the children. She lived with several siblings right at the end of the village. They had a small house with a cowshed. She asked me to come to them so they wouldn't be alone, and I did that. I packed my things into a cart and moved in with them. We disguised ourselves at that time, dressing in old clothes and scarves. We wore dirty old clothes to make the soldiers think we were old women. At the time there were not one young woman among us!

When I returned to my own apartment later the door had been kicked in. Soldiers had kicked in the door and stolen anything of value. The silver for example, everything of value. They also took all of the alcohol. I had hidden the good porcelain in the cellar but they had stamped on it and destroyed it. They broke it all on purpose. I only dared to go back home a few days later.

It was very difficult to find anyone to repair the door. There was no one who would have been able to fix it. The lock was okay but all the wood was broken. So then we lived there with no light, no water, no electricity, no men. Completely without anything. We locked the house but an agent, a sort of caretaker, came and he let the Russians in. You were not allowed to lock your door against them. They came mostly at night and one night they came to our place. My son was ten years old at the time and he was sleeping in my husband's bed. I went out to them. They were shouting and you could hear them from miles away but you couldn't understand them because they were speaking Russian. However I could see that there was an officer among them. If there was an officer there it was not as bad because if the soldiers didn't behave themselves they wee severely punished. So of course I was really pleased to see an officer there. They came into my living room and then into my bedroom and they saw the small boy lying in my bed, on my husband's side of the bed.

They pointed at him and said "Small man, small man!" Then they left.

They laughed themselves half silly about the 'small man'. But I have to say, they were very fond of children.

One day I was out on my balcony, the kitchen balcony that looked over the garden. My neighbour was on the balcony opposite, and she whispered across to me "The Russians are coming!"

It was too late to lock the apartment so I hid in the corner of the balcony. The Russians came into the house and they looked everywhere but thank goodness they didn't find me on the balcony. I was really frightened.

Were all the women so scared?

There were women of course who were not frightened and they had lots of advantages. They had enough food and also milk. They got everything from the Russians that they needed when they slept with them.

Were there many rapes?

Once the invasion was over all women who had been raped had to register and they were examined to see if they had caught a venereal disease or if they were pregnant. If they were pregnant they could have an abortion, they didn't have to carry the child. That was done in a hospital by Russian doctors. They had very good doctors I must admit. There had been a great many rapes, especially of the young girls. Eight or ten men would rape one girl. That was dreadful. It was dreadful the things that happened. But if you knew who had done it then these soldiers were punished by the officers. But we had other occupiers, and the Russians were not the worst. The worst were the Poles. There were some real animals among them. You just can't imagine.

Did the children suffer from the war?

The children suffered in that they were hungry. They didn't suffer so much under the Russians because they were given food occasionally. The Russians had a fantastic respect for their superior officers. The simple soldiers were completely uneducated and came from overall, including Mongolia. They hadn't seen electricity or water that came out of the wall (running water), or watches or clocks. They came from furthest Siberia. They really didn't know anything.

Then I moved to a different city where the Russian command was stationed. The Russians were there in a camp but they were allowed very little leave. The Commander was a good Russian.

When did the men arrive back home?

Oh that was very varied. Some were home relatively quickly but for some it was years before they came home. Others never came home.

Were there difficulties when the men came home?

The men had become feral because of their years in prison camps. They had had very little to eat. Many were crippled and some were very sick.

Did the men find work?

Yes, mostly they had to work in the forests. The Russians dismantled all the factories and took them to Russia and there was nothing left in Germany. They took everything that could be used. The women had to dismantle railway tracks. If you refused, you didn't get any food ration cards. Then you didn't have anything to eat. That was tough work. That was on the railway line from Leipzig to Dresden and still today that line only has a single track.

The Russians vaccinated us against all sorts of illnesses, we didn't know what we were being injected against. I found a doctor who wrote me a certificate saying I did not tolerate injections. You could arrange such things if you had connections..

What is your reaction when you see war reports of TV, like the Vietnam war now?

When I see refugees with children I always see myself. It reminds me of what I went thorough at the time, and we were luckier than most because we didn't have to flee. The whole of the eastern area was evacuated. It must have been atrocious. I know of one instance, a family from Breslau. They had a child in intensive care with meningitis but they had to take her from the hospital and evacuate. I know this girl and she is still affected today. It was like that for thousands f people. It was ghastly.

Did the women suffer in the war as much as the men?

They suffered differently but certainly not less. There was nothing to eat, they were frightened of the soldiers, they were frightened for their own menfolk. They didn't know whether they were alive or dead or whether they would ever come home. The women suffered a great deal.

When my father gave a sermon in the Nazi times (and later under the communists) there was always someone there taking notes. If he had said a single thing against the state he would have been deported to a concentration camp immediately. One was spied on everywhere and it was the same where ever you lived.

When did you move from the East to the West?

Well, the war ended in 1945 and in 1957 I came to the west from the eastern zone. Things were still not fixed over there and today things are still not right. They can't read what they want to, they can't travel where they want to. Of course, there is no comparison to the post war period.

At the time there were a great many fortune tellers and soothsayers. Everybody knew one. One went to these women, mostly it was old women, and then we would 'oscillate'. There were many men in camps or missing and question was 'Is my husband still alive.' You took a photo of the missing husband with you and that was put on the table. Then the wedding ring was held over it on a string.   If the ring went in a certain direction that meant the husband was alive. After a time every ring would start to oscillate.

Something else I will never forget. We had very nice neighbours living in our apartment block. They came from Berlin and had lived in America for twelve years. I talked to them a lot. They had been to one of these soothsayers and had asked if there was going to be another war. Everything was so uncertain between the Amis and the Russians. We all thought that it would start again and they would be at each others throats. But this soothsayer said 'No, there will not be another war in Europe. Only after fifty years.' I often think of that.

Seven or eight years after the war I had a phase when I thought I could hear bombs falling in the night, although there were none there. But I could clearly hear the noise, that whistling that they made. I would wake up drenched in sweat.

Many many years later I visited Dresden again. I knew Dresden well, it is a beautiful city. But when it was bombed it was awful. At the time there was not one man there in uniform, There were only civilians. There were thousands from Czechoslovakia and from Schliessien. They were everywhere, at the Zoo, they had small children in prams. So many people died there, people were simply wiped away and you no longer knew who they were. They bombed the zoo. The animals died and people were running around burning from the phosphorus. One heard that the Englishman who dropped the bomb had lost his wife because of the Germans. His whole family died because of the Germans.

ANNA MARIA H. 1915: DIVIDED LOYALTIES

Anna Maria H. born 1915, Lived in Bad Teplitz, Schoenau (Sudetenland) during the war.

> **"My mother-in-law can no longer cry. She is empty. I can, thank God."**

You were a member of the party?

I really resisted joining the party. It was my father-in-law who insisted I join, not so much my husband. My father-in-law really pressured me to join.

Oh, when my daughter was born I really wanted my sister to be a godmother. I only have one sister, one sister and four brothers. We loved each other dearly and we both wanted her to be god mother. It was my dearest wish. But when my father-in-law heard about it he was horrified. '

Good God,' he said. 'You can't have the wife of a Jew as godmother for Brigitte!' Brigitte was my daughter. I was forced to have my sister-in-law, my father-in-laws daughter as godmother. That started something within me that really hurt and my sister was so disappointed. She wept and said "I am not a bad person just because my husband is Jewish.' And my brother-in-law was such a wonderful man, so helpful and decent, so gentle. My sister was so affected by her experiences that she became very ill and spent a lot of time in hospital. She had asthma and couldn't breath – it had all psychological causes. My brother-in-law looked after her. He washed her and managed her sick-bowls. I mean, which man does that? My husband certainly wouldn't have. I could bet you anything. Maybe he would have done it once or twice, but not over the long term. My husband had demonstrated that he would stand by me but not if I became very ill with vomiting and so forth. But my brother-in-law was so very good. And that these people who had never done anyone any harm were so vilified by Hitler.

Again and again it was said that the Jews were responsible for the first world war and and second world war, but that is not true. If Hitler had accepted them into the army instead of persecuting them, if he had taken German Jews as soldiers I am certainly they would have fought bravely for their nation and their country. Because there are a lot of Jews in Israel who are homesick for their home in Germany. The English Jew Morgenstern was the first person who begged that Germany should not be destroyed. He was a Jew.

Did you understand what the concentration camps were?

Yes, one knew. Because I had Jewish friends who were sent to concentration camps. They didn't make any exceptions. I could show you letters I have from Jews saying that I was a loyal friend and that I sent packages to them in the concentration camps, food packages. I sent them to Felix because he wrote to his father that he was hungry but his father had nothing to send as he was a Jew in Prague. So I sent packages to him and when the new Czech rulers came in, he sent me a letter so that I had something to prove that I was a decent German.

Also my brother-in-law was Jewish and many Czech friends. Even the straw cutter, he was the Chairman of the National Commission, I was good friends with him as well.

In the apartment house there was a neighbour and she was friends with a Czech. I was friends with him too and she told me that she listened to foreign radio and told me the frequency. I had already been listening to it before she told me but I didn't dare say so. Then we listened together to what the English said, because they broadcast in German.

And you didn't tell anyone?

Good grief no! I couldn't do that. You couldn't talk about anything you had heard.

My sister had lots of Jewish friends and told me that her girlfriend Finna Marek was in hospital for a knee operation. I said I'd like to visit her but she said that would be difficult because the Jewish hospital was behind a building that housed the National Socialist (Nazi) Party office. I said that didn't make any difference to me because I was a member of the party, me myself. I had to become a member because my husband was a member and my father-in-law was a staunch member and it was impossible for me not to join. My father-in-law said, 'Your husband is a state employee, works for the employment bureau and if you don't join he will have difficulties'. I didn't want to join but I did so because of the difficulties. Why should I fight it, so I went and joined. I did the membership swearing in ceremony, the party troth. I did indeed hold my hand up but I did not speak the troth and I never wore the party insignia. Instead I kept it in my handbag. So I told my sister I would get in, see if I didn't.

I put on my party insignia and I bought myself a big bowl of ice-cream, it was summer, and I went through. I was stopped by an SS guard who questioned me and asked where I was going. I said I had an acquaintance in there and he let me through just like that. Once I was in the hospital I took off the insignia again because I didn't want to visit Jews wearing a party insignia. I went in and distributed the ice cream. They were so happy, they cried for joy because none of the Germans were nice to them at all. Finna Merek told me that she had had her operation without any anesthetics at all. She was just bound down. The doctors were Jewish but they had no pain killers nor anesthetics They were all operated on fully conscious, without anesthetics. I told her that next time I came to Prague I would bring some. I had a friend who was a chemist who was also in the party and was good friends with my husband. I told him about it and he was humane and gave me a tube of painkillers and I took them next time I was in Prague.

But I also experienced something gruesome as follows: I traveled one day with the tram in Prague and there was a Jewish woman standing there. She had a star on. An SS man got in, saw this star and said to her 'You don't belong in the tram, how dare you travel in the tram, as Jew. She replied that she couldn't walk very well which was why she always took the tram. The SS man said, 'You are being impertinent" and gave her a push and she fell down. When she was lying there he said 'You old Jewish fetel, now you are making a theatre and he kicked her in the face with his heel so everything bled. I was so appalled and I wanted to scream at him that he was doing the whole German population a disservice, but I didn't dare. My sister was married to a Jew and my husband was a member of the party and ultimately I was as well. But that triggered something inside and at that moment I hated. Not the German people though, I was one through and through.

But that he permitted himself to do that!

Yes!

My father-in-law gave me a Hitler bust for Christmas once. He thought he was giving me pleasure but I put it in the kitchen cupboard and there it remained. I couldn't talk politics with my father-in-law but it was easier with my husband. He didn't do anything against my sister, actually her helped her. He brought her food from the black market. I can't blame my husband, that would do him a disservice, but my father-in-law he was an ass. I asked him once how many Jews he would have for breakfast and he said 'I'd eat one and a half million each day and they would soon all be gone."

My mother-in-law was very nice, she was from Romania, and she said 'But Papa, you shouldn't say such dreadful things, you know that you hurt Anne's feelings.'

So it was best not to talk politics at all. I didn't allow myself to be bailed up by him any more.

Anyway, my father-in-law was convinced that Hitler would win the war until two weeks before the end. He was absolutely sure, you can't imagine, he was completely blind and my husband as well and I had always said we'll loose this war, we have to lose it, it cannot turn out well because one single nation, the German nation, wants to control the whole of Europe. They want to eliminate all the Slav peoples, all the Jews, my God, we'd have the whole world against us. The small states who stood by us, they didn't really count and we couldn't depend on them anyway, we saw that when Italy and Austria changed sides. It was fortunate that Germany lost the war. It was lucky. If we had won it it would have been completely impossible, it would not have worked out.

Did you know other people who thought as you did, for example friends or family?

My whole family, my mother and all my brothers were social democrats from when we were small. My father was a member of the Social Democratic Party, SPD we say today, he was a very active member. My mother was also active in her home town. She was in the council and always active. So from when I was a child I was German, but for the Social Democratic Party, the workers party. The communists didn't count at all where we were.

Were there women whose men were communists?

No no, there weren't. Although my family was German I had two years Czech schooling because those were the Czech rules and not of our choosing, My father was employed in a German firm that was later confiscated by the Czechs. The world war one legions to whom the Austrians and Hungarians and also the Czechs belonged, fought together in the first world war and then in the end the Czechs fought against the Austrians and Hungarians and those were the so called legionaries.

The factory where my father worked was confiscated and given to the Czech legionaries and they said, well you eat Czech bread so you should send one of your children, we were six children, to the Czech school. So my brother Franz, the middle boy, was sent to the school because the older ones had already left school. He was at the Czech school for two years and when he graduated there were only myself and my brother Rudolf left. My father said that since I wanted to have a career in business I should go to the school. So it was my turn.

Was it difficult to be German or to be a Social Democrat in Czechoslovakia at this time?

Two sorts of Germans developed at this time. One group were the people who gathered around Hänlein. As Hitler to Germany that was Hänlein to Sudetenland. Konrad Hänlein was the equivalent of Hitler in Sudetenland and he gathered a troop of Germans around him and these people eventually became the local National Socialists, Nazis. I was a German too but not in the sense of National Socialist but my husband was, automatically. When the acquisition came, SHS is what they called themselves. These Germans called themselves the Sudeten-German Home Front. When Hitler marched in my husband got a medal, a medal of honour. The SHS was the spearhead that made the union of German and Czechoslovakia possible.

When the war began, what was the first thing that happened.

At first people were very enthusiastic.

Did you notice changes?

There were changes but it took a while until people noticed them. People thought it would be a lightening-fast war that would be over in six or eight weeks. But it lasted one, two, three, four years and longer and people became depressed.

Did you notice a war was on where you were, for example bombs.

No, Bombs only fell at the very end, but hardly any at all in Sudetenland.

So was the only difference that the men were called up?

Yes, and of course that doesn't suit any woman when her husband is conscripted into the military. There were perhaps a small group who wanted to say their husband was one of the first who fought in the war but most were not very enthusiastic. Just as I was not very enthusiastic. I would much rather have had my husband at home and I would not have been at all offended if he had been rejected. I wanted to be German but I didn't want blood to flow.

So you questioned the war?

On no. Each year from 1941 to 1944 I went in April and May to my husband in Kennekrätz then six or eight weeks to my sister and then a week with my husband and then home again.

So you lived alone?

Together with our doctor, I lived alone. My in-laws lived nearby and my own parents in the next town.

Did people helps each other more now the men were away?

No you couldn't say that. They weren't helpful, just the opposite actually, many were envious of me. I would almost say that people resented that my husband was a city employee and I got 80% of the salary because most other women just got a small pension from the state. They were not helpful.

Someone denounced me too. One day a man from the employment bureau came and told me I should do something for the fatherland; asked if I couldn't get a job. I then went to the employment bureau and said I couldn't work as I had a young child to bring up. But they knew a lot about me and said, you have a mother-in-law who could look after the child. I told them my mother-in-law was very anxious, although she was good to the child. But she had tried to commit suicide and had had a nervous breakdown. I can't trust a small child to her. No I certainly can't. They had to accept that, but said I had to do something. And I said yes I understand exactly because my husband is the Human Resources manager here at the Employment Bureau.
They said, 'Are you Frau H?'
'Yes of course.'
'Then why didn't you say that earlier,' they said, 'that changes things'.

So that was the end of that for me. I was never approached by the employment bureau again. You see what sort of wrangling there was? If I had not been the wife of the human resources manager then they would have given me no option and said I had to work. It would have been an order. I went to a factory only once, as a volunteer to pack bandages. I stayed two days and it stank so much of ether and I had to vomit. I couldn't cope and I had to go home. I didn't want to go. Not because I didn't want to do anything for our soldiers but because I wanted to be free.

Were their problems during the war with accommodation or money or food?

No, there was no problem with accommodation in my home town and everyone got enough from the state that they could live, so no one had financial problems. Of course I was in a much better position than my neighbours because I got more than double the income of the people who lived above and below me whose husbands were not employees of the state and only got a pension for their husbands who were away.

Wasn't that uncomfortable for you, with the neighbours?

Yes. The neighbours didn't like that and they told me so. One neighbour said "you can't talk, you are swimming in money, we have to be frugal and our husbands are fighting on the front line and your husband sits in the interior.' The were jealous. One woman even said to me that in her opinion my husband should die in the war. Her hate must have been so overpowering that she wished for my husband's death. But the opposite happened and her husband died and my husband came back, thank God. But I was sorry that he died because he was a good man and his wife cheated on him during the war. There was a lot of cheating during the war. The woman who lived upstairs cheated on her husband with other soldiers and the women who lived below, this woman of whom I am speaking, had a child that people doubted was her husband's.

Why do you think women did that? For money?

No, certainly not for money because no one was in financial difficulties. It was simply the sexual experience. I don't know, perhaps I am abnormal but

I didn't ever think of doing the same. I was completely loyal but I was not rewarded for my loyalty, whereas the other women were disloyal and their husbands were perhaps more loyal. But no, it was not a financial consideration. We had enough food and no one was starving.

Women would have become more independent having to do things by themselves?

Yes of course, and I became more independent too.

And were there problems with the men because of that?

I would say that it didn't suit my husband particularly, that I was so independent. He said to me, 'Now I am here and now I am responsible for this and that. I am taking responsibility.' And over time I changed back. Actually I had become so independent I was quite capable of living without the help of a man. Yes, but my husband and I found each other quite by accident and he took over the reins again. He took over too much actually so today I am dependent again. Once again I have no self confidence and I would warn women against letting their husbands take complete control. I don't know if other husbands are like mine. My husband plays the big man and criticises me if I do anything independent at all. I have got to the point that I can hardly buy a new coat by myself because I am no longer used to it, Papa always has to be with me, even to buy a pair of shoes and that is one step too far.

My daughter is much more independent. She goes and buys herself a fur coat and that is the end of that.

So there was no solidarity between women?

No, although there was some solidarity because women said to each other, your husband is away and my husband is away. But it depends how you view solidarity. They showed solidarity because we were all grass widows with men on the front, but if there were problems, or social problems, then people didn't help. If someone was sick no one else offered to cook or go shopping for them.

Why not?

I don't know, I am not sure if that is part of the German mentality. My daughter, for example, belongs to a catholic community and there people are perhaps more helpful and I would say that my daughter and her husband are very active in this community and very helpful. But I have noticed that although my daughter had three children, if she gets sick no one in this community offers to help or says 'Can I bring some food over.'

Once the war was over, what was the feeling?

Yes well naturally we were really frightened the Czechs would take revenge because so much injustice had been done to the Czechs in the German Reich. It was especially so when Heindrich was murdered. The SS Lieutenant General Heindrich was murdered in Prague. I was in Prague at the time he was murdered. It was really bad. Every day Czech citizens would be court-martialed and shot, and only because they had said quietly 'He deserved it. Why did he make such problems for the Germans." Because Heindrich was barbarous. Himmler and Heindrich were beasts, they were not men. I remember my nephew, my sister's son, had a Czech friend who was the nephew of a famous footballer in Prague. His mother was a widow who moved from Prague to Brünn. On the day that Heindrich was murdered she was in the train and all she said was 'It served him right!' What she didn't know was that she was sitting next to a Gestapo officer in civilian clothes. She didn't know whether he was Czech or German. So he caught her and made her come with him and in ten minutes she was gone. Summary execution! Just because of that. You can imagine the boy, Jichi he was called. I notice things that are callous, I really feel them. Today it is not so bad, I don't notice things as much. But the boy Jichi he developed a venomous hate.

How old was Jichi?

He is over forty now but at the time he was small. He was ten or eleven years old when his mother was shot. But he grew up and he hated the Germans because he himself hadn't done anything. But his uncle, the brother of his mother swore revenge and I can imagine he was dreadfully angry.

I can tell you the partisans of Prague they foamed at the mouth. That was told me by the Chairman of the National Commission. He was completely powerless. I had wanted him to give a key from my apartment to my sister so she could take the furniture which was all new but he told me it was fruitless, he had had all his power taken from him and the partisans were foaming at the mouth. So I left him the key and he could give it to whomever he wanted, even to the Czechs and they could do what they wanted with it. And that was what happened. A Czech acquaintance took everything from the apartment that was there to take. Those were hard times.

They were upset because they knew what was coming. I too listened to the BBC on English radio.

Wasn't that forbidden? Weren't you afraid?

You'd go to concentrations camps. That was forbidden

In my hometown, where I lived, there were so many suicides every night. The sister of my friend and her son lived in a different suburb where a whole household committed suicide. There were seventeen people. The women were too scared so a man undertook to liquidate them and shot them in the mouth so there were brains everywhere. That was murder and among them were the my friend's sister and her son. She told me about it and was completely exhausted.

Why did that happen?

People were so shocked and were scared stiff of the Russians. During the war Hitler's propaganda machine had told of such gruesome happenings that people thought if the Russians came they would all be raped and shot anyway. And that happened in some places. One hundred or two hundred in a night, not all together. Later we found out about it and how much is true you never know but there were hundreds of suicides.

Don't think that my brother-in-law who was a Jew had it better be the Czechs. On the contrary, he had exactly the same misery there as with Hitler. It was not much better, just like the Russians today. In the beginning it was not as bad, but it got worse with time. My brother-in-law was beaten because he spoke German. He left of his own free will.

Which year was that?

That was 1945. On the 8 May the troops had marched in and on 15 June, five weeks later, we had to leave our home.

The worst thing after the expulsion was that I was alone. My upstairs neighbour took me with her because the partisans than came from Prague to Deblischoenau, not the Czechs, but the partisans, they came and ravaged the place and we had to leave. It was said that our neighbourhood would be evacuated on 17 June 1945 and we had to give all our money and savings books up, everything but ten marks. We were threatened with death if we didn't obey but I didn't obey, I kept eight hundred marks for myself. My father-in-law worked at the bank in Deblischoenau and he gave me the money and if it had been up to him I should have given everything up except for ten marks, but I kept eight hundred marks for myself, but I couldn't fritter it away. .But I was alone. My mother and brother could not come because my brother had a profession that was needed and they didn't let him leave, nor my father-in-law until they had a replacement.

So I was alone and my neighbour upstairs said she would slit her wrists that night so I slept upstairs at her place on the floor and kept an eye on her. I said to her she had no right to slit her wrists and kill her child, that was wrong. I looked after her and she took me with her and her whole family. I had family too in the German Reich so at least I had a goal, somewhere I could live. That was Dresden. The next day the partisans came and they hit us in the back with their rifle butts and said 'Go home to your German Führer" so we had to leave.

Did many women and children have to leave their homeland?

Every day a certain number. That was a great migration. You have to remember, there were three million Sudenten Germans who were expelled. That was a migration and many people killed themselves, hung themselves in the woods.

My mother-in-law took her own life. When they didn't need my father-in-law in the bank any more they took him off to a concentrations camp and my mother-in-law committed suicide. I had been expelled already so I wasn't there. I heard about it at Christmas time, 1945. I got the first post from relations on Christmas eve and they wrote that I should not be shocked but both my father-in-law and mother-in-law were no longer living.

Were you frightened of the Russians, or by the English or Americans?

No we had papers from Sudetenland. I had my identity card from The Reich and I had a travel visa from the Czechs. The Czechs only gave travel visas because they wanted to give the appearance that they were not trying to exile the people but that the Germans were leaving of their own free will. They wanted to show the rest of the world they had clean vests. So they didn't talk about expulsion but instead gave you a travel pass. You could take ten kilos and ten mark notes. Yes, with ten ten-mark notes. They had done exactly the same thing to the Jews.

Did a lot of women sell themselves for food?

Yes, many women sold their bodies.

What did other women say? Was it just understood?

I would have to say that was not so common in Sudetenland that women sold themselves, I was not there long enough to know. But in Germany I got to know a lot of women who sold themselves to the Russians because they had nothing to eat. They were forced to do it, not that they wanted the experience, but because they had no other alternative. After the war no help, really none, was given to the refugees. It was probably not even possible because everything was disrupted. You have to imagine that in the DDR there were only Russian command posts and in the cities only

Russian commanders and the Germans had to obey. They put communists and communist fighters into all the government positions and they were very critical of the refugees. Because they knew they all came from the Sudentenland and were all Nazis so they didn't help them at all, not even a little bit. You just had to box your way through. I have to be honest and confess I stole fruit from trees, fruit that was still unripe, and my neighbour kept watch in the fields while I dug up potatoes. I was sweating from terror because I knew that if I was caught I would be sent to Siberia. It was well known that if you broke the law you would be sent tot Siberia.

I'll tell you one thing I did as an example. The pub where my neighbour was living had an attic and you could climb up there. I discovered that there were great balls of tobacco hidden there. I saw them and I thought to myself, they have those from the third Reich and I could sell some. At the time tobacco was very rare. So I took some leaves and hid them in my purse. Then someone from the pub came in. He had not seen that I had taken anything but I had done so.

He said, "You've stolen tobacco!"

"No I have taken nothing, I swear to that," I said. But I had taken some, at least half a pound.

An oath is something sacred for me, and even today I suffer from having told a lie because I only say I swear something when it is true. I got sugar, it was was brown sugar, not refined, but at least I had sugar and that was very important. That was what you thought the whole time, how am I going to get something to eat today.

Did other women understand others who sold themselves?

Oh it didn't come to that. One sold tobacco to the Russians and traded with the Germans. I don't know if they would have understood because the whole thing was not open, very secret, that was black market and whoever was caught was punished severely. My husband sent me cigarettes from the English prisoner of war camp. He sent me one hundred English cigarettes and we sold those, one for ten German marks and then you could buy yourself something to eat on the black market for two or three hundred marks. But it was all very risky with high penalties and prison sentences. It was not possible to have direct contact with the Germans because everyone was frightened of being betrayed. You could only go to that corner where black market articles were traded. I was too frightened to go, but the friend with whom I was living, she had more talent for that and she sold or traded all the cigarettes and she even traded with the Russians. One even bought schnapps, very expensive schnapps from the Russians then traded it for other things with the Germans. Later I lived at a butchers. The butcher's apprentice was accused of stealing sparkling wine and was forced to leave the apartment. Later we found this wine and we sold it for five hundred marks a bottle. So that is how we always traded. We couldn't do anything else, we were forced to act illegally. It was self preservation. I had to look after my child.

There were no other possibilities!

No exactly right. It was survival instinct, you did what you had to and I can imagine that many women gave themselves to the Russians just for food, just to save their own lives. I remember once where I lived the Russians came by creating chaos and came right to us and they wanted to buy schnapps. They were so drunk.

Then one day there was an announcement from the Russian command that all German women had to go to the doctor to have a test for sexually transmitted diseases. The Russians said that all German women were bad and passed diseases onto the Russians but it was the other way around, it was the Russians had the most sexually transmitted diseases, so they said. I was not very knowledgeable about these things, I was always a bit backward. I am still not very informed about these things but people said that the Russians were immune to these diseases. To this day I don't know if that is true, but anyway you had to bring your written confirmation from your doctor to say you were not infected. I was not infected because I never had sex with anyone but my husband, to this day.

Where was your husband?

At first I tried to find my husband by writing a letter to Herr F. in Lugau. to ask whether he knew where my husband was. He was a corporal like my husband and they had been at the same place for years. I wrote a letter and sent it there and at the same time my husband wrote and sent it to the same place, to the Erzgeberge (Ore mountains). My husband wrote that he didn't know where his wife was and since they lived just on the border he asked whether they knew where the Germans from Steppenschoenau had been evacuated to. This is what Frau F. did, she sent the letter my husband had written to me and the letter I had written to my husband. So I knew his address for the first time and my husband knew mine. He sat down and wrote several letters with the same content. There was the Russian border, the English border and the French zone. That was what it was like at the time. And that was how I first got contact.

What did you do then? Was he in a prisoner of war camp?

My husband was in an English camp and he was well looked after. First he was in Belgium where it was not so good for the first months, but then he was sent to Westphalia, where they were virtually their own boss. The German officers had guaranteed that there would be no deserters and although they answered to the English the German officers were in command. They were clothed there and got very good food and if something was worn out, like shoes, they were able to swap them for a new pair. They really had it good I must say. My husband sent me jams, ham and cheese from his own rations.

On 4 January 1946 my husband went over the Russian border illegally, from the English to the Russian zone, to the DDR, to Hallische Saale, but I was not at home.

I had traveled to the Erzgebirge again and lived with my brother in the Czechoslovakia. My brother was a hairdresser and spoke perfect Czech. He was a very sought after hairdresser and they didn't want to let him go, they offered him Czech citizenship. I had had contact with him and he had put five thousand German marks for me in Zwickau on the German border where I had to pick it up. So I went from Halle an der Saale to the Erzgebirge, and picked it up from Frau T. where he had left it. Then I wanted to see my brother who lived only three kilometres away from where I was with Frau T. She said that her son Dieter, who was about nine years old at the time, would take me there.

Dieter had belonged to the Hitler youth and she said, "Dieter don't go the dangerous way with Frau H., go the long way around. It might be a bit longer but it is safer."

But what did Dieter do? He promised his mother to do that but he didn't hold his word and went the shortest way.

I didn't know that and asked him, 'Dieter you are not going the dangerous way are you?"

'No, no Frau H.,' he said. 'We are going the right way that my mother said.'

Then suddenly he said "Duck!" and he said 'Those over there are Russians!"

The Russians stood there with their weapons at their feet. We crawled along for some time until we couldn't see them, then he said 'Now we can stand up again."

I said to him, 'You took me the dangerous way didn't you?"

"Yes Frau H." he said, "the other way would have been far to far. Kilometers further."

So that was how I got to my brother.

Our greeting was very heartfelt with lots of tears. They didn't live in their own apartment at night. Originally they had lived elsewhere. They had fled to the Reich, but they had seen the misery there, so they packed up and went back to another part of Czechoslovakia and were living in an apartment that had once belonged to other Germans. He didn't have an extra bed for me so I slept in the children's bed. He didn't tell me how dangerous it was until I had left. Every night there were raids on the

Germans and if they had found me they would have arrested me and him too. I only discovered that later.

Was it difficult for you in Dresden?

Yes very difficult. Where I was in Dresden, the woman wanted to slit her wrists. She took me to her nephews place where I lived for eight weeks. That couple slept in one bed and they took their child out of its bed and it slept with the mother, and my child was laid in the child's bed.

But there was a problem getting food. There were food shortages and we had nothing because we didn't have any ration cards. At the time there were still ration cards but we had no residence permit. Without a residents permit you couldn't get food. They had to share what they had with us. They were four people and then there was me and my child and my acquaintance and her child. There were eight people. So she had to share the food and the husband was rather steamy. He always tried to come in.

Now I have to relate something terrible. The woman, I was certain, was a very good wife, A. she was called.. She left every day and came home at midday. She went off every day with a neighbouring woman who had an illegitimate child. She came back before lunch and then she cooked. It took me a long time to realise that they were going to the Russians to give themselves sexually.

For money?

No not for money, for food. No one would have done anything for money, food was what was important. They did it for food. One day the woman came and she had a rash and boils on her legs. I asked her what it was and was really quite anxious. I was quite fastidious and never sat on the toilet seat before putting newspaper on it. I was always that way and I taught my child to do the same. And I have to say, they had a very ordinary toilet with two boards and a hole between that you stood or crouched over. So she had these boils and went to the doctor. I asked her what the doctor said and she replied that the doctor said you could only catch what she had only through sexual contact. And I was frightened and I left there of my own free will.

But the husband had even killed the cat so we had meat. He told me I should help and I said, oh god no! I screamed in terror - it was a huge male cat. But he did actually kill it and it was so tough that he put it in a bag and hit it with an axe. Anyway he killed it and had it roasted. The others all ate but I would have vomited even to think of eating it.

I thought to myself that I couldn't let my child eat it. I would sooner starve. My friend the countess, she was called Margarete, said 'she doesn't know, and it is important that she stays healthy' and she ate it as well. But I didn't eat it. I would have rather died. It was so horrible.

But I knew she had a sexual disease. Later I realised she had sacrificed herself so that we could eat. And I have often thought what good people there are. And I have to thank her because I was a complete stranger.

Anyway I left with my acquaintance who stuck to me through thick and thin. The woman who wanted to slit her wrists and her child. The Dresden people said she could remain there, but she said no, where Anne goes, I am going too. Then we left and we walked kilometers every day, from town to town, trying to get a residence permit. It was impossible to find anywhere to live until we got to Birnau in Sachsen, a locality where they said if you find a place to live we will give you food. I found a room with an elderly couple that I rented and finally I had a certificate. I could sleep there. My friend and her child and parents rented a large room in a guest house and that is where they set themselves up. They were given some milk. Those people had a cow or perhaps two and so my friend got milk for her child. I didn't get milk but my child was six years old and from the age of six they didn't get a drop more milk. In their sixth year they go about a quarter of a liter. And they got a half liter or a whole liter from these people. I didn't get a single drop.

I cut a great heap of wood for the woman where I was living. That was men's work. She had goats to milk. At least every morning she put a little milk in the coffee for my child. But I had to work very hard for that milk.

And then they told me I had to leave because I didn't have any menfolk who could work, so I had to leave there. We went to Mittenbergen which is near Halle an der Saale, that's where I ended up. And there I caught nits. I caught them twice during my flight as a refugee. I cried, cried bitterly I had swollen eyes. I went to a delousing establishment and they said to me I shouldn't cry, that they could tell who bred lice and who caught them. Those were very hard times.

In Helmsdorf I had the following experience. I went walking with my friend, she with her child and I with mine. She had her child in a pram and we went out a while over the fields. And there was some woods, just a small patch. Suddenly I heard the sound of a motor, then it was very quiet, then I heard voices. I said to my friend that that was not the sound of German people, those were Russians. Then I look and see two Russians. Quick, duck down, into the ditch at the side of the road. My friend said 'no, into the woods'. They were about 100m away. I said, no that's wrong, but she ran and I had no option but to follow her and the Russians saw us. Two Russians. We ran to the woods and hid but it was too late. They came after us and they each had two pistols, just like you see on television, these antique pistols with wooden handles and very long. They held us up with these pistols and wanted to rape us. But I speak Czech and many words are the same as Russian, and said 'there are two children here.' There were two Russians one of which was Asian, a Mongolian type face and the other was perhaps a white Russian. Anyway you could see the difference. The Mongolian-looking one had very bloodshot eyes. Maybe from lust, I don't know. They were about 21 or 22 years old. I was twenty nine at the time and my friend was thirty. I said what about the children and the Mongol said 'Shoot them'. I could see the other Russian was more humane and I turned to him and said , Du Karascho, Du Karascho". Again and again.

What does that mean?

'You are good.'

Then he said to the other one, leave them alone. He wanted my friend, she was a real characteristic type and he wanted to have her immediately. I would have given my life for her. I was more forceful than she was, her husband had been killed and her nerves were shot. She just cried. He was about to hit her on the head with the butt of his revolver and I stopped him and screamed at him that he should stop. I yelled, and we had learned this from our experience with the Russians, I yelled 'Machine is kaputt.' In German that means that the sexual parts are not in order, she is sick, sick in the abdomen. And he wanted to hit her again but the other one stopped him. Then I said, Gretel, take your child and go away. Go and don't look back and run and run. I wanted to send my daughter with her but she said she wanted to stay with me. My daughter clung to me and wouldn't go. And that was my good luck. I said that I would bring my child home then return. And he said tschechilaswow and I understood that. It means 'Word of honour' I said tschechilaswow, and shook his hand and said in Czech, I'll bring the child home and come back.

The other one said 'If you don't come we will shoot you dead, you'll be killed, guaranteed.'

I took my child and ran to catch up with my friend and she broke down. She couldn't breath and was so agitated. We came to an electric fence and both of us got an electric shock. The fence was for the cows but I didn't know about them and in the area many of the electric lines had been damaged by the war. I got a shock and I thought it was the overhead electric wires, but actually it was only this harmless fence. Still we were shocked. We ran home and they waited for us in the woods. We had left the push chair in the woods and we were completely exhausted. Although we were exhausted we were afraid, what if the pram is gone. We went back the next day. We put on scarves and went and collected the pram. That was terrible. They had asked … if I had only known what they meant when they asked where the commanding officer was. The Russian commander lived in the next door house and they would have run away because they were frightened of him. It was forbidden to rape the women. But I didn't know that and I said he lived a long way away. That was the wrong thing to say.

Those were the sort of episodes one experienced. You know, now I am really agitated. When I talk about it I am so affected again that I relive the whole thing. Those were harrowing times in Dresden. Those were the sort of experiences I had.

Then I left Dresden for Helmsdorf. In Dresden we had food ration cards
and there we had ration cards too but I didn't know how long we could keep
them so I didn't de-register myself there. So I had two places of residence
and I was always stressed because I thought that it might be discovered.
And one day an aunt who lived in Dresden came out and said to me that the
police had paid her a visit looking for me. I suppose they discovered I had
double ration cards. They told her that Frau H. should come to the police
station so they could question me. In the night I sweated a lot, my nerves. I
got a fever and shook like a leaf, thinking that if I am arrested my child
would be sent to Siberia. I was scared stiff. We experienced really horrible
things, I could tell you stories about what happened to us for hours. One
doesn't remember them spontaneously and especially not if you are
nervous.

Did you have a problem with the police about the ration cards?

No. I went there but they were actually very polite. I didn't give them time
to bring up the ration cards. I went in and said I wanted to de-register from
there. He asked me a few things then wrote the certificate. He asked where
I was going and I said I didn't know. I asked him to write 'Unknown
destination". He actually did that and that was the end of that episode. I
was still anxious because I didn't know if there would be repercussions.

You had a child. Do you think the children suffered from the war?

Yes they did, they did. My daughter always came to the bank with me
where we withdrew money. After we were expelled she asked for things
and didn't understand when I said we had no money. She couldn't
understand at all. Suddenly from one day to the next we had no money.

Do you think the women suffered more than the men.

I think the women suffered physically and psychologically more than the
men. It depends on your inner attitude. For example, my husband, I think
he thinks differently to the way I do. When I see these gruesome pictures
from Vietnam then I say 'That is murder." If I see bombs burning children
or when they are wounded and the women are screaming then I am really

upset and cry, but not my husband. My husband is not interested in these things at all. I ask myself sometimes, and also my husband, why were you a national socialist and he simply says, I am German.

Because they had children?

Yes, I think that is because of the way women think. Women in general are more feeling I think. I speak from my own experience, I am a very soft-hearted person. There may be other types of women, and indeed there were very many women who, for example, prayed to Hitler the way they would pray to Jesus Christ. If they saw a pair of blue eyes they fell into a faint. With Rudolf Hess it was the same.

I had a brother who said it this way: "You know I saw Rudolf Hess and looked him in the face and was quite fascinated. The man radiates charm and he hypnotises people" and my brother was not a National Socialist sympathiser.

Now I can understand how the women liked the man and I can imagine how women reacted. I am not to be bought, neither psychologically nor in my thinking. I am not to be bought, I think for myself, and that is the difference. I think if women had a say in politics then they would not start wars, they would sort it out politically.

IRMA A. 1914: RESISTING IN SMALL WAYS

Irma A.: born 1914, lived in Hamburg and Berlin during war

[This interview was recorded by hand rather than on tape]

In 1933 I lived in Langenhorn, a workers' area in Hamburg where the communist and socialist movement was quite strong. Hamburg has a history of independence. One always had the feeling that Hamburg didn't really want to belong to the Reich, it was the Hansastadt. When Hitler came to power many of the people living in my area were taken away to concentration camps. We had a very good idea of what the concentration camps were. We believed that you had to work hard there, got bad food and were quite likely to die. We didn't know the extent of the atrocities though.

When these people were taken away from our area a group of people including myself collected money to give to the families affected. I luckily left Germany for England in November, but all the other people who had collected with me were arrested. I didn't realise we were so close to danger.

My mother wrote to me from Germany while I was in England and ordered me to visit the German Club in London otherwise I might have difficulties when I returned home. That just shows you how frightened people were. I did go once but that was all. I said it was too far away from where I was living.I went back to Germany after a year.

On the first day of the war there was an air raid as I was coming home from work - it was a single aircraft, then it was quiet for months and months. I was working in a paint firm. The war didn't change much except that when the men were called up I was allowed to handle the ordering and the telephone. Before I simply had to write letters.

Women were not allowed to work before the war and that caused resentment. They often needed the money. During the war there were more women working but they didn't, to my knowledge, replace the men in the high positions.

I had actually wanted to be a nurse but Hitler got in and then I couldn't. I went to England instead but came home again because my mother was ill, and then I look a shorthand typing course. I started smoking as a direct result of the political situation. Hitler said that the German woman 'doesn't smoke' so I started smoking. But it was impossible to rebel in more than these little ways.

There was a joke at the time about Hitler sending Ribbentrop to India to ask the oracle what the future held. He came back and said, 'I see a great victory but Germany must believe that'. You have to say it in German, "Ich sehe einen grossen Sieg, aber Deutschland muss daran glauben". And that had a double meaning. I liked this joke and often told it until one of my colleagues said, 'If you tell that joke once more I will have to report you'. She had found out how much I liked it. You had to be very careful. You didn't do any good anyway being defiant.

Just before the war I joined the red cross. I got a notice that I had been called up and had to report with 48 hours provisions and a change of clothes. When we got there they told us it was not a red cross job, they needed telephonists and teleprinters and that we would have to live there at the hospital. I was surprised but I didn't like my job and was quite pleased to get away. I had been living at home and looking after my father. Both my brothers had been called up.

After our training they told us that we really hadn't been called up and needn't continue. But by then I wanted to go. I think they may have changed their minds in the middle. They had rung up my firm and asked if they were entitled to keep all their workers. They were not. So I got called up and once I was there they told me I was there of my own free will!

I met my husband at the house of a very pro-Nazi family. He knew that I was in the services and he thought, 'Oh, she is one of those'. He was introduced to me as a Sudetendeutscher. They were generally very pro-Hitler so I thought, 'Oh, he is one of those'.

We eventually started telling each other political jokes and found out who we were. He was a half Jew, so although we got engaged we weren't allowed to marry.

He was not allowed to be a boss. Later he was not allowed to work in the drawing room. He had to supervise the foreign workers, funnily enough! He got along very well with them.

I was sent to Belgium to work as a telephonist. We were kept very strictly. On the whole the Belgians were very nice to us, but not always. In Holland it was worse and in France. We had little contact with the people as a rule. Only with the shopkeepers. We felt we were just there to do a job. We lived in a boarding school where we had taken the main building. We had to do P.T. in white shorts. The nuns made the school children look away when we did our P.T. I think we showed too much leg!

I think the girls became more independent. So many of them had lived at home until then. Quite a lot of my friends had problems when their husbands came home after the war. They were used to having their own money and paying the bills. There were problems especially when the men had been prisoners of war and had been away a long time.

Our house was damaged in 1943 in the raids. We only got a new ceiling after the war, the whole of it had fallen down.

I was lucky with the raids. I was in both Berlin and Hamburg but missed the big raids. I was in Berlin in 1944 during the raids - I went to see my fiancée there. I was in the suburbs during the raid and when I went back into town to look for him, I couldn't find him. His house had been bombed away. They had been in the cellar having a sleep, so they were lucky. You got two days off work if you were bombed, and a new flat to live in.

When we came to England after the war and they told us how badly England had been bombed, we thought it rather ridiculous as we had come from Hamburg and Berlin. The actual destruction was so much less than in Germany except for a few towns.

One day during the war my fiancée met a friend of his who was a Nazi. This Nazi told him that he had had to stand guard on a road with his back turned, while heavy lorries went by. He had no idea what it was until one day one of the lorries turned over. It was one of those in which they directed the exhaust into the back so it killed people. He was just so disgusted, this Nazi. That was the first we knew of what was happening. The rest we only found out after the war.

If you are told something often enough you begin to believe it. Goebbels kept saying that when a Jew was nearby you had a funny feeling. After the war a cousin of mine remarked, 'It's funny there are already so many Jews and half-Jews around.' My husband asked her how she knew they were Jews and she replied, 'Well you know, one does get a funny feeling.' We were most amused. My husband didn't tell her until years later that he was a half Jew because she was such a simple and harmless woman.

My husband came over to Hamburg from Berlin near the end of the war. We met a policeman we knew on the street and he told us that Hamburg would capitulate, that it wouldn't fight. Of course we were very pleased.

My husband wanted to register - that was in April, 1945, in Hamburg. He found a man sitting with his feet on the desk reading the newspaper. He said, 'Heil Hitler' and the man said, "What do you want?" My husband said he had come to register and the man said, 'You must be crazy!' He took him along the corridor to show him a yard where all the papers were being burnt.

'That's where all the papers are', he said, 'and now you want me to start more papers.'

With the end of the war some people were very afraid that we would be treated very badly. But I was happy because I was engaged to a half Jew and hadn't been allowed to marry.

After the war we were very lucky because my husband had an uncle in the British Army who posted us two pounds of coffee every month. That was worth much more than my husband's salary.

Between the wars I was a pacifist - I come from an old socialist family. But I think I changed. I found the war necessary. Hitler couldn't have been allowed to go on. But the older I get the less political I get. I am becoming more and more disgusted, not with politics but with politicians.

FRAU X. : LIVED IN HAMBURG DURING THE WAR

Only part of the recording of Frau X. is available. She was recorded on one of the tapes that was used twice and most of her testimony was deleted.

My daughter was born in a hail of bombs. The windows flew out and we had to hang curtains and bed sheets over them. Once a mine blew off the whole roof while we were in the cellar. During the very first bombing raid a bomb fell on the children's playground and 17 children were killed.

Did you live in fear?

Yes of course. You never knew if you would make it out of the cellar, and whether your apartment would still be there if you did.

In March 1939 it started. We all had a cellar but we had to get bags of sand to put out fires that started. That all had to be in the air raid shelter but often people didn't worry. Then bombs came through the stairwell roof and fell into the stairwell, blocking the way out of the cellar. Heavens, we were nearly suffocated because of all the smoke. It was dreadful and so hot. Luckily I had a leather jacket. I grabbed the thing with the jacket, although on the wrong end.

I was not in Hamburg during the heavy bombardment. I left earlier.

Did people still go to work regularly?

Probably. I think there were two large air raids and then everything was rubble. Then people could no longer work.

What happened.

I don't know. I was no longer there. I can tell you that the more important buildings had to be reconstructed. The hospitals and munitions factories. I had to go too, everyone had to. Even to the last, we fixed the Elbe bridges with the Russian prisoners of war. That was my last work for the war effort.

I looked after others because I had enough. And then later everyone worked to fix things up.

…..............................

One could not go there even when the bombers were gone because there was no oxygen. Most people suffocated, were glued to the asphalt which went soft. We met a 12 year old boy in the street with a bicycle. He wasn't meant to be there. He was scratching among the debris. We asked him what he was looking for and he said he was looking for his mother, We used to live here and my mother must be lying here somewhere. It was all rubble. He couldn't see anything but he said he had already found his brother and had him in his rucksack and now he was looking for his mother. He cleared away the stones. Some things like that you don't forget.

I have the impression that the war was almost worse for the women because they had children?

Yes, especially when war is at home. The men went away to fight but the women had to fight the war at home, the bombing raids that we had. That was the worst. They came from above and we had no defenses against them. On the front it is different, you have weapons, the men were together.

ELSA W. 1913: LIFE AS AN EVACUEE

Elsa W.: born 1913. Lived in Hamburg then Sundhauser (1942), then evacuated to Griefstadt-Turingen in 1944

> **"My father said to my mother, Don't you dare vote for Hitler. He wants war, that's all."**

[Handwritten:

My father said to my mother, 'Don't you dare vote for Hitler. He wants war, that's all.'

My mother would have voted for Hitler because everyone else was. She had no idea about politics How could she? She was at home until she was sixteen, then married and behind the cooking pot with a room full of children. That's how it was for women in those days. They didn't have any idea about politics. They voted how their husbands told them to.

There were some women in the National Socialists who were worse than the men. There were a lot of people before the war who made lots of money. People who delivered goods.

Girls had to do work duty: it was one year long or otherwise you wouldn't get a job. I married in 1935 after 3 months. My mother-in-law was at home and had to be cared for. We got a costume at BDM we were so poor. My husband would never have allowed me to work once we were married. What a scandal! We had a loan.

The rich could pay for an abortion and then have only one child but the poor had little money so they had to go to illegal abortionists. Often they were in so much pain that they told someone and they were sent for a long time to the asylum. It was worse than prison.]

In 1939 when the war started, what did the people think?

That varied a lot. For me it was dreadful. Firstly I had to let my husband go and secondly I was alone with the children. That was the hardest part for me.

And other people, were they glad?

Yes, I think others were glad but I never was. I was never happy about it. My husband was called up but not my father as he was too old already.

So the men were away. Did the women know what to do?

Yes, those who didn't have children worked. They were obliged to work, but I had three children so I didn't have to work.

What sort of work did women do?

That varied. Some factories were changed so they made war materials.

How often did the men come home?

It depended on whether they were still in training. If they were in training they came home every three months for a few days. Then they were sent away and it depended where they were sent. My husband was sent to Holland. He was in Endhoven in the local headquarters.

What did you notice most when the war began.

We had food ration cards. They were introduced as soon as the war began. Women with small children always had enough but two adults who ate a lot, they were always short. Later towards the end of the war it got even worse.

Did the children go to school?

The schools were open of course but mine were too young for school. I went to Schneverdingen because of all the bombing. We had to go into the cellar at night. We didn't have a chance to sleep at night. I went to Schneverdingen of my own accord and found an apartment with strangers there. They had a furnished apartment which I rented from them.

What did you experience in Hamburg before you left?

There were a lot of bombing raids and I had to flee into the cellar with the children. That was dreadful. I lived on the first floor.

How often were the raids.

Sometimes they were every night. The alarms would go off and I had to go into the cellar with the children. That was why I moved away.

People were frightened?

Yes of course. We had to go to the cellar clothed

Was it a large enough cellar that you could sleep there in beds?

No. There were wooden pallets we could lie on. When the alarm was over we went back upstairs.

Later you were in Thuringen. Was that also your own wish?

No, I was evacuated there. I couldn't go back to Hamburg because the place where I lived had been bombed. I would never have been able to go back with the children, there was nothing for me there, everything was bombed or had burned.

Why did you leave your furnished rooms?

Well I was in hotel and that became too expensive. There were a group of us that were in Sundhausen of our own free will and we were evacuated to the village of Griefstadt as a group.

Did the State pay?

We had to pay our own rent. There were various farmers with big houses who let out furnished rooms.

You got the money from your husband?

Yes, the rent money.

Was it easier to find food in a village?

Yes, initially it was easier but later it was very difficult. There were no potatoes. The major had to go around to the farmers. The farmers gave nothing of their own free will even though their cellars were full. The mayor came with me when I had nothing and went to him for help. I said to him that I needed some food for the children but the farmers wouldn't sell me anything. So the mayor came with me and the farmers changed. 'Yes, you can come here for food, yes you can come to us!' That was what they said then. I paid for everything.

Didn't people pull together?

No. We had been bombed and were interlopers in the village. They were the wealthy farmers. They had food, they had everything and we had nothing.

What did you do when you had so little

Well I had ration cards.

I meant, what did you cook. Did you have vegetables only or was their meat?

That was all measured out, but there was not much to have. Three children don't eat much though and the quantity was the same. That was how it was for five years. It was only later that we had nothing at all.

When did you have nothing?

After the war. There was nothing more to have, but the farmers still had food. They had eggs, they had fat, they had sausage, they had everything. I sewed for the farmers, for their wives and daughters. Dresses and skirts and blouses. They gave me peas and sausage. I had so much I couldn't eat it all. The people who had no land but wanted something sewn, they paid me. I took cash from them and food from the farmers. From that moment on I had enough to eat.

In the cities of course it was much worse. They often had nothing at all to eat. We could also go into the field during harvest and eat ourselves full. My youngest would come home for dinner and I would say, come and eat. He would say, Mama I'm full. I've been in the fields. He had eaten so many carrots and peas until he was full.

Did you listen to radio during the war?

I didn't have much time. I sewed a lot and I knitted for the children because you couldn't buy anything.

Whoever had a radio could listen to it, the Volksempfaenger. It was forbidden, but actually we never listened to it. We put on music or something, or listened to the news when it was broadcast. But when the war ended there was no news broadcast at all. I had been longing for the end of the war.

[Handwritten:

When Italy capitulated I said we should too. I was informed on by one of the women. But I was lucky because I sewed for he local policeman's wife and I knew the policeman.

He said to me, 'I have looked right through this rule book to find something that applies to you.'

He found a paragraph in the rules that applied to me – my husband had died in the war. He called in the woman and told her what could have happened to me. Later she apoloigised. She probably didn't mean it either.

He came from America. He said they had sat by the radio and cried when he heard them say 'Komm Heim ins Reich' Come home to the Reich, we need you!" When they came they were disappointed. He said he couldn't believe how he had had 'sand in his eyes'.

When the war ended, were you happy or sad?

I couldn't be happy, I had lost everything. I had lost my husband, lost my apartment, I was with my children who knows where. My parents were not there, I was completely alone with the children. For me, everything just kept going. Why would I be happy? What for?

When did your husband die?

He died in 1942. I was always alone wherever I was.

Were women more comradely with the men gone?

No!

Were some of them happy to be alone?

That varied. Some were no doubt happy to have husbands away with whom they didn't get along. . Some, the war brides, had not known their husbands long so it didn't really matter to them that they were not there. They aged during the war. Some remarried, some went out to work again (they had a pension) and managed quite well. But a woman left with three small children can't go out to work She had to stay and home and live from her war pension and that was small. Those who remarried got compensation. Those who had never married had to find work and from a pension.

Did anyone help each other, for example when food was short?

No, not much changed. Everyone had to look out for themselves. Everyone was frightened they would starve. People looked out only for themselves, more than in good times. One went off over the fields.

Swapping became normal. Whoever had something to swap was okay. Especially the farmers, they had food to swap. They got carpets for their fat, real carpets and a pair of shoes for a pound of fat. That was how it went.

I stayed in the countryside in Griefstadt. There was no possibility of change. First the Russians came. We were the Russian occupied zone but we never saw them. No one did anything to us. Then later we were told we were in the American zone and the Americans marched in. That was a Hurrah for the children. There were chocolates and biscuits. The Americans distributed them.

Was the war a bad experience for your children or did they not notice much?

They were too small to notice.

Did the war change you. How would you think about a new war?

I wouldn't want to live through another war, bust despite that there is war everywhere today. Poor people, the things they have to bear is dreadful. They experience for many years what we only experienced for four years.

I always think that people who lived through the war experience it differently from the way I do, who have not lived through a war.

Yes, that is true. But my children didn't experience the war, they were too small. For me it is different. I think war is dreadful, any sort of war. A mother always thinks differently, thinks about her children. I once saw a picture on television, I almost cried. There were bombs falling and small naked children were running. They didn't even have a shirt, nothing on, and they ran for their lives. They had no father, no mother, they just ran, they didn't know where.

You could experience that in Hamburg too, a city completely bombed out.

Were there special problems when the men came home?

Yes there were problems with some, new cuckoos in the nest.

The women had probably become more independent?

Yes, that as well. You heard that often enough. Some women had other men living with them at home. The husband came home years later and the wife had lived with a different man for years.

I suppose people thought they might be dead soon anyway.

Yes, everyone thought they would be next to die. Everyone tried to find advantages where they could.

Your generation, women especially, were not brought up to be independent.

A lot of women had to work. The men were no longer there even if they were married. There was a lot of work available after the war. The war had changed things. We had lost four million people and we needed replacements. We had foreign workers and the women had to work too. So the women all learned professions. That was not the case before the war.

So women became more independent?

Perhaps. The children, they grew up without fathers really. They became more independent. But we women learned a profession too. I was a secretary as a young woman. Once I married that was over. That would have been a scandal if a married woman had continued working. A man would never have allowed that. Now it is a scandal if a married woman doesn't work. Women with small children go out to work. But at that time, even a woman without children should not go out of the house to work. It would have been a scandal for the husband to have a wife who worked, except in cases where there was very little money. And probably if the wife was a teacher or some such. There were a lot of female teachers in our school, but they were all widows. None had a husband, or they were too young to have a husband. It was different then. The wealthy had nannies to look after their children.

The childminders were sort of married off. That was my mothers fate as well. My father said that his wife was not to clean the dirt from others houses, even though my mother was never a cleaner. She was too weak. She could only look after the children. She told us so often that she took the children to the sand pit and she played in the sand just as they did. She was only fifteen years old and half a child herself really. From there she married.

Why did you come back to Hamburg eventually?

I had to show I had accommodation there before I was allowed to come. If I hadn't had a place the authorities would not have known where to put me. Someone found a place for me in Hamburg and wrote to me that I could live at such and such. I had to show that to the authorities.

And why did you come back?

Because I am a Hamburger. I wanted to be in Hamburg again. What would I do with the children on a farm? Milk cows?

Even though it was more difficult in Hamburg?

No that was all over. People lived in cellars and built again. They built huts as well. That was not too uncomfortable. The English who came here couldn't believe that the workers could live in such hust and make them comfortable houses. The houses were often made very cosy inside. When you were inside you couldn't tell you were just in a hut. That is a characteristic of the Germans. They make whatever they have pretty. Everyone had a small garden out the front. You could plant vegetables. We lived for two years in a hut and then I was allocated an apartment. I was in Hamburg and I had three children so I had a right to an apartment. That was in the Lindenallee. Two women also lived there. It was a four room apartment and two rooms were already occupied. One of the women lived with me. Of course that was a bit cramped. We found a room for her and she moved out The other old lady stayed with us. She was very nice and she looked after the children for me. She later died.

You didn't leave Griefstadt because of the Russians?

No we didn't see the Russians although we were told we were in the Russian zone, and we were. Then the American came. I stayed in Thuringen. I was seven years in Thuringen in all. Now it is Russian. It was later swapped with the Russians for Berlin. But when it was Russian then there were no soldiers. It was the DDR.

CHARLOTTE N.1913: POLITICS AND SUFFERING

Charlotte N. born in 1913, lived in Genthin near Magdeburg (100 km from Berlin) during the war

What did you notice when Hitler took power?

In the first years you didn't notice much change, I mean in 1933-36-37, you didn't notice any changes really. One had the feeling, I'd like to say, that part of the population felt it was coercion that the youth had to join the Hitler Youth movement, that children had to be part of that. They were simply drilled. The same with fatigue duty for women, although I say to myself sometimes that it might be good if we had compulsory work today.

It was like this, my ex-husband (we divorced after the collapse) was very interested in the House Ludendorf. Do you know about it? They were against socialism. Ludendorf was a General in the 1914-18 war. General Ludendorf lived in Tuzting and distributed a lot of his writings there. At the time he published a weekly newspaper that came out on Mondays. It was a political paper. General Ludendorf was absolutely against the church and very pro German nationalism. He was a German Nationalist. His wife, Dr Matilde Ludendorf was a philosopher. That was his second wife. He did some good things, especially in the 1914-18 war. Whoever was interested in his views found them very persuasive and my husband was very enthusiastic about them.

At that time I was classy, blond and tall, in other words pure-blooded! Very 'northern' as the Germans say. That is why it all happened.

General Ludendorf published a lot and Frau Ludendorf published really good things as well. I remember she published a book called 'The German woman, servant or partner?" I wrote to her about that book, because the other books from General Ludendorf made my husband crazy.

I always said that if my husband had been Catholic and had put the energy into the catholic church that he invested in the House Ludendorf, then he would have been named a saint within his own lifetime. My ex-husband didn't have an easy time under the Third Reich because he openly declared his allegiance to the House Ludendorf. It was difficult for him, and he spent some time in prison.

I did a lot of things with him. Because of the difficulties we had in Genthin we even wanted to swap the practice for one elsewhere. My ex-husband is a dentist. We had organised everything, organised to swap our practice with a practice run by a colleague on the Bodensee. It was all organised but the Gauleiter (at the time Hitler had Gauleiters) intervened. The Gauleitung wrote to us that we were not politically reliable and therefore we were not allowed to move. It was not possible. Well, then the war broke out. Dentists got their marching orders fourteen days earlier, because they had prosthetics to take care of. A dentist needs time to make a prosthetic after a tooth has been pulled. With a doctor or a surgeon it is not so difficult, but a dentist can't make prosthetics so quickly so they had to give dentist fair warning when they were called up. But with my husband it was different. He was called up and had to leave within two days. That was because in our house there was a Free Mason, and Ludendorf was very much against Free Masons. Herr B. was a cavalry captain in the 1914-18 war and then in the second world war he was in the army administration. On the morning I was taking my husband to the station we passed Herr B. in the hall, then when I came in again he said, 'Oh you have just taken your husband away.'

I replied that I had and he said, 'Oh Frau N., your husband is staying in his profession but he will be building bridges that are a bit bigger.'

They had sent my husband to the bridge building unit and after talking to Herr B. I realised that this was victimisation.

So anyway, he was called up immediately and was a soldier straight away.

After that I worked with dentist replacements. I already had two children. The war started I 1939 and I had my first son in 1937, my daughter in June 1938. The war broke out, but I visited my husband and then I had a third child in 1940. Later my husband worked in Berlin as dentist for the police service. He used to write to me that he would shoot his boss then shoot himself. I got a lot of such letters. They were horrible and gruesome. Then I visited him. My husband is a very difficult man. He is a highly intelligent man but an impossibly difficult fellow and he probably had difficulty wherever he was with the military.

The trainer there was, by chance, from my home town and went to school with my brother. He looked at me and said, 'Well what are you here for? I said that my husband was here, Dr N. Well the trainer was a small minded man and now that he knew who was my husband he nabbed him during exercises and shouted at him 'You academic pig' and so forth. That sort of thing – really awful. I used to tell my husband to turn the other cheek but he botched it and the others botched it. The war years and those letters were a real burden for me – that was gruesome.

Later we had a friend in Genthin, the mayor of Genthin, and I told him I didn't know what I should do. Actually he had a bit of bad luck too. He met a girl and she got pregnant. Even a mayor is a man, of course that is clear. This girl ran around Genthin bragging that she was having a little mayor. That was not acceptable and awful for him. He was moved to Berlin and got a very good position there. In the Third Reich you had to work 12 months before you got a permanent position.

When I had had my first child, the woman who later became his wife was my first dry nurse. Those were the connections. I visited he and his wife in Berlin and he said to me, we'll find a way for you. He did help smooth my path.

I had an appointment with someone high up in the hierarchy of the army in Berlin and told him what was happening to my husband and said it was not really fair, that my husband was not in the best of health and I wondered if he could be moved to a position where he could actually practice his profession. I praised my husband to high heaven, which didn't actually reflect what I really felt about him. This man pressed a button and a young fellow came in and was asked to get the file on Dr N. I thought to myself, oh my God, they already have a file on him.

So the file was brought and this officer said to me, Frau N., I am very sorry for you and I find it is fantastic that you want to paint your husband in such a positive light, but in reality things look a little different. However, because of you I will have him moved from the bridge brigade. Then you will no longer have this burden. A short time later my husband was moved into the army health division and treated the soldiers. All because he had written me such letters saying he would shoot his superior officers then himself. Even during his education his superiors had lodged complaints against him. He was such a difficult man. In addition I was expecting another child and we already had three children. The officer was very nice and through his efforts I was successful. After the war this whole story made things difficult for me.

Did the women think the same way as the men?

Yes, they all did. I have to say, in the beginning, I mean at the time of the take over of power and everything around that, that was greeted by most people with approval because before that there was so much unemployment. I was born in 1913 and the war was 1914-18 and then afterwards this inflation and all.. You wouldn't believe the destitution and the unemployment. Nearly one out of two men were unemployed. I often said to my children, children, when I think back to when I was a young girl, Fridays were the day that unemployment benefit was paid, and people stood in long queues, right around the block and past our place and what did they get for unemployment payments. They were all unemployed. After the take over of power was the third Reich, and what did they do? They gave the people work. For family men that was manna from heaven. They saw to it that people had work and things got better.

I have to say too that during that time, we young girls could be out on the street until one or two in the morning and nothing would happen to us. No one did anything to us. That simply didn't happen. You could go out on the street and not be in any danger at all. I was a young woman, in 1933 I was twenty years old and I liked to go out. My mother was very strict and when she said I had to be home by ten and it was already ten past ten, then I didn't dare go home at all. Instead I went to my sister. To get to her house I had to go right through the Tannermuende forest. They had a big asparagus plantation on the other side. That is a forty five minute walk and I walked that walk quite alone at 10:30 at night. I was never harassed, not once. You could do that sort of thing without a problem because the penalties of harassing someone were very severe and people didn't dare. Previously that was not so, no oh no! So in the beginning that was a wonderful freedom and we saw that people had work. We'd none of us had work, none of us, we had nothing. We just lay around. Ten pennies were a fortune to us! At twenty we were cheeky and happy if we could buy three cigarettes for 10 pennies! That was a big thing for us. In the beginning there was no one who didn't accept it.

In the beginning my husband accepted it too but then he got interested in the House Ludendorf and later there was this fight because Ludendorf was absolutely against the church and Hitler was a Catholic. At the time Hitler told Ludendorf that he would fight the Catholic church, that he was also in favour of that, that they would be fought. Ludendorf and Hitler were together on this.

I have to say at the outset, when that began with the house of Ludendorf, that part of it had interested me. But my husband was driven crazy by this house of Ludendorf, this whole thing. They say that religion can drive you mad, but it was the House of Ludendorf that drove my husband crazy. But because of that I was never really confronted with the whole of National Socialism. I was treated like an outsider.

Were the women politically engaged?

No, I would say the women had no idea about politics. There were women's meetings where this or that might be done, craft and the sort of thing that has become popular again today. But that was increasingly done under pressure and the other women suffered from that. Not me, because I had already been branded, I was the wife of a Ludendorfer. Whenever I went anywhere they made eyes at me and stared dreadfully. They thought to themselves that they had to be careful in my presence, that they didn't dare say anything, that I was certainly not a German and proud of my fatherland.

The other women were sort of kept together, there was this Blockwart (warden) who drummed up the women. They met at evening gatherings and they had to rip up old clothes for bandages and that sort of thing, because everything was used. The women were more or less forced to do that. That was not work done of their own free will, although I must say that the women did sort of do it of their own free will because they thought of their their husbands, and that was why they did it. There were craft evenings and we got food there. We had ration cards and I have to say that during the war the food distribution was good. You got what you needed, but the rations were only just enough so that you could live. At the beginning of the war the people cried 'Hallelujah

Did you have the impression that war was the only way for Germany?

No, we did not have that impression. You can say that we were of two minds. There were some who said that it was forced on us but there were others who said we had picked a quarrel. I can tell you what I personally experienced and heard from my sister-in-law, who I later brought over to stay with me. She had lived 20 kilometers from the Polish border and heard things from the postal service. The postal service vans drove right along the Polish border.

My sister-in-law said the postman said to her, 'Frau R., what do you think it means. I drove along the polish border and I saw trenches being dug all along the Polish side. Nothing was being dug on our side. What does it mean? They are building on the Polish side.'

War had not yet been declared. That is what she told me. I say to myself that we common folk will never really understand the reasons for the war, even though we lived through it. I can't make a judgment, simply because I was forced, through my marriage, to be an enemy of the National Socialists. I could not conform to the National Socialists. Impossible. That would have been against the beliefs of my husband. That is why I heard less about it and I saw less. People tried not to talk about it in my presence.

And I tried not to too.

Did you work during the war?

Yes, I worked in the practice. The men were all away. Although the men were away, women had to work a great deal. Well, it was true that some received compensation, but what do material things matter at all, when you are under emotional pressure. There were so many happy marriages that ended miserably because the men never came back. Even today the women have not coped with that.

We always had to work and I worked the whole time in our dentistry practice. I always worked with the replacement people because my huband was away. One got support but it was far too little. In order for our practice to function I had to work, there was no other way. The women became completely independent because of that.

You see where we lived, that was the route that was overflown when warplanes flew to Berlin. Then we had a munition factory in the area of Genthin, in Alt Plato, and they were searching for that. That's why there was always an 'alarm level one' in our area. The town square was undermined, by that I mean there were lots of tunnels built below it. It was ridiculous but we always had to go down below with the children, we were not allowed to stay above ground. I would have preferred to stay in my apartment. I always said to myself that if we got hit by a bomb then I wouldn't know about it and if the bomb hit the shelter when we would be just as stone-dead. You couldn't do anything anyway.

Of course it was dreadful, but through that we were educated to be very independent. People all changed during the war. There were so many tragedies and you were always worried about your family. I lost a brother. Because all of your relations were in the war you were always worried.

You have to consider, in 1940 my son Gerbert was born and in 1939 the war broke out. He was not even 24 hours old when I had to go to an air raid shelter. I was taken to the air raid shelter. The doctor had come and I had said 'I want to go to the cellar, and he said I couldn't go to the cellar in my condition, but I insisted, I want to go to the cellar! They said the children would be taken to the cellar but I had to stay in my bed. I said I would not stay, so they took me down to the cellar as well. Now you can imagine, a woman who had just given birth and the child screamed of course. The doctor said to me, Frau N., you'll have to get a dummy for the child. If he cries like that in the damp cellar his lungs will be pumped full of that cellar air, so please get him a dummy, even if it is unhygienic. Then every night, and even during the day, we were in that cellar. I was so exhausted I got an abdominal infection and my doctor said to me that I had either to find a place for myself where it was peaceful or I should book myself a place in the cemetery. My sister was with the red cross and we organised for me to go to East Prussia. It was completely peaceful there, nothing was happening at all. I went to East Prussia then and I returned there every year. I went between times to recover. After four or five weeks I had to return though because there was the Practice and I had to live off something with the children. I had to live of something, somehow.

Also, you developed a different attitude to life as such. During the war with all the alarms, there were times when you did not really value life any more. After some time you made light of life itself. Over time we started to play betting games in the bunkers. Nothing mattered any more,. You took the money out of the bank and took it into the bunker. What did you need money for any more? You couldn't do anything anyway. Because we had the feeling that nothing good would come of it for us.

For the last two years of the war we said to each other, 'friends, it is getting worse and worse. It is only getting worse.' We didn't ask ourselves what would become of us, we thought there was no way to save ourselves. We realised the end was coming, somehow we could see that. Ah, God, a year and a half before the end of the war we realised there was nothing more that could be done. We became completely apathetic. One simply didn't value ones own life. We no longer cherished our own values. If the children broke something, valuable porcelain for example, we no longer thought that it was a tragedy. We thought 'whatever'!

If the children came and said they had broken a plate I said to them, 'Why are you crying. It just doesn't matter. It is completely unimportant. Whether you drop a plate today or whether a bomb drops on it this evening, it is all the same.'

That is how one changed. Of course later it was better anyway because we had to forget everything. And, you know, later we had absolutely nothing. There were tears about a single slice of bread. I had to say, I am so sorry to have to say this child, but you had better leave that piece of bread for tomorrow. That's what I think of when I look back at the war.

Because of the practice we had food so I didn't have trouble in this respect, the children were not in need. But one simply didn't value anything. Nothing mattered! We couldn't care less because you had no idea whether you would be alive and able to get out of the air raid shelter after the sirens.

I used to sit in the bunker with my children close beside me and say, 'Stay very close to Mummy so if a bomb hits us not a single one of us survives. Then we are all dead and none of you survives alone.'

That is what the children said too. They said, Mummy its droning, and they would quickly gather around and sit very close to me with their arms around me. We sat there tightly, in a very small clump and then they always said when a bomb hits, at least we are all dead and none of us survives. That was how we thought. We no longer valued life.

When it all ended and the Russians came then we asked ourselves why we hadn't simply ended it sooner. Then one stayed alive, one learned how to manage life again. Then finally one became human again.

What did you do in your free time during the war?

There was no night life really but despite this, during the war, how can I say, I had new acquaintances and other friends of mine that I still had because I still represented a practice and we had parties and celebrated all sorts of things. As I told you, we lived as if there was no tomorrow, we didn't want to miss anything. We lived every day as if we would be dead the next because we thought, tomorrow you might not be here. Where ever there was an opportunity to have a party, then we had a party. That was wicked I have to say, that was wicked. But it was just we women by ourselves, we partied. There were no men there because the husbands of all the women had been called up. Except there was one man there, that was a man who had artificial ribs. He was there. So when there was an opportunity, we partied.

Did you have anything to do with the underground in the war?

No nothing at all.

What did you listen to on the radio?

You couldn't listen to foreign radio. We were suspect and always watched. They never let us out of their sight, especially because of the way my husband was. They walked outside below our windows in the evenings. We could never have listened to foreign radio. That was impossible, quite impossible. We had to report so often to the local authorities. They held us on a short leash. We had got a certificate saying we were not politically trustworthy so they made life very difficult for us. They really did!

Because my husband had been employed by the constabulary he was automatically a member of the SS even though he had certainly never had anything to do with the Third Reich. If you wanted to accuse him of that it would have been very unfair. It was quite the opposite. When the war was nearly at an end, in 1944, I was with my parents-in-law in Templien in der Uckermark. My husband was on the front in a mobile unit that had a lot missing. That was in July 1944 when the assassination attempt was made on Hitler. My husband had been ordered to got to Berlin to re-stock his mobile unit and Genthin was on his route to Berlin so he stopped in Genthin to see us. You know in the war the post didn't function as well as it should and I was not even there.

He rang Herr B.'s doorbell and said his family was in Templien with his parents and asked whether he could leave his mobile unit in the yard there because there was valuable equipment inside and he didn't want to leave it in the street. Herr B. had a large yard with an entrance way. It had once been a brick works. So Herr B. and his wife opened up the gateway. When the mobile unit had been parked they asked him how things were going. Being the sort of man he was, he apparently said the front was going backwards. In 1944, that was how things stood. Whatever else he said I cannot tell because I wasn't there, but on 20th July he drove on to Berlin and it was on the 20th July that the assassination attempt was made on Hitler. My husband was in Berlin and one day earlier he had made that statement in Genthin. In the evening he drove on to Templien which is not far, about 40 or 50 km and he arrived where we were. He had holiday, furlough of 8 or 14 days or something like that. But anyway, he arrived. My mother-in-law's cousin lived a few houses further along and she said to me, you know Charlotte you and the children could live at her place because she is away. My mother-in-law was elderly so I was happy to accept the offer and said, that great! So I moved and then my husband arrived. We lived there for two of three days, I am not sure exactly how many. We were having an afternoon rest when the bell rang and there were soldiers at the door. They had been to my in-laws who said where we were. They wanted Captain N. My husband had the war grading of captain.

I told the soldiers my husband was sleeping but they said they had to talk to him so I asked them to wait a moment and went to wake him. I said to him, Lothar there are people from the army here who say they have to speak to you. He dressed quickly and as he came into the room they rushed at him, ripped off his epaulets and said he had to come with them.

I said, oh my God, what has happened but my husband was speechless because he had no idea. They put him in prison in Templien. I went to the prison and discovered they had treated him like a felon. They had taken his shoelaces, his braces etc. Treated him like the worst criminal. I asked what on earth had happened. But they said they couldn't talk to me.

I was still living in Templein but because of the agitation the children and I moved back in with my in-laws. Then three or four days later, very early one morning, it was about four o'clock and still very dark, I heard my husband whistle outside. We had a special whistle. I looked out and saw my husband chained to a watchman, and I said, 'Lothar, what had happened'. He replied that he was being taken to Berlin to the SS court.

I said, ' what have you done?'

He said, 'I don't know!'

Then he asked me to see if I could find out what had happened.

So in the following days I ran around to all the agencies and they had all been moved out of Berlin so I had to go all over the place. I ran around like a crazy and I can't remember where I found the unit he was with. But I did find them and I spoke to his superior. I said, tell me what on earth has happened. Then they told me that it was suspected that my husband had taken part in the assassination attempt against Hitler.!

I said, that is completely impossible and explained why. Then I rang home in Genthin and the girl who helped me picked up the phone. She said she daren't speak with me because the phone was being monitored. I had no idea was had happened. No idea! Then in Berlin I learned that my husband had made some sort of comments and that my apartment was being searched. My husband had wanted to return via Genthin and he had left his steel helmet, his rifle and some hand grenades, the things a soldier carries, at my place to pick up on his way back. That was found and then they wrote a report that he wanted to start a front in Genthin and attack the army from behind!

But things were clarified. After a chat my husband was suddenly released. He was never formally interviewed. Suddenly after a cosy chat, he appeared in Templien! I was still at my in-laws place. He would have been locked up four or five weeks. That is how long it would have lasted had they pursued it. You know, and this was the real problem, the whole thing made life for both him and me very difficult later. Genthin is, after all, a small place with a population of only fourteen thousand.

Anyway, my husband was back in Templien and now we took our holiday. We had a holiday house on the island of Kirchmuehle which is near Genthin and I said to my husband, you know Lothar, it would be best if we go to Kirchmuehle for these few days, and that is what we did. We came back on a Saturday evening and my husband had to leave again on Sunday.

When we got to the train station in Genthin, there were the women from my women's circle group. I don't know why they were there. They turned their backs on us and wouldn't look at us. Former patients spat at my husband in the face. They all believed that my husband had something to do with the assassination attempt but actually he had had nothing to do with it. It was because he had always been outspoken and never hidden his views. He had, for example, said we should negotiate with the English and the Americans. I was frightened because so many people were Hitler followers. But my husband was not. He went back to Berlin and was there when the war ended. Then he came home of course and I was in Genthin with the children and was pregnant again. In 1940 I'd had Gerbert and because my husband was often home, I had Gerbert. That was in 1945. My husband was in Berlin but visited every Saturday and Sunday, and I was highly pregnant. My fourth child was born in July 1945.

In May the war had ended and what we experienced after that was gruesome I can tell you. We had already had to deal with the air raids and the bunkers were really primitive at the time. It was late in my pregnancy, I sat there with the children in the bunker and my friend who was a pharmacist said to me, you can't stay here in your condition.

How much did you hear when the front was retreating?

Oh yes, people said, it is crazy, what stupidity. They should give up, they should surrender. They are just slaughtering us. Oh yes, we said all that!

Also when the English and the American bombed us, the discussion would start. Then people said, our side doesn't stop, even when you see they can't go on. They should put a stop to it, it is madness.

At the end people were very much against Hitler because it was such a disappointment. There were of course, always some idealists who said that we would get there in the end. I always said that they'd be winning the war even with the enemy standing in front of them with a pistol. Hitler would still be saying we are winning the war. He would drive the whole population into misery.

I have to say that in Genthin most people were against national socialism. But despite that our local leader blew up the bridge that crossed the Mittelland canal so the Americans had to retreat. We would have had occupying troops instead of fighting troops and the misery would not have occurred.

What was the mood of the people when the war ended?

We weren't really surprised I have to say because we had seen it coming.

We hoped in Genthin that the Americans would come. We celebrated and said, don't worry children, we said, the Americans are coming, the Americans are coming! We were frightened of the Russians. Then the Americans arrived in Alt Plato and the Group Leader in Genthin ordered that the bridge be blown up. So the Americans said, why would we bother to cross the river and they withdrew to Fischbek, and then they withdrew to behind the Elbe River. They withdrew to the Mittelland canal. Then the ceasefire was announced.

My friend was with the navigable waters company and had contacts with the people who had motor barges, some of which had built-in living quarters or offices. We rented one of these boats and she made sure the things we needed for a birth were on board and told me not to worry, if something happens, we are prepared. I was seven months pregnant. There was this chaos around Genthin, then a ceasefire so we thought the worst was over.

Then we decided we needed to leave Genthin because the mayor had declared it an open city – can you imagine? So we said, we must get out and we went to other friends in Seedorf which was a small village. Our friend there, Hildegard von G. had a property there. That was the daughter of Superintendent S. and I was friends with the other daughters as well. We all went to Hilde von G. and stayed there.

What did the people think when the mayor declared Genthin an open city?

They were all frightened. They were all frightened! Then I inquired at the pharmacy the next morning and they said we had not been declared an open city, but we left anyway.

So we were in Seedorf and thought we would avoid everything. But what we went through was enough. We all sat in the cellar and there was shooting above us. I had brought my sister-in-law and her three children over from Eastern Prussia in October 1944 and she was there too. I also had three children and was very pregnant. Then there was also a Berlin refugee with her three children. Hilde von G. had five children. Gisela K. had two children. We were all there. Gisela K. was in town at a guest house. She had her small daughter Barbara there and a little boy of seven months old that she was still breast feeding.

After the shooting the Russians stormed the village and overran the guesthouse and on that night they raped Gisela Kuno seventeen times. This woman was still breast feeding and had milk in the breasts and her son lying beside her. The Russians bit her on the breasts and trampled her son to death during the rapes. She arrived the next morning with her dead son and Barbara and had a vial of cyanide in her hand. She said, Charlotte, come lets us make an end to all of this. Superintendent S. was there and he said, children do not judge so that you yourselves will not be judged. Then I talked to her and said, Gisela, this will all end.

Then people from the canal came and said the Russians had been there. Then the Russians came into the house and we all sat there in the cellar, me with my children Gerhard and Gertraud. These were not the fighting troops but the ones who had been released from the concentration camps. They came into the cellar and said, 'You, blond woman, come!' I had very blond hair at the time. I took my three children by the hand and he wanted to take me out of the cellar. He said, kids away! And I said, where mother goes, the children go! I went up five steps with the children by the hand and this pig turned around and kicked me in the stomach. We all catapulted down the stairs, my children screaming of course.

Both children, without another word, went to the old copper that was in this cellar and put their hands below, into the ashes from the wood that had heated the copper. I wondered what they were doing. They spat in their hands, put them into the ashes then they came and stroked it over my hair and they said, Mummy, no one will ever again see that you are have blond hair. That is what these small children said. Gisela K. was in the cellar and she had always said, Charlotte don't be afraid, I'll look after you. This woman saved my life. When the Russians came she sat in front of me like a wall. This woman was raped and raped again. She wore trousers and a jacket but they didn't have time to undo her trousers, they ripped them off her. The good Lord should punish me with blindness if I tell a lie. This woman had a thick layer of blood on her back from the rapes. They had pushed her onto a coal heap and taken turns raping her. That was dreadful, so awful.

Then the officers came and said rape was forbidden. People said we should leave everything upstairs as it was so when the Americans arrived they could be shown what the Russians had done. In our dreams! As if! The Americans never came. More Russians came and it became worse and worse.

We came out of the cellar when the officers said the soldiers were not allowed to rape us. The another Russian officer came with a translator and said that German women were allowed to defend themselves. Then a woman came in and said he should go upstairs because the daughter of the superintendent was being raped again. The officer went upstairs and threw the soldier who was raping the women downstairs. That was in the afternoon. But in the evening the horde came again. They knew exactly that there were eight women in the house. One was sick, that was me. So there were seven healthy women – three Stephanies, My sister-in-law, the women from Berlin, Hilde von G. and Gisela K. We had barricaded ourselves inside but they got in anyway and demanded that the women come. You come, they said. My sister-in-law was with me and at that moment she reacted rather egoistically and hid. So there were only six healthy women and me. It was a huge house, and she had hidden and they wanted the seven healthy women. I called out, Gerda come out, you are putting us all in danger. Then I went down and said, I am the seventh woman, I am the seventh! But they said, you are not the seventh. They dragged the six women off to the woods which surrounded the village and which were on fire. They raped the women there then they let them go and said, go home, nine o'clock is curfew. The women ran and the soldiers shot at them as they ran. I was alone in the house with the superintendent and all the children and we waited for the women to come back. Oh the misery. I can tell you, what we experienced you couldn't fit in a book.

Then a neighbour from Genthin came over, Genthin was about 18 km away, not very far, and he said he thought Genthin was becoming calmer than where we were. A Russian command post had been established in my apartment. I wanted to go but my sister-in-law didn't want to come with me. But the women who had always been raped on my behalf, she said she would come with me. We had to walk along the middle canal, there was no alternative way there. We put Barbara in a deep pram and I took a large stick and tied a white flag to the top and off we walked. Gisela K. had Barbara and Gerhard in the pram and I had this flag because there were Russians everywhere. There were cows everywhere. You can't imagine what it was like, several hundred cows that had not been milked and they bellowed. That hurts a cow, when it is not milked for several days. The Russians were there guarding the cows. When they saw my white flag they took pot shot at it. When we got to Genthin I counted 27 holes in this flag. Twenty seven times a bullet went through the flag. That is how we got there.

Seedorf was on the other side of the canal and we had to get over it to get to Genthin. The bridge at Alt Plato was gone and we had to get over the canal. How could we get over. There was oil or petrol on top of the water, and I thought that if someone threw a match we would all die. A boat came from the other side driven by a Mongol Russian. I said to Gisela, do you think we can trust him? She replied, we have to get over regardless. As he took us over he could see I was very pregnant but that Gisela was good looking. He also noticed that Barbara belonged to Gisela. When we got to the other side he took the child by the hand and led her away. Of course Gisela followed, and that was what he wanted, that the mother should come so he could rape her.

Then as we got to Genthin we heard the screams. Women were throwing themselves from the balconies because the Russians were chasing them. By the time we got there it was curfew.

I went to the house I had previously lived at on the Marktplatz. The name had been changed to Adolf Hitler Platz during the Third Reich and that was where I lived. I wanted to go inside but there were Russians posted at the front with rifles. What do you want? They asked. I said, I live here. You don't live here, it is the command post, they said. The apartment, in fact the whole house had been seized and was now the command post. Then I went next door to the guest house and asked if I could stay there because we had just come from Seedorf and my house was occupied.

The justice department was on the Marktplatz and behind it was the prison and all at once the prison door opened and Irmchen came out. That was my home help girl whom I had brought over with my sister-in-law from East Prussia. She called over, Frau N., come over here, we are living here. So that is how I came to be living in the prison, We got one of the prison cells and that was where I lived with the children. No table, no chair, no bed, no cushion no towel, no nothing. Everything was gone even the floor tiles. We had naked earth. Irmchen sat there in the empty room. The building was a really old old house, with shallow window ledges and outside in the yard there was an old well with a pump. They used to build the wells in previous days with a *Brunnenstein* which was large flat round stone.

In the evening we took rope and wire and wired the doors shut so that we could be as secure as we could make it. We had no curtains for the windows. The Russians made a fire to roast a suckling pig and they sharpened their knives on the *Brunnenstein*. We didn't have anything, not even curtains, so I took the children and Irmchen and we all crouched below the window sills so that we would not be seen. So we stayed there in the prison and then I heard from Irmchen what had happened there.

The local doctor lived in the apartment that was above mine. That was on the Marktplatz where there was a small market and a bank. The family of the manager of the firm lived above the bank. On the first night Herr T., Frau T. and their daughter were all shot in the cellar. The Director of the bank shot them The director shot them because the women been so raped by the Russians that they didn't think they could survive. They had themselves killed because they thought, this is the end, this is not a life, this is too awful. But Frau T. woke up. She had not been shot dead but had only had her eye shot out. She crept over to our apartment where our housemaid Irmchen was. Irmchen laid her in my bed and quickly went up to doctor Oberlat upstairs. At that moment the Russians came and they thought Irmchen had shot the eye of Frau T. and they wanted to arrest her. But doctor Oberlat explained what had happened through a translator. When I tell you these things you must think I am telling tall stories but it was so horrible, it was awful. And then Irmchen was left alone and had no one. Then I came back from Seedorf.

But I must tell you that in Seedorf, when I was seven months pregnant, I was lying upstairs in a room with my children the Germann and Gertraud and also Gerhard was lying by me. I also had the four boys and another girl. The door opened out. And they always said that they had respect for children so I had Gertraud lie on a mattress in front of the door. She was born in 1938 and this was 1945 so she was barely seven. A solder came with six others, saw Gertraud and said, kid gone or I'll break her. So I took the mattress and Gertraud away from the door so he could come in. And he raped me, even though I was seven months pregnant. I kept saying, I'm sick, I'm sick, please please, I'm sick. And my children were all there. He just said, if you don't do it voluntarily I'll send soldiers. So then he left me and sent in the six soldiers. And I was seven months pregnant. Can you imagine? That was what happened in Seedorf.

Once we got back to Genthin I looked for an apartment, and I found one. When I think of that apartment even today a shiver runs down my back. This apartment had belonged to a locksmith and his wife and two children. Above them in the Lindenstrasse lived a court employee. I mean, they all had to do their duty when they were employed by the State and they had him on their black list. He lived there with his wife and 13 year old daughter. They were upstairs in the apartment that I got, the parents and daughter and two or three other children I think, though I am not sure. They all went to the couple upstairs and they built a sort of alter and wrote a letter saying they were leaving life of their own free will and they all signed it. They they all slit their wrists. Their blood ran right down the stairs and into the apartment that I got.

The things we lived through. If I knew that the Russians were coming again then you should cut me in pieces rather than have me live through such things again. The things I experienced were terrible. I always said to our Germann, don't go outside, don't go outside, but you know how children are they did go outside. You know how curious children are and living in an prison was an adventure. One day Germann and Gertraud went upstairs to explore and came back green in the face. I asked Germann, what is wrong and he said, Mummy there are lots of dead men lying upstairs. They were German soldiers all shot and piled high in the room upstairs. You just can't describe the horrors.

The Russian fighting troops were really were not cultured. When they pulled the chain to flush then they washed their hands in the water that was flushed into the toilet. It runs away, they said, the water comes out of the wall and runs away. Those were very, very poor people and had never seen such things. I mean, you have to put yourself in the mindset of these people. We used to have large kitchen alarm clocks and we saw soldiers who tied these onto their belts and walked around like that. They were proud of their clocks, very proud. There were many people who lampooned them but there were many young women with children who said to themselves that they would rather go to bed with the Russian soldiers than starve. So they were bought for food.

When I think about it, I have an acquaintance who has a potato chip factory, but at the time no chips were made, all the potatoes were used to make schnapps, only schnapps. Only potato schnapps.. the Russians came with their cars to collect this potato schnapps. They got blind drunk. You have no idea. If the Americans or English had done to their own comrades what the Russians did when they were drunk!. You just can't image it. We had our own tavern where we would meet for coffee and we met there once and there were Russians at the next door table. They had a bottle of potato schnapps on their table and were drinking that. In the tavern they had sort of behaved themselves. Then one of the Russians who had been drinking turned his eyes up and fell off his chair. He lay there on the floor. The other Russians, and I swear this is true, they took their comrade by the legs, one leg each, and they dragged him out. This tavern had seven stone steps on the way out and as they dragged him out of this tavern his head went bang, bang, bang, bang on each of the stone steps. They dragged him out and left him lying on the pavement. We were horrified and though his skull must have cracked. That's how they treated each other. People who have not experienced what the Russians were like would not be able to believe it. And the things we experienced afterwards.

My whole apartment had become the Russian command post. Millions of people lost everything in the war, I know that, but I had had my own apartment and after the collapse, when you see two or four Russians manhandling the piano onto a truck, then off they drive. Others came out with things from the dining room and others carried armchairs from the living room. The fourth brought things from the bedroom. You know, we had looked after our things, we had cared about our homes and loved them and were happy when they survived the bombing, and then you see your things being treated like that, things going in every direction, it really hurt. And you are left sitting in prison and sleeping on the bare floor.

Suddenly there was an announcement at the market place that whoever thought they had been harmed by the Russian troops or had furniture taken, should meet at the market square at 11am and we would go as a delegation to the Russian command and ask where the things were. So that is what we did. . I said to Frau O., lets go too and see if we can't get something back. So we went to the Magdeburgerstrasse and stood there too. We stood there for an hour and a quarter in front of the private apartment where the Russians were and for that hour and a quarter the Russian officer addressed us in Russian. We had no idea what he was saying, absolutely no idea. Later the translator translated what he had said for that hour and a quarter. He said, if we thought that one of the red army had taken something and we knew where it was then we should go and reclaim it.

Now I knew that in the bank opposite, the building where everyone had taken their own lives, I knew a Russian family lived there. I had been told that my piano and my bedroom furniture had been transported there. Frau O.'s furniture had also been taken there. So we did as we had been told to do, and rang the bell downstairs. A Russian soldier came down and we said, excuse me but we had been to a talk and had been told that if we knew where our furniture was we could reclaim it. Then a translator came and translated that. The Russian officer said how dare we come into his apartment and say that his furniture was ours. Such things happened. Those were the stories.

What was the opinion of people at the time?

The women and mothers just sat there and cried. They said, why didn't the Americans come. Why didn't the Americans come! They were angry with the Americans and said, they must have known how the Russians would behave. Why didn't they save we helpless women from what we had to experience. The man who blew up the bridge was arrested later and died in prison. He didn't deserve anything better. Imagine what the women and children would have been spared. Here in Genthin and also in Seedorf, we women just sat and cried. We sat and shook and cried. We had tobacco that we wrapped in newspaper and smoked. You know I just can't describe it. I don't think we women were normal any more. We had made our peace with life and sat wondering why we were still alive. We couldn't look to the future. At the time we couldn't even feel for our own children. That was an impossibility; it was all much too much. We had just eaten and had cut our tobacco and someone passed by whistling 'In the Night one doesn't like to be Alone' and Gisela K. said, oh God, there is a German man whistling a German song. But when I looked, it was a Russian. He came in and made Superintendent S., this old man, sit on the sofa and his two unmarried daughters lie on the ground in front of the sofa. Then he had other Russians come in, that was not just one, but two or three. He hit the superintendent on the head with his revolver and made him watch his daughters being raped. If he tried to look away he was hit on the head with the revolver. That was what the old superintendent was made to do. That was what it was like. From then on we women and children kept together,. No one dared to be in a room by themselves. We all stayed together. The Russians raped the women whether they had children in bed with them or not. When we all sat together and cried then Ruediger, the oldest son of my sister-in-law, said to me, Aunty Charlotte why are you crying so much? Are the Russian soldiers so bad? They just rattle a bit with their belts then they lie down and sleep a bit with mummy and then they go away again. That was how the children thought. It was just as well that they didn't understand it.

Did you notice any effects on the children later?

Yes, I did. Our Germann was twelve at the time so he understood I what was happening. They knew about rape and you saw that with their spontaneous effort to disguise my blond hair when the soldier said, you blond woman come with us. Both of them immediately thought, how can we save mummy. They spat in their hands and rubbed as into my hair and said Mummy, no one should see you have blond hair. The children understood exactly what was happening. Later in the west my daughter once saw some American soldiers when we were out walking, two American soldiers with weapons and with grey-green uniforms similar to those the Russians had worn. They didn't take any notice of us but my daughter fainted. She was as stiff as a board and foaming at the mouth. The soldiers came and stared. I could see mortal fear on the child's face. The soldiers asked if they could help but I asked that they just walk on, which they did. Once she came to herself she started crying and screaming, mummy why did you lie and say that there are no Russians here? She thought they were Russians and collapsed, stiff as a board. She was eleven. I said to her, Gertraud those are not Russians, they are Americans. Then Germann said, they spoke English, they didn't speak Russian. They are Americans little sister, you don't have to be so upset. She suffered, and continues to suffer. She gets migraines and cannot have children It simply sits too deep within her. It has got better over time. The first time the children saw soldiers that was a nightmare. You could see that. If other children said, look the Amis are coming, my children ran away. They didn't want to see any soldiers. They weren't old enough to know that it couldn't happen again. These poor children had seen such dreadful things. It was all too terrible.

Did the children suffer physically from the war.

No, my children not but other children the same age as my little girl were raped by the Russians. Ten, eleven, twelve year old were raped. They died. They were kaputt from the rapes. Where we were the doctors in the hospital did nothing but abortions for something like eight full days. After that it was illegal but there were always sympathetic doctors who performed abortions even though it was dangerous to do it secretly. My own children were not touched by the Russians.

Once my children came in white as chalk. They had played in the Lindenstrasse with a child who stuttered a bit and as some swallows flew over the by said 'schwaebchen' and a Russian who was there thought he said "schwein' (pig). They took the woman to the NKWD and locked her up. I don't remember how long they locked her up but the children came in and said, Mummy the Russians are coming again.

How long did the really awful times last when the Russians came?

They said they were in control from the beginning but the rapes happened continually. That lasted as long as I was in the East Zone. You didn't dare go out in the dark, that was impossible. People didn't stop at anything because they had nothing. They went into the woods and gathered wood. That's where the Russians raped the twelve year old girls. The children died and no one cared. No one cared at all.

One hears a lot that the Russians were good to children.

No, No! I would like to add to that apology the story around the Mittelland canal, Genthin on the Mittelland canal. There were boats that had a lot of spirits stored in them and people were so stupid they took the spirits into their own houses where the Russians found it. Over in Travamuende my sister asked a Russian soldier why it was so terrible on our side but calm over there. The Russian she asked was a young student, one of the Russians that were decent, and there were decent Russians as well. He said that the troops on the Travamuende side were the occupying troops but the troops on our side were the fighting troops. That was the difference and that was why it was so terrible on our side. The fighting troops didn't stop at anything. Later we had the doctors write us a sickness paper to say we had venereal disease but the Russians just said in German, we too, we sick too! They thought it was a protection when the certificate said we were sick and they said, we are too!

When I came back from Seedorf I noticed that Irmchen seemed withdrawn. She was 23 years old and came from a place in Eastern Prussia where they had no electricity or flushing toilet. She had never seen electric light when she came to us. They had nothing, nothing at all! Because it was so very rural. I brought her back by train and that was her first train trip, at 23 years old. She was frightened because she thought the train might tear itself apart. She was such a harmless girl. When I left for Seedorf I asked her if she wanted to come with me but she said she'd be fine because she spoke Polish. But she looked strange so I said, Irmchen has anything happened to you. She kept repeating that nothing had happened to her. The poor girl was embarrassed to tell me.

But one day she said she had been raped buy the Russian soldiers and she was now pregnant. The doctors at the hospital performed an abortion for her. Even this poor girl who had never been touched by a man had to bear the shame of being raped by the Russian soldiers. My mother-in-law was sixty nine years old but she was raped and they broke her arm as they raped her. That was what it was like! That is the sort of thing they did. It is impossible to describe what it was like, you just can't imagine such things. Gisela K.'s little boy died on that first night when she was so raped and the fourteen month old son of Hilde von G. died of whooping cough in the cellar. We put these two little corpses in an officers suitcase and put them in the shed. We used these two little corpses to protect ourselves from rape by the Russian soldiers. The Russians got a shock when they saw these little corpses and turned away. Then some very brutal Russians came and said, in the earth, in the earth! Meaning we should bury them. It was just dreadful.

What did you eat?

In May was the collapse, in July my son was born, in September we got butter for the first time over there in the Eastern zone. This butter was full of mold. We kneaded it under the cold tap to get rid of the mold so we had at least a little fat. I had had my son in July and there was nothing to eat. Absolutely nothing.

In the Mittelland canal there was sugarcane. It had been sunk. Later it was pulled out of the canal. It was full of canal water, dead fish and all sorts of other rubbish but this sugar water that was distributed. We also made substitute coffee (Malzkaffee) out of barley grain. We roasted the barley grain and ground it up and from this I made barley coffee with the sugar water from the canal. That was my food, that barley coffee. I needed it so I could feed my child. That was my fourth child and the first that I could breast feed. The first three which had been born under comparatively normal conditions but I had not been able to breast feed them. But with my fourth child, need brought me to the point of breastfeeding. But what did I have. I had nothing to eat, only this barley-coffee that I cooked up and added that sugar-stuff.. I have to say I drank this stuff by the bucket full, just for the nourishment. Only for the nutrients. I fed my child for nine months just drinking this stuff.

The Elbe bridge had been blown up so the Russians built a concrete bridge over the river that they used. Germans, engineers had to help demount the things the Russians confiscated and they transported all the things that had been demounted from the other side across the bridge past us. We all watched where they were going, he is going to there, the other is going here, and so forth, Some of them secretly gave me a little food.

One thing I know for sure. Gerhard is born on 29 July and on 2 August and eleven thirty in the evening there was a knock on the window. I thought it was the Russians again. My sister in law was with me and I said , Gertchen go and have a look who that is. The man said 'I come from Ternamuende. That was where I was born, so my sister-in-law let him in. He had brought us a bread, a can of liver pate sausage and a little raw chocolate for the children. So there I was on the second of August, eating a slice of bread with liver sausage. I can tell you, I nearly died from eating that liver sausage. My stomach was no longer able to digest it. I just can't tell you how sick I was after eating this bread. There was another who came with some potatoes in his backpack.

We lived in the back apartment and in the front there were Russians and they ate white bread and butter. They brought it out by the bucket full and threw it in the rubbish cans. Then they watched to see whether our children scrambled after it. I used to say to the children, I know hunger hurts, but do me the honour of not showing that you are hungry. They never took one of those pieces of bread. The Russians thought we would get our dinner from the rubbish bin.

Just once my Gerhard and my Gertraud came in with tears in their eyes.
They cried dreadfully and said 'We have stolen, Mummy, we have stolen!"

I asked them what they had stolen.

The caretaker, K. they were called, they had got all sorts of things from the
Russians, amongst others a pig and a pig stall. They also got potatoes and
they cooked them for the pigs. And I had no potatoes for my children. In
front of the pigsty there was a bucket of potato peelings and a couple of
whole potatoes. They were already cooked and were there to cool down
before they were fed to the pigs. And my children went and each of them
took a potato.

After they ate them they came to me and said, 'We have stolen,. We have
stolen potatoes from Frau K.'s bucket, potatoes that were for the pigs. I said
to the children, children that was theft of food, I cannot condemn you for
that. That is not stealing, I know that hunger hurts terribly.

Whoever had something in those days didn't share it. I lived in the new
apartment and after Gerhard was born my eldest became very sick. He got
pneumonia. At the time the doctor said, 'Frau N. I am very pessimistic'. But
we managed it, we managed to save Germann, but he had a reversal and the
doctor said he could guarantee nothing but if the boy had a quarter of a
pound of butter every day, then he might get better. But where should I find
butter? Then I remembered an acquaintance, Frau M., who had a small
shop.

Frau M. had been the one woman who supported me when all the relations
were saying my husband was involved in the 20 July plot, that was during
the war and before the collapse. Indeed her husband shot himself because
of the Nazis. He was in the party and, I don't know the exact details of
what happened, whether it was ration cards or something, I am not sure.
But anyway Eugen M. shot himself and this woman had to live through that
and now that I had my own troubles she helped. She was a former patient
of ours. She had helped when I was ostracised in Genthin when my

husband had left again. This woman sent me a note on which she had written 'Dear Frau N., By coincidence I have received a wonderful roast and I would like to invite you to dinner. Do come, and bring your children.'

Her daughter Christa and my Gertraud were in the same class at school. So a little friendship developed between myself and Frau M. So now my Germann was sick and Frau M. said, "Frau N. I will do whatever is in my power to do."

She had things in her shop for sale and I said to her that I would help her in the shop. We became friends and used the Du form of 'you'. So I helped her and I said to Dr Mueller that I couldn't work as I had to go to help Frau M. I helped her in the shop and we even went to Berlin once.

In Genthin we had a sugar refinery. The workers there used to tie their long johns to their legs then fill them up, the space between the underwear and their naked bodies, with sugar. Then they came to us, to Frau M. in her shop. We would stand the men on paper and undo the bottom of their trousers and the sugar would trickle out. We were not shocked that it had been stored against their naked bodies. We had sugar and we were happy! And we also took this sugar to Berlin. That was after the collapse that we went to Berlin and we hocked this sugar.

We had a Jewish family there, and they gave us small leather flowers or a belt. You can't imagine how inventive people were in making things. Things were made out of every bit of rubbish. I was good at handiwork and if I found any bits of wool I crocheted small flowers or a purse or things like that. We sold them in the shop to Russians. We didn't take money for them but said we wanted butter or we wanted food. That is how I was able to get butter. I gave the butter to my son. My doctor said 'Frau N., that is a miracle gift. Today our Germann is a big strong man, his sickness didn't leave a mark.

Just when I had sort of survived my son's illness my daughter became ill. She caught shingles. In this case the doctor just said, I can't help you with this. At the time we had what we called health healer. Do you know them? They were mostly old women. In my despair and since there was no medicine, I called on one of these women and brought her to my daughter. She recited an incantation over my daughter, and whether you believe it or not, she healed my daughter. It might have been just chance and she would have got better anyway but I feel myself that she healed my daughter.

Frau K. had white bread and she gave a crust to the children, it had been lying around and was completely dry. But they didn't mind, they stood around and chewed on this old dry crust. But then I started working with Frau M. and at least I could get food for the children. Then later I got most of an apartment from Hilde von G., she gave me bits of furniture and so forth, but later I had to leave that all behind again when I came to the west.

Frau M. had connections and I benefited from those. I don't know if 'freibank meat' is something you know about? That is meat from sick animals that had to be killed, so the meat may not be healthy. There was a butcher in our area who got this meat and sold it on to very poor people during the third Reich. After the collapse we were more than happy when we got a piece of this meat. We were happy and celebrated that we had this meat and had something to eat. We were happy when we got frozen potatoes that you had to grate to eat. Or we ate them as pancakes, although we had no fat. We grated the potatoes, sprinkled on a bit of salt and cooked them directly on the stove top, on the hotplates. They tasted wonderful, especially for the children. As I said to you, we had no potatoes, nothing. We walked for miles when someone said there were potatoes somewhere. When you heard of anything you did anything to get some. That was awful, that was really difficult. When you saw what was put in the rubbish, all the things we didn't have. We didn't have the daily bread for our children, that was so hard, so so hard.

Did the women hold together during the war?

Yes, yes they did. Later though, when everything was legislated you couldn't expect a lot of help. In the East zone everyone was frightened of everyone else. That was a catastrophe, no one dared say anything. I had friends there and because I always has personnel in the practice I had stuff. I shared things with my friends during the war but when I was thrown out of my apartment not one of these four women, who were still in their own homes, thought to ask me if I needed this or that. Those friends didn't share, but the friends I made in Seedorf, they did help. The daughter of the superintendent told me to come and get what I needed. They gave me furniture when I moved apartments. They really helped. Those were people with a heart and a soul. The other friends didn't help at all. If they had lost everything too they might have been different. People become egotistical and are frightened that they might have to share. They probably thought it easier to avoid me completely now I had nothing. If they had visited me in the prison cell where we were living, they would have had to offer something but they were probably just happy to have saved what they had. One friend of mine who had lived in America came back from America to marry in Germany. The Russians refused to recognise her passport. They ripped up her American passport. Those people left for America again later.

And then later this whole story with my husband. I wrote to him that he should come back because everyone in Genthin knew he was not a Nazi. A man from the communist party even stopped me in the street and said, where is Lothar, where is Lothar? I said I didn't know. He told me that Lothar should come to a meeting because they had found all the papers and seen that life had been made very difficult for us and that would be published. But my husband couldn't come because he had belonged to the police and although we didn't realise that he automatically joined the SS when he worked for the police, that was how it was. Also he didn't want to live under the Russians. I wrote to my husband that he could come back but he wrote back saying it was me who was entirely responsible for him not being able to return. You had to go to Berlin because you wanted me to be a captain. You wanted your husband to be a captain. And previously he had written that when I didn't do something he would shoot his superior and then himself. Now after the war he writes that a simple soldier wasn't good enough for me. In my opinion a street sweeper can be a decent person, and being a decent person is the important thing.

Were there problems when the men came back?

There were a lot of problems and I think there was never as much discord and quarrels as at that time because the women were challenged, they had to stand up for their rights. It was not the case that only the men were at the front! I think that what we women suffered on the home front was much much worse. To clarify, of course out there on the front it was awful, but what we had to go through with the children and the fear, when you continually thought that you might be killed leaving the children to fend for themselves. That was frightful too wasn't it? It is no small matter to have to flee the house with the children a couple of times every night and head for the bunker in the market square. Then just about as soon as you were out again the whole process would start again.

I think there were many misunderstandings. I mean, the men were convinced they gave their all at the front. We women were also convinced that we had carried our equal part at home and that we really achieved something during the war. I know of many marriages that broke up, that failed due to this. I know of one example from my inner circle where the woman had a child and afterwards was sewn. She had an abdominal operation and was so damaged by that that she didn't want to have anything more to do with her husband. During the war she met an occupation soldier, a Frenchman. She had an operation because of this Frenchman so she could be together with him. She hadn't done that for her real husband. Then after the war her real husband came back and she said, no, under no circumstances, I no longer like you and so forth. There were dreadful quarrels. It was legalised many years later.

Also it was the case that some women comforted themselves by taking other partners and they forgot that their menfolk gave their best as well. The mentality of people can be very varied, and there are a whole lot of things that happen.

But I also have to say that women were given an insane load due to the rapes. If the rapes had not happened a lot of marriages would not have gone down the drain. They somehow lost all feeling because they had been raped by strangers, by these Russians and they were different afterwards. Some were complete bums afterwards. I know for example, one of the women who was there when the Russians bribed the women with butter and so forth. In the apartment we were later allotted there was a Russian family upstairs who lived like lords. We lived downstairs on the ground floor and we could see the rubbish bins from our kitchen. And now, hunger, hunger,

hunger.

Why did you move to the west?

The husband of my sister-in-law had been in an English prisoner of war camp but was released early and had luck as he was put on as a teacher. He wrote to my sister-in-law and told her to join him. In the first weeks you could still go over so my sister-in-law left with her children. My husband was in the English zone and had landed in Oldenberg. He wrote to me that I should give Germann and Gertraud to my sister-in-law to bring with her and that I should keep the yet to be born child. I did not do that of course, and luckily I didn't because my sister-in-law wrote to me that she was shocked at her brother that he was not intending to come home and that he had wanted to keep two of the children and leave me two. I wrote to him that there was no sense in his suggestion and that you didn't bring children in the world just to leave them without a home. I said that I my opinion he could do what he wanted, that I didn't want to pry into his private life but that it was very important to me that the children had a parental home. He wrote back that he considered the iron curtain as fate telling us we should live apart. Oh well, as stupid as I was then, I thought that somehow things would work out.

We still had the practice and I have to say that I had replacement personnel there right through the war. The last one was a very old man who had fled Prussia and this man, Dr Mueller, he made it possible for us to rescue the equipment from the practice. Dr Mueller had the translator from the NKPD in his practice. We opened the practice again in the Lindenstrasse in the name of my husband and I got approval from Halle, which was where our city administration was, to keep operating the practice with replacement personnel. So now I wanted to visit my husband.

But I made the mistake of becoming politically engaged. The party that is SPD in West Germany was the LPD in the East and I protested with the women from the LDP against the things that were happening. I also tried to get things done for other people. Then it got too hot for me and I slipped up and said that if the Americans, English and French had no control over the Russian zone then we were as good as in a concentration camp. At the time if you wanted to speak publicly you had to have your general concept approved by the NKPD before you spoke, but in my frustration that just burst out of me. In the NKPD there were always spies. That was what broke my back. Then I had to leave. Actually, it was alright for another year but then I fled illegally over the border.

I could write a whole book about fleeing illegally over the border! A translator from Eastern Prussia even traveled with me. She wanted to get away from the Russians too. She had friends in the English zone. My mother stayed with the children and I went to the west to see my husband because he wrote that he thought that the iron curtain was fate telling us we should live apart.

I had the feeling that he was very happy to see me when I got to Oldenberg. He told me that he had a practice there. He had a living space in the basement and a practice on the mezzanine. It was all really well set up. He said to me that when I cleaned there next day I would see a woman, I have forgotten the name of this woman. He said that I should not speak to her and not to answer if she spoke to me. I didn't respond but when I was cleaning next morning the landlady came and said I shouldn't throw the water down. I apologised and said my name was Frau N. Oh, she said, a lot of people have said that! I said, I am very sorry, but it is true but if it is any consolation, I have come from the East zone. I asked for a minute and I got my passport and showed her my Russian passport.

This woman started to cry and I asked her, why are you crying? There must have been a lot of women, which is why she called me Miss.

When I asked why she was crying she said that when my husband had moved in and there was a good relationship between the people living there she had asked him if he would like to bring his wife and children over from the east. Apparently the four children were too many for him because he had told this woman that his wife had had an accident and was a cripple. Now there I was, standing whole and healthy in front of her. My husband talked a lot and I, stupid cow, stayed with him for several days. That is when I got pregnant for the fifth time!

I was active for the LEP and I was often woken at night, I can't tell you how often, I no longer remember, but often, and then I would be interrogated. I was taken to a dark cellar. You sat in this cellar and suddenly very bright spotlights would be turned on from a corner. You were floodlit and then the asked shock questions. They thought you would blurt something out. They put a photo album in front of me and asked do you know this person or do you know that person. Of course I didn't know anyone. I said, no I don't know them. You have to know them, they said. No, I don't, I said They wanted to know who this or that was. I did know some of them but I would never have told them. What I had been through was so awful I had decided that regardless of what people had done, I would never betray anyone.

Then one day this little translator came to me. She was the one with whom I had gone over the border with secretly when I visited the west. She said, Frau N., there is nothing else I can do. Either you leave or you will be removed from your children. You must leave! You must leave!

I had done a bit of planning and my friends over here had got me a passport, although they got it illegally. How I got over the border sounds like a fairy tale if I tell it. I had a passport for myself, an English one. I took my children by the hand in the East zone and walked with my bags and with the children through the tollgate. They said to me, why you here English, why children, why children?

Then I was a bit naughty with what I said to the man on the border. I said, you know I brought my children here to grandma. The children had to eat their fill. Now they have eaten well I am taking the children back home. Then the fool said, good good, you go you go.

I thought to myself, dear God, please don't punish me for the lie I have told. I didn't know any other way to get the children over the border. I said that as if there was nothing to eat here in the west and I had had to take the children to the east to feed them at Grandmas. The blockhead believed me and let me go. I had been through so much that at that moment all I wanted to do was save myself. It was not easy, but you just had to pull yourself together and remember. How often I thought to myself, nothing matters any more. There's no point, you'll never achieve that. You wont get that. Impossible, you will never manage that. But the one consolation is that my children are good to me. That is a comfort. A real comfort!

I had to leave the East, there was no alternative, so I took my children and left and arrived in the west completely penniless. I had some relations in Bayern who told me I could come with my children to them, but when I got there and they saw us all, they decided they didn't have room. I also had a friend here in Wiesbaden and I asked her if she had room and that is why I ended up in Wiesbaden. I handed in the divorce papers from here and so I was divorced here in the west.

Yes, well, that was my life. I got a provision from the government and then I got a job at the Census Bureau which I built on. Today I am 63 years old and my children are all married. Normally I just don't think about it, but when I start thinking about it so much comes to mind again.

But when I got to the west I had nothing once again. The children had the clothes they were wearing and nothing else.

Then came the currency reform. The few things I had to barter I turned to money in the East and I sewed it into the lining of the children's coats. So I got it here but it didn't help me because then the currency was reformed and everyone got twenty marks. You had twenty marks and otherwise nothing. I tell you, I stood at nights and washed shirts then ironed them dry so the children could be clean at least. Because I didn't want anyone to notice, even with the little money I earned,. The other children who had lost nothing couldn't imagine what it had been like for us in the East. They had everything again and then my children would come and say that Bjorn had got this or had got that.

You can believe me when I say I went to bed hungry every night. Even when I had the job in the Census Bureau. I didn't dare eat in the evenings. That would have cost far too much money. That would have been impossible. I thought to myself that I should be able to do it so the children didn't notice anything was wrong. I said to myself, the children should not suffer just because you are divorced and because we are as poor as beggars.

I put all my resources into pleasing the children.

Later I had a colleague at work whose wife said, 'Oh bring some fruit to Frau N.' They had a large garden with fruit trees. So then I had fruit that I preserved. I also went to the baker and on Saturday afternoon when I finished work I went and cleaned at the bakers. That way I also got some bread. I did all sorts of things, whatever I could. I had the goal that the children should not be hungry.

How much child support did you get?

Nothing in the East. Absolutely nothing! Dr Mueller had the practice and he paid me a rent because I had approval to continue the practice with substitute staff. That was how I was able to continue to feed the children. But when you live through such terrible things and all the rapes, then you don't think of this sort of thing. In Seedorf, money lay around in heaps. The children came with their savings books. They didn't know if they had any value any more. Having Dr Mueller gave me a life. I had a life and could live quite well.

Then I came to the west and I got child support. I got 150 Marks from the support agency. None of our friends had room for me and I was pregnant when I arrived. My fifth child was born in the west. We were living out of Wiesbaden in a garden hut, a dreadful old place. A real old garden shed. I met a man over here who wanted to marry me. He said he had put in for a divorce as well. But then one day he said he couldn't marry as his wife had come over from the east. I was in such despair, sitting in this old garden shed, that I considered killing myself and all the children. But the police were told and they could see the condition of my mental health. They saw to it that I got an apartment and that is where my child was born.

The children were too small to take it all in. I applied for child support but I couldn't have lived without the bit of help from friends. I asked at the child support agency if it wasn't possible to get some support from my husband. I was divorced in 1949 in a rapid process and in December the child was born. My eyes had been opened during the last visit I made to my husband. They showed me the most awful photos. When I saw in what sort of positions he had himself photographed with other women I realised there was no hope for our marriage and I wanted to be free.

Then through an accident I got a job in a large insurance firm. My child was born on 6 December and at the beginning of April when he was five months old I took a job serving lunch at an insurance company. I myself had had staff previously, but that didn't bother me. I got fifty Marks and I bought food cards, but I didn't eat there. Instead I took food home. The cook there was a decent person who said, Frau N., send your Germann and take your food home So my children ate this food for lunch. They didn't eat the soup, we had that for dinner with a piece of dry bread. The child support took 27 Marks from the fifty that I earned, so I had 123 plus 50 Marks but I had too pay 70 Marks for rent. I had five children and had to go serving to feed them. I went in the mornings at eleven after I had got my child ready. When he was sleeping I rushed off and served the insurance people. I could be home again by one thirty so I could feed my child again. I did that for eighteen months.

Then I heard that the Census Bureau was looking for people who could work from home and I started there.

The man to whom I delivered my work said to me, Frau N., you are bringing your work already?

Yes, I said, I have finished it.

He said, you are not paid per piece but per month so you needn't work so hard!

I said, but I have finished the work. He aid, well I'll give you some more but please bring it back on the first.

They thought that if I brought the pile of work back after a week it must be full of mistakes!

When I brought the next lot of work back this man said to me, Frau N., if I hear that they are looking for workers I will make a big effort to make sure you are employed by us at the Census Bureau. That was how I got the job. I started on 1 June 1952 and worked there until April 1974.

Once I had that job things improved but before that, I can tell you, I lived through bitter times, very tough times. You know when you sit at the table in the evening with growing children. Germann was born in 1937 and in 1949 he was twelve years old and really hungry. The others as well. When you have to say, Germann please leave that slice of bread for tomorrow

At the time we lived in the Nerostrasse and an American family lived at the end of the street. They had a boy the same age as Germann and he liked us a lot and he took our children there. They always got something to eat there. The couple was really delightful. They gave the children clothes as well. They were the couple who managed to get us an 'action for Christmas, parcel as well. They would come over themselves with parcels and I was in tears and thought, a lord, that we will be able to eat until we are full again. That was wonderful. After what we had lived through with the Russians which was so dreadful.

My husband had told me when I visited him in Oldenburg that he had such difficulty. Later when everything was finished between us I wrote to the dentists association in Hannover and said that I was divorced and I would like to know whether my husband was practicing and that he had never paid me a single thing. They wrote back that they couldn't do anything, they could give no information as that was not possible.

Then me at work one day my children rang and said a telegram had come. The telegram was from the dentists association, asking me whether they could make an appointment to meet me. I immediately thought something had happened to him. Had he shot himself, was he in prison, what could have happened? I rang them and the dentists association asked if it was suitable if the President of the Association came and saw me. I said of course. I still had no idea what was wrong. He came on a Saturday, and this gentleman brought his wife. At the time I lived in a basement flat in Nerostrasse. I lived very simply but I had tried to make the apartment look cozy and loved. So there was this gentleman with his wife and I asked whether I could offer them something. They said no.

Then they asked questions. They wanted to know whether my husband really had written his doctorate. I said that yes, he really had because I typed it up for him. The doctor title was truly his. He studied both medicine and dentistry but when he graduated he worked as a dentist and stopped his medical studies but when he worked in Berlin during the war he took them up again and graduated with a doctorate. He dictated it and I wrote it up on Saturdays and Sundays. I received the certificate notifying that he is a Dr med. Dent.

They told me how he was behaving, but I knew that already because one day when I was serving lunch in the insurance building there was one Director who stayed back in the Directors dining room. There was a dining room for general staff and a small neighbouring room for Directors. This man said, excuse me, but are you the wife of Dr. N. from Oldenburg? I said, yes I am his ex wife. He told me that if I was interested he could tell me about my husband, so I went with him upstairs to his room. He told me how my husband behaved. At the time of ration cards, instead of lining up with everyone else he would push in in front of all the old grandmothers. If they complained he said, Excuse me, you don't seem to know who I am, I am Dr N.

Such crazy things. He also told me all the court proceedings he had started. I had had to make sure the divorce papers were sent by my lawyer to my husband in Oldenburg and it turned out that this man was the person who had had to process my divorce suit and this office was the joint plaintiff for all my ex husbands court actions. That was why he knew all about them. That is how I discovered what a shining light he was.

The gentleman from the dentistry association, I have forgotten his name, asked me what I earned at the Census Bureau. I showed him my pay slips. I was really happy to be earning 318 DM with my five children. I thought I was doing really well. He looked at everything. When his wife saw the children she started to cry. She said to me, how is it possible? A wife and five such enchanting children from a man like that. It is surely not possible that he is the father of such beautiful children. I said, oh yes he is! She said, we can only hope they inherit the genes from their mother and not their father. When the meeting was over the gentleman said he would tell you the reason why they came. He said, we apologise that we didn't bring any flowers and we hope you will forgive us and hope that you will take this and buy some for yourself. He pressed money into my hand. He gave me a 100DM note! I was jubilant. Then they left and I didn't hear anything for a week or ten days.

Then I came home one day and Germann said to me that the postman had been and said that I had money at the post office.

I said, what do I have? No, I wouldn't be getting money. That is not possible.

Yes Mummy, he said. You've got money to collect from the post. And do you know what? This gentleman had organised that I got forty marks a month per child from the dentists association hardship fund. That was 200 DM and they backdated it five months!. I had been sent 1000DM! I was able to buy the children new shoes and some clothes! Until then I had had to buy food on credit. You try and feed five children on 123 DM plus 50 DM per month!

When we first arrived I didn't even have a change of underwear for us. When the children went to bed I would wash their things then iron them dry so I could give them clean underwear in the morning. That's what I did. When I started at the Census Bureau we started work at 7am. I worked in Kastel and had to be there at seven. I returned at 7:10 in the evening and the children were alone the whole day. I would quickly go shopping and in the evening I would wash and iron dry the clothes and do the cooking so the children had something to eat next day. My day ended at 2am and started again at 4am. You can imagine what sort of state I was in. During the worst years I couldn't see the steps. We had a day off for housework but I didn't dare take it because I was just a casual worker and I wanted a permanent job. I was trying to be perfect. I would not have dared to call in sick.

One day I took the bus, then waited to change to the tram to go to Kastel and my legs wouldn't hold me up. I fell down and couldn't get up. I had not dared to stay home as I thought I would loose my job. You can imagine, concentrating on work all day then worrying about what you had to do in the evenings. I wouldn't wish one day of my life then on even my worst enemy. I wouldn't wish it on anyone. It was very hard. That is why I ask myself today how I coped.

I retired two years ago at sixty years old. I finished on the first of April and on the 25 April they operated on my spine. My spine is completely ruined. I make an effort not to let it show. I don't like people noticing. I am telling you only because you are interested but otherwise I wouldn't burden anyone with the information. I am too proud for that. But really, what I had to live through was not so simple!

Do you look at TV war news?

No! I can't look at it. I can't watch sad films or criminal series. Even when I watched the opening ceremony of Olympics I wept. I sit and shake and think, what about all the trouble spots in the world. I cannot watch misery or hungry children. If I see a child in the street with a runny nose, I go and wipe it. I have my pension now so I can relax, but there is still so much poverty in our country. Recently I saw three little boys in Karstadt eyeing a large basket of chocolates. I said to them, don't take any, you will cause your parents so much grief when you are caught. I said to them, choose something for yourselves. Do you want a bar of chocolate or a bag of lollies. They chose a bar of chocolate and I went to the cashier with the three boys and asked what it cost. I paid for it and then I said to the boys, now take it and leave the shop as quick as you can. The shop assistant said, I have never seen anything like that before. I replied, how sad that you haven't seen that before. Would you have me wait until the children took the chocolate and were caught by your shop police? We can't know what these children are suffering.

Hitler liked the idea of women having lots of children!

Yes, he had bats in the belfry. I actually had to hear that from my husband as well.

Personally I had to deal with so much. I was treated like a worm, trodden on like a worm. Particularly in my marriage. You know, if you have to hear that you were only married so your husband could have big blond children. When one is treated like a birthing machine! The first child in 1937, the next in June '38 and then not in '39 but another in 1940. That was horrible. I am glad today that I was so strong and left that situation. If I had gone back to him I would have been the proud mother of ten children today! So at least I know what I have today and I don't have to beg permission for anything or thank anyone. And my children are so grateful. Sometimes we talk about things and sometimes when one of them complains about something, the others say, just remember what our mother went through.

Many women lived through those times and continued to live!

Yes, and you know, sometimes when I was here alone and I thought about it all, I said that it was almost impossible what people can live through. You wouldn't believe how often in life I had said, that's it, I can't cope with anything else, I simply cannot go on. But then we got another hit. Again and again impossible situations.

My boys said to me I was just lucky one didn't have to walk around with a sign listing all the things I had had to deal with in life. It is impossible the things in life you have to deal with.

RUTH L. 1911: A CRITICAL BERLINER

Ruth L.: born in 1911,lived in Berlin and Pommern during the war.

Were people enthusiastic about the beginning of the war?

Not in my circles. They were skeptical if anything. Berlin is a critical city. Maybe in the smaller cities people were enthusiastic. People were very pessimistic and those in my circle were sure that the Nazis had provoked the war. I am not a member of a party but my tendency is towards the Social Democrats.

I married in April 1939 and my husband left in August. He was conscripted and had to leave. That was the blitzkrieg, the lightening fast war of Poland, then when Poland had been taken it was war in the streets of Berlin. I was working in Berlin and I went with a couple of friends and bought some new clothes. We said to each other, who knows what will come. I was working as a secretary and we were then not allowed to give up our jobs,

Hitler wanted women to have babies?

Maybe that was so in Nazi circles but not in the circles I moved in.

Women and careers?

The men had all been taken away and women had to take their place. On the trams and so forth. But the higher positions were always occupied by men. A few of the younger men left but otherwise from 1939 to 1941 everything was the same as before. There was full work output.

Women had to be independent. In 1941 I left my job. I had enjoyed working but in 1941 my son arrived. Then at midnight there was an air raid warning. One knew, when one had a baby that there would be air raid warnings. The nurses laid the babies in the arms of their mothers then we would be taken to the cellars – each woman with her own baby. The hospitals were pre-warned.

My husband was in Russia, I didn't know where. But I wrote to him that our apartment had been damaged and he got two days leave. He fixed up the apartment because apartments that were damaged were liable to be plundered. If anyone was caught doing it they got a death sentence. Our house was repaired at the beginning of 1942 and we could cook in the next door apartment.

In 1943 there was an appeal by Goebbels for women with children to leave Berlin. I had a relation to the east in Pommern and I wrote to her and asked if I could come and she replied that of course I could. So I left with everything I could carry. Berlin was more difficult. For example I stood for several hours to buy a salad which I then cooked like spinach for my son. You watched where queues were because something special might be available there.

Women helped each other. We travelled for hours on the tram to pick cherries, but you had to be careful because if you were caught by the SS you would be punished. The people who owned the trees were compelled to deliver the fruit to the state and then it would be distributed. The shops were just distribution channels, they couldn't sell what they wanted to.

In the countryside it was still very quiet. I helped with the harvest, collected wood and chopped it up. It was easier to get food there too.

My husband was killed in 1943. He was due to come on holiday but didn't arrive. On the second day of the holiday I went to the railway station because I thought he would arrive but I ran into the leader of the local group, the man from the Party, he gave me the death certificate. I thought, now my life is at an end. I couldn't imagine how I could survive, but one did survive.

I went to Berlin as often as I could to save things from my apartment. The fight for Berlin threatened and I thought I would be much safer in Pommern. At the time we couldn't imagine that we would be overrun. Berlin was very dangerous as it was bombed continually. There were a lot of people still there who had nowhere else to go and others who just didn't want to leave.

I never listened to enemy radio but I did other things. We had a couple in our block, the man was an officer in the air-force and the women was very forward. We were thrown together because of all the alarms and sat day and night in the air raid cellar together.

We discussed the war situation and I asked her 'Frau X, do you really think we can win this war?" She went into a fury. If she had reported me I would have been taken away the next day. She was indignant that I could doubt that we would win the war. At the time I didn't realise the danger I was in. Only much later did I become aware that everyone was being spied on and that anyone could be sent to a concentration camp for saying something like this. That was the funny thing, that they kept it so secret. My second husband was in a concentration camp through the war, and when we think about it, I don't know. I do know that our doctor, he was Jewish, and he was taken away and never returned.

Berlin was such a big city and everyone lived for themselves. One day my music teacher said to me 'you shouldn't come back,. You might already be watched because I am Jewish you know." He left sometime later. The Kristalnacht was deplored, at least by people in my circle.

In 1945 we were told we were to evacuate [from Pommern]. We left in minus 15 degrees cold. I buried all my silver, and I have never been back! I didn't have a car or anything like that and the was train no longer running. One day a column of cars came through the village and I asked an officer where they were headed. He said Berlin. I asked him if he would take me with him in his jeep and he said okay, we'll do that. We put my bags in his jeep and I climbed in with my two year old son. I had three coats on. Then we left. I didn't know where my relations were. After 10 days in an open car at minus 15 we arrived in Berlin. The officer had cared for us and we found accommodation with a family. This officer always brought us something.

In March 1945 I traveled with the tram into Berlin from Oranienburg and there was an air raid alarm. When I came out of the cellar I asked what had happened and which area had been bombed and I was told that Oranienburg had been bombed. My son was there in Oranienburg. I went part of the way back as far as we could, by tram and then ran along the tracks. I was not alone, there were lots of other people running back with me. We weren't just jogging, we were running. We were afraid. What has happened. Then I saw our house from a distance and it was undamaged. Thank God, I said. They were all still alive.

The in April 1945 we were told for the third time that women and children should evacuate. I went to this SS Officer and said 'Where can I go?' They told me that there was a special train, only for SS wives, that was travelling to Bayreuth. I went with them. My husband was not SS but he had been an officer before his death. Then we sat for ten days in a train without windows. The SS had diminished. There were still some who believed in a final victory. We were strafed as we travelled.

We were each given an accommodation docket. I was sent to a village in the hills so I sat on the station and waited for a train to take me to this village. A train arrived full of soldiers. One single soldier climbed out and I thought to myself that he looked like my brother. It was my brother! He had been sent to the east in an anti-aircraft unit. He was deputy leader of an anti-aircraft gun. He lay there and saw a Russian tank and he crawled away and got a bazooka. That was a weapon that you threw then it exploded. Although he had never shot a bullet, at that moment he had a job and he threw the weapon and hit the tank. That stopped the Russians breaching the German defences. This heroic act was rewarded with four weeks holiday and that saved him. Then he looked for me, asked everywhere where I might be, and finally he found me. So he came with me to the village. The farmers there are poor. We were given a big room and that was where we lived. I made a stove with stones and old tin cans.

We had a very bad relationship with the farmers. They also had very little,

270

but they had more than we did. They had lots of bread. They were really nasty, they didn't give us eggs or a single slice of bread. The vicar said that people should help the refugees but that didn't help. I appealed to the mayor but the mayor said I would be deported if I made a fuss. He was a farmer too. I knocked on doors everywhere looking for an egg. I picked blueberries. Once when I was taking a walk in the fields I saw a hole in front of me thought, ' I don't believe my eyes'. It was full of hens eyes, I don't know how many, ten or twelve. I looked around to see if anyone was watching then I gathered them up. They were a rarity. I returned often to see if there were more but there never were.

My brother was there and suddenly after 10 days the American marched in with tanks and armour and so forth. The farmers hung white flags out very quickly.

Then we moved to Lübeck because there was nothing in this village and we couldn't last through the winter there. We traveled in a coal train. It was incredibly dirty. We were weary of life. We went to my step mother and she greeted us with the words 'Oh! You've come as well.' Her whole house was full of displaced persons from the east. I found another apartment with the help of my stepmother. The city was overfull. There were people living in every cellar. Then in Lübeck I played dance music on the piano, together with five men, to earn some money. We travelled from one place to another. I also played piano behind scenes in theaters. I played 'Parle mon Amore' among other songs.

I didn't have much experience with the black market because I was too afraid to try, but other people were very adept at it. I did go out to the farmers with a set of officers boots and material for suits but they were so spoiled because people were offering them things from all sides. I came back with a pound of lard and a piece of bacon fat. The farmer had lots of wild ducks and said he would send them to us if we sent two cartons of cigarettes. He did send them to us but they smelt so fishy when we cooked them we couldn't eat them. The ducks had fed only on fish. And for that I had sacrificed two whole cartons of cigarettes.

Despite all of this, that was a time I wouldn't have missed.

ELLEN VON A. 1910: THE FALL OF BERLIN

Ellen von A.: born in 1910 and lived in Berlin during the war.

> "God how we hated the SS. The SS were pigs. Not the soldiers of course, the soldiers hated the SS too. One morning at the grocer's I said 'good morning' instead of giving the Hitler salute and I got hit on the head from behind."

What was the atmosphere like among the people when war was announced? Were people happy?

Horrible. We were in the dark at the time it started. In front of our place was a very elegant and respectable Jewish eatery where we got our wood. I saved a beautiful small girl that wanted to run across the street. I didn't know it was a Jewish child, and it didn't matter to me what child it was but I wanted to save her.

But then the SS came and two nasty women said 'She saved that brat,' and they wanted to arrest me.

I said, 'Firstly I want to see your papers, and secondly I am the wife of a high ranking officer so you will wonder what happened to you and I have the duty to save a child, that was how I was brought up!'

They threw the poor child onto the street and drove off. I went and picked up the child. She was bleeding and I took her to my place. I went over the street to her parents but they had all been taken. Later they were all gassed.

Was that before the war?

No that was already when the war had started, but this incident was a few months before the war and they all wore their stars.

What was the atmosphere in Berlin later in the war?

It was dreadful. We had to leave repeatedly in the night.

Were people anxious?

Oh yes, people were very fearful because we were bombed out a couple of times. That was when the war was in progress. They emptied my apartment, stole a Gobbelin. It was six meters long and four meters high and they cut it out of its frame. Today it would be worth two hundred thousand marks, but the Germans stole it from me.

When did the German's steal it?

That was before the war ended, when we had to go to the bunkers with wailing sirens.

Did the German soldiers steal it?

No not the soldiers, the German women. There were only women there, the men were all away.

How did the women get it out?

I was bombed out a couple of times and the doors didn't close properly and I shut them with wire. They cut them out of the frames and I never got them back.

When Berlin fell we were all lying in the cellar and the Russians came and they spoke German and said 'Stand up!'" but those first ones didn't do anything to we women.

Later they bound a couple of women to trees with a branch up their
vaginas. Oh the things I have experienced!

The Russians came and they had to manage effectively on a litre of water a
day for everything, drinking, washing. Everything was broken. One of the
street pumps was broken and spouting water and we stood in queues and
got a pot full of water.

We had nothing to eat so we ran everywhere looking for food. In the
evening I went through the ash-bucket. Some still had potatoes and that sort
of thing and I secretly took them and cooked them in a pan. The food I had
had in the cellar was all taken by the Germans.

I had beautiful jewelry from my in-laws and stupidly I put it in a small case
and thought I would use it as a pillow, but I had been seen and some nasty
girl told the Russians 'the woman in the cellar has stuff' and everything was
taken away. The last watch I had was upstairs and that was gone but what I
had downstairs was worth half a million. I wanted to have it back and they
threatened to shoot me.

Now the Russians came and set up commandos in the street where
everything was organised. I was in our courtyard and a Russian came and
said, "You woman, some to the General."

I asked why.

"You come to General!"

So I was taken up and he spoke excellent German and there were a whole
lot odd tables with their equipment and listening devices etc on them and
also cooked herrings among the dirt. That was a sight!

He said,"Give me your ring and I give you food!"

"I am not hungry!" I was starving, imagine not being hungry.

"You eat then you undress," he said, or something similar.

You wouldn't believe how my heart was racing.

I stood there in front of this General and said " Sir, for that you don't need intelligence or skill to take a woman who has not done anything wrong and take her like a animal. I take you for a gentleman, and I see that you are a General. Do you still want to have me?"

He looked at me, then looked to see if the door was shut, then he let me go.

I really gave it to him although my heart nearly beat out of my body, but I praised him and that impressed him.

I went back to the cellar and he sent a Russian to me with a piece of bread and butter in newspaper. That was okay, at least I got something, and I was allowed out of the cellar. All the others had to stay in side.

I had reminded him of his honour. ' I am speaking with a gentleman and my husband is an officer just as you are'. And 'You don't need intelligence for that". I could see that hit the mark. I saw the change in his face and the other officers all turned and looked out the window. They looked at me from head to foot, then they left.

He was not alone?

No there were four or five there, but all officers. I don't know, but later when my husband came back from war and I told him about it, he said 'If you said that you would have hit him like a hammer in the stomach and he would have been so ashamed.'

'I think I am speaking with an officer and General,' I said, and then it was over. No one wanted anything from me and actually I was looked after. When I was in the courtyard or in the street and one of the others harassed me the General's man would tell them off. He had got an order to protect me. When I said I don't have water, he went and got it for me.

And the other women?

The were still in the cellar and were not allowed out. I had permission to go our once, I had got it from one of them. They were so clean when they arrived, so white, and with many different languages, a sometimes not quite correct but you could understand every word. They were very polite, but not the others later!

This officer was among the first?

Yes, they were the first. And then the order came from Stalin that all women could be taken and they were raped willy-nilly.

I have heard that all women were raped. Did any escape this?

Well they took all they could. But I knew a very friendly couple who ran a make-up shop and they took me in. They had a cellar behind a table with a carpet over the top so it couldn't be seen and when we heard the Russians coming, drunk and noisy, we all disappeared down into the cellar.

Once I had to watch while they raped a woman who was at least eighty. Four or five of them, one after the other. They stood in line with their trousers open and watched as they waited.

Like animals?

No much worse!. An animal just does it once and this was completely different. Those were not humans these were subhumans, that is how they behaved. Then suddenly, no Russians dared to do it. Suddenly an order must have come from above, that's enough, and suddenly it stopped.

How long was it like that?

About three months, no about two weeks, and then you could go out again, but you had to be careful on the street or you would be locked up.

When women in big cities like Berlin had n food or money, did they giver themselves to the Russians in order to live?

Oh yes, that was very common. I would have rather eaten grass!

What did other women say about those who gave themselves?

Dim witted, they said, we have enough to eat, those are stupid cows. That is the last thing you should lose, you can lose your hair and your teeth and your purse, but your honour and your name, that is the last thing I would giver away.

I can understand if women had children to feed that they might choose this path!

One thing I have to tell you is that I climbed over a fence and stole carrots. I did that from hunger and later the others supported me. I was very thin, just as you are, and I could get over the fence and I did that. That was hardship that caused me to do that. I got over the fence in my high heels and I didn't only take carrots for myself but for the others, then I gave them away.

The fourteen year-olds who still wore their hair in plaits were left alone, but those who were fifteen were taken. And there were a lot in the street because of the alarms and the bombs.

Once a Russian said to me "Here woman, I give you a cow" and left me with an cow. It was May. The cow was starving but there was some grass under the trees nearby. It was May. What do I do with an underfed cow, I wondered. There were no men and I was not capable of slaughtering it myself but perhaps someone was and I was thinking I would take it to where I was living so we could have meat. But then five depraved women stole it from me and ran away with the cow.

In the city?

No, more on the edge of the city.

Did everyone steal at this time.

Yes, those who lived though the fall of Berlin.

What was your experience with the bombing? When did it start?

That was the last two years. We were hardly back home and the sirens would go again and it took me 10 or 12 minutes to reach the bunker nearest my place. Then a part of this bunker was destroyed.

Then I was unlucky when the Russians were there. I needed something from a shop and a Russian said he would take me there, but when I jumped down from the car I broke my leg. But they were nice and made me a plaster cast. When the war finished hundreds of bodies lay in the Serpentine Place and the women had to take hold of them and throw them on wagons. And there I was with my leg is a cast but I couldn't just stand around.

So you had to do what the Russians said?

Yes, first the Russians, then the English. They were pigs too.

What was your experience with the English?

The Russians were replaced by the English troops. They weren't as bad as the Russians but when they could corner a girl, they did.

Yes I heard of all the rapes that caused such fear.

Yes but the Russians were worse. You can't imagine how many were infected. They all had to go for an examination afterwards. But that was later when things had calmed down. I had to go too although I had not had anything to do with a man. My God, one after another we had to go into the room.

How was the clean up organised?

The women had to do it, it was mostly women who had to clear the streets. I told you about all the bodies in Serpentine Place. They were all thrown together onto special wagons. They were taken to the cemetery and were thrown into long trenches that had been dug there. And it was May and in the heat, how that stank. We all wore these masks, made of fabric and dunked in perfume or something so you could bear the smell and weren't infected. That carried on calmly and we were all given tea and a half pound of bread at the end of every day.

Did you still have food coupons?

Yes you got coupons to starve. We got new food coupons. When you worked on the street to clean up you got a class two card, or a bit more.

What about the children?

The children got them too and they were treated well. I have to say, the Russians are very child-loving. They took the children out and played with them. To their own honour, they liked the children and never did them any harm. That made me very glad When they had an apple or something they would call a child over and give it to them. That was really nice of the Russians. Mothers would send their children over to see what they could get, and they always came back with something, maybe a piece of dried bread or something.

And the English. How did they treat the children?

They played the enemy and were impertinent, really rude. They'd throw a cigarette butt on the ground and if someone reached for it they would be kicked and they took joy in it. They had special ways to be really mean.

Later the black market developed in response to the famine. The Berlin rail station just teamed with people. I still had some beautiful lace linen and I took a packet to the station to swap for food. Someone asked what I had I said two sheets, two pillowslips. He said he had a goose all neatly packaged up. and I couldn't believe my ears . We went around the corner to swap our parcels.

Was that forbidden?

Yes everything. It was all done secretly. Sometimes they pretended not to see, I observed that too. So anyway I swapped my linen and took the goose home. When I unpacked it I found a swan! They must have caught it at the lake where there were dozens of them. They packed it up so there were only a few feathers visible and they are the same as a goose. I came home and this swan really stank. I didn't have a pot or fat or anything like that.

Can you eat swan?

No, and I can't describe the revolting smell. When I think about it today it still makes me want to vomit. .I fed it to the poor dog. I like animals and when I saw this dog looking so mournful in the street I took the bag and fed the dog. That was my best experience.

Did you dare go back to the black market?

Yes later. People had no cutlery and I still had beautiful cutlery in the cellar. I took small packets, Stumpen we called them, to the market and swapped for two carrots. I swapped it all that way. I was caught once and they wanted to arrest me. That was the Germans. That was after the war when the Russians had gone but the English were still there.

He wanted to take me in so I had to think quickly. I helped an elderly man a the time carry his packages. I looked after him and helped him carry things from his cellar and he paid me in cigarettes which I used to swap for food. So when they wanted to arrest me I offered the man a couple of cigarettes and they let me go. That sounds like a fairy tale but it is the honest truth.

So everyone went to this corner to secretly swap goods?

Well people walked beside each other and just said one sentence. "I have such and such!" and just carried on walking. I said, 'What do you want?" "Do you have coffee?" I said "Do you have fat?. And so it would go on. Then he would wink and you would quickly swap packets and look to see no one had seen you.

How do you think you would have been punished if you had been

caught.

It was forbidden, I didn't know anything else – only that one could be arrested. We did it from hunger. I never stole, I always had something to give, I just wanted something else.

You said you were bombed out twice?

Yes twice. Once everything was repaired. The second time, after two years I got an apartment. I slept in the corridor. That was a pretty apartment.

Did the bombing change things?

Not, Berlin, I changed a lot. I no longer talk to people who had a lot and lost nothing. They say oh stop, it is just not true! I have learned not to talk about it to such people. I was so stupid at the time. I see them today, they hid their jewelry behind the oven. Or in the curtain rails, the ones that have metal curtain rings. They pulled down the curtains and left the rods tightly screwed to the walls. They didn't tell me or I could have done the same thing. And when it was all over the boasted that they had saved everything. They took down the rails and out poured their jewelry.

They were prepared!

Yes, but if they had told me I could have done the same thing. No, I don't want to talk about it. It was all so dreadful. Even today I can't stand to see suffering, I weep when I see it. It was so gruesome, the women screamed and were raped and they stood there and couldn't do anything. It was impossible, so many men and the blood just flowed.

If you see other wars, for example of television, do you empathise?

Yes very much. I want to protect all people.

I have the impression that women had special problems because they had children?

Yes, and they had no protection. I wonder about the women who lived through the war who say another war would be impossible.

There was one mother with four children. The youngest was 18 months old and cried all the time and I took one child to help her. I like children and I said she should give one to me and I would take her to the bunker and we were no sooner there than the bombs started falling. There were arms and legs everywhere, but the bombing only intensified. I was so angry with the English, I must say.

That was inhuman, they didn't need to do it. It was inhuman, they knew that there were women and children there but the bombs just kept coming. Excuse me, but they were swine. But they weren't as bad as those who stood there to rape women, used them and then discarded them like old shoes. But many women gave themselves to the Russians too.

For food?

Yes for food and for their children. I understand that, when the children are starving. She gave herself to some man and he gave her a piece of bread for the children, I understand that.

Yes, I would understand a woman with a starving child doing that.

Yes it is understandable but there were also some who just got drunk.

Maybe it was all to much for them?

Yes, it was certainly all too much. It was really dreadful, the fall of Berlin, but the first troops who came were polite. The ones who came later, those were the real beasts in human clothing.

The men were all away at war. Did the women show some solidarity between themselves?

Oh no, one was jealous of the other when the child had something the other didn't. They didn't help each other.

And after the war, when no one had anything?

Yes, then they helped each other. Then we helped each other. As I said, I went to the rubbish tin and got potato peelings. And everything was broken so I collected wood. I collected branches from trees and made a fire in the courtyard and boiled water. I had nothing. We got one liter of water the first two weeks, then three liters then five liters. I didn't wash myself for weeks on end. You needed the water for drinking so you couldn't wash yourself. I looked like a pig. Everyone was like that, not only me. When you really stank then you washed yourself a little here and a little there. Washed your face and rinsed out your eyes. Water was like expensive perfume. When I think about it now, running around for a fortnight with the same undies and socks. I didn't take them off once. I didn't have time to change, things kept happening.

And you didn't have other clothes?

Oh, I sent everything away when we were bombed. I wore wooden shoes, a pullover and an old wide skirt. That was all that I owned. Also two handkerchiefs and a few other things in the cellar but I wasn't able to get in there because it had been barricaded. That was where I had some other underwear that I could change into.

How did he women help each other?

When one women had a problem we went and helped, or looked after the children if they went collecting or begging. I looked after children and then they brought me back bread. We held together like grim death when the Russians were there. But people stole each others bread. It was only a crust, but you had to hold onto it.

Did people know why there was war, did they think it would end quickly?

Yes, we thought it would be over quickly.

We didn't know but we heard later that they [Jews] were locked in their own synagogues then benzine was poured and they were set alight.

Did people know?

We didn't know.

How much did you know? For example when people did something they weren't supposed to and were taken away. What did you know about the camps?

We thought at first that they had been arrested and were being deported. We learned what had actually happened only later.

During the war or only afterwards?

No during the war. I also hid a Jew and later I was fine because he made sure I had every thing I needed. I hid him in my broom cupboard.

For how long?

For about half a year. I shared what I had with him and he gave me a Jewish ring. At night he had to move and I had to hold watch that no one saw him because I would have been shot if he had been discovered.

HERTA T. 1909: WAR AND ITS AFTERMATH

Herta T. was born in 1909 and lived in Stettin[97] during the war.

"The worst during the war was that I could not be a human with feelings and wishes. I just felt like part of a machine that had to function only to win the war." (From Herta's letter saying there were no mistakes in the text.)

You know, in the first world war the men went into the war singing, on trains decorated with garlands and signs saying "God save England' or 'God destroy France'. I was in school then and we got days off when the troops won victories. We used to call them 'Conquered Death' days. We often got days off when there was another victory. After the war there was the revolution and the houses in Berlin where I was living got shot at.

The second war was quite different. Nobody was glad about the war and nobody wanted war. But you know, we in Germany are, what can I say, we feel intimidated – we are convinced that no one will grant us a thing, every one begrudges us, and that is why things like this happen. The French and the British are the same. People are convinced the others wont let us prosper; we dealt with the unemployed and now we are past the worst of things and now they will come and take it all away.

If you live in a country that was never invaded like the USA then it is different. But we felt we had to invade before we were invaded. Israel is like that today. I will be curious to see what happens in Israel. Everyone is saying that Israel will have to win a war to have 20 years peace. If they

---

97 The fortress city of Stettin on the Baltic sea was contested in its history, between Sweden and Prussia. The city of Stettin is now in Poland and is called Szczecin

can't win, then that's it – they wont survive. If you are surrounded as we were with two fronts, with Russia on one side and the others on the west, then you don't have an option, you have to begin somehow and take the others by surprise, otherwise you wont survive.

Did people think that war was really necessary and it was their last chance?

It was really dreadful when Hitler took over in 1933, or earlier even. We had this world financial crisis but no one understood that conditions were difficult everywhere because the papers didn't write about it. Occasionally you would read that others were having difficulty as well, that it was a worldwide crisis that and we couldn't do anything about. We had seven and a half million people without jobs and we have only sixty million people. I don't know what percentage of the working population that would be, but with seven and a half million unemployed and youths hanging around everywhere you can imagine what it was like; the insecurity, the burglaries. It was like a postwar period when no one will give anyone else a chance. There were a thousand things you had to be careful of, things you take for granted today like security.

In 1930-1933 the government failed. It was non-operational and simply didn't function. It was not supported by the people. Hitler was the only one who was listened to by the people.

I was in high school when Hitler took over and I must say that at first people were disgusted. I remember a teacher who said we had our lives in front of us and we would have to adapt or we wouldn't survive, but that he was too old. He was probably about 35, that teacher. I am sure he would have adapted later too so he could keep teaching. Then later in the adult education school (Volkshochschule), you know the free education option, well everyone was in the party. Germany was quite different by that time.

The Americans will never understand it; they think Hitler was just a murderer but he wasn't a murderer in the beginning, he brought us work and bread. Of course there were jokes made at the time and I suppose a lot of people must have known what was going on but somehow we just didn't realise what was happening. I remember one joke that went through the newspapers – that there was a new milk bottle factory or baby-stroller factory but however you put the pieces together the product was a machine gun. But by that time Hitler was in power and there was no going back.

We lived in a well-to-do suburb of Berlin and in the beginning a group of us volunteered to support the house-girl scheme. We went around to the women who lived locally and said to them "Things are going well for you. You are earning enough and you could make things simpler for yourselves by taking on a girl to help you in the house. They are unemployed and doing nothing and you could teach them how to run a household."

So these women took on a household help and the first thing they did was give the girls a bath. Then they sent them to the hairdresser and bought them clothes and then they showed these girls how to run a household. I think some did really well, but some of them were not success stories. But later when the factories needed workers then I think they probably all left to work in factories. That's how it started, it had nothing to do with anti-fascism. But no one in the USA understood that. It is hard to describe what it was like in those years when we had so little freedom.

I didn't have any children of school age. If you had children at that critical age, say between 8 and 12 years old and in school, well they did a lot of gymnastics (today there is not enough gymnastics) but if you were a musical child then you were angry with the government.

Mostly we just didn't realise what was happening. We were so cut off and didn't realise our newspapers were restricted. You know there was burning of books, but somehow we were oblivious. The newspapers became more and more censored, but we didn't really notice because it was done slowly. It is the same with food. If you are used to cake and then suddenly only rye bread is available, then you notice. But if you are living in a country that has cake on the menu, but the cake becomes worse and worse and one day it is simply rye bread, then you hardly notice the change. It's the same with milk if it is slowly watered down.

The evil thing is that we are so afraid of the Russians and that also had something to do with it. They have always been involved in our wars, in 1914 and also earlier, the Cossacks in East Prussia. We had heard from the many Germans who lived there at that time what happened to them. This time, I don't know if you know what happened in Berlin, but the Americans held back and regardless of your age, whether you were 16 or whatever your age, if you were a woman you were there for the Russians. The girls and women in Berlin at the time had years of suffering afterwards. They raped really young girls and made them unfit for life really. Theoretically abortion was against the law, but the German doctors, you know, they did abortions. I know that because although I wasn't there I had a lot of friends in Berlin. When the Russians marched in it was unimaginably dreadful. These assaults sit in your bones, sit in the bones of the whole nation, and you don't forget them.

It is the same with inflation, my generation is scared by the events of the twenties. I was young in 1922-23 when suddenly all our money was worth nothing. The older people who had saved all their lives and had money in the bank or shares, suddenly they had nothing and they had to queue up at charitable organisations and be looked down on by them. Then they were living as their cleaning ladies had once done. The same thing happened in 1948 when again suddenly the financial system failed. We had a currency reform; the old money, the Reichsmark, was gone and the Deutschmark was introduced and everyone had the same, forty Deutschmarks. Suddenly everyone was exactly the same. You see they can organise such things and it worked. Maybe the Americans organised it.

Anyway once again all our savings were gone, but this time it was different. Anyone who owned something could sell it. The farmers had rooms full of radios, silver and Persian carpets and whatever else they had collected from city dwellers in exchange for food and now they could sell it. People who had relied on their saving now had to work, so everyone was looking for work.

We had fled by that time to the countryside near Nuremberg. We'd had nothing at all so we had had to look for work. We did whatever we could to earn money and the locals looked down their noses at us. It was really bad but then came the currency reform and suddenly everything was different. I worked before the currency reform and was independent, but suddenly we were treated quite differently because suddenly our money was worth something. Suddenly we could buy things. It made such a difference. Suddenly the day after the currency reform the shops were full of vegetables, full of meat and everything else. The day before there had been nothing in the shops because money wasn't worth anything.

One thing you shouldn't forget is that twice we lived through periods when money became valueless. We saw that life continued but only when you had a skill, when you had done some sort of apprenticeship and had something to sell. You see my husband was a civil servant in the air force and suddenly in 1945 that was gone. There was no salary, no German Reich, nothing. It is hard to imagine. But suddenly nothing functioned and only later did things start again.

We waited three years, or was it more, and then all civil servants got jobs again. They weren't in as good positions as previously, but they had jobs that fitted their eduction better. There are things of more value than money. In the USA they think the President is responsible when their shares loose value.

What it was like when the war began.

After the first war I lived in Berlin. In August 1939 we were in Berlin at my parents place. They were away and we were having a holiday at their place. My first child Gerda was 8 months old and I was seven months pregnant.

We had a nice apartment in Berlin but up three flights of stairs. When war was declared my husband was transferred to Stettin because a new building authority was being established there. The V2 was being built in a factory in Penemuende north of Stettin. There was a hydrogenation plant there, where they made synthetic benzine and both of these factories were bombed. You saw the planes fly over Stettin and you knew where they were going. My husband was transferred to the building authority in Stettin and they had to build a fake factory there, one that would deceive the planes. They built one factory that was the true factory and another one in the woods somewhere that was just made of cardboard and plaster and such like.

In reality our factories had so many foreign workers. They were called *Zwanksverschleppte* which is forced displaced persons, and they came from everywhere and of course they didn't want to see Germany win the war. In the first attack on the hydrogenation plant at Poelitz the bombs also hit the fire brigade station and afterwards it came out that the foreign workers had run around in the woods with torches and shown the planes where to bomb. So this fake factory was completely useless.

My husband was in Stettin but I stayed in Berlin because I didn't have an apartment there.

So on 1st September I was at my mother's and she said, "No, you don't go back to your own apartment, that is much too difficult for you. You have to queue so long for food vouchers and you wont have any one to help you. You stay here.".

So I was not in central Berlin but at my mothers. The had a house and garden and she still had a maid she was able to keep. So the children were well taken care of and there was no problem. At Christmas time we moved to Stettin because my husband had been allocated somewhere to live there. He got a house which was subsidised by the air force because he was working for the air force administration. The house was owned privately but the investor got cheap money to build and for that he had to rent some of his houses to the employees. The house was in a completely new street and didn't even have kerbs. Just a sand track to the houses. We were on one side with the air force and on the other side were the navy because Stettin is a harbour and there were a lot of ships there.

Did you work?

No I didn't work. Only after the war

Was your husband always there?

Yes, he was there at first. Then he was sent to Paris in France for two years and then to Russia, in the Crimea by the Volga. He was an electrician and built electrical facilities for airports. He was not at the front but just behind it. He was away and I was always alone, just like the other women. Everything went well for the first three months, but after that it was extremely difficult. I don't know if doctors know how to help better nowadays but in those days there was no help at all. There weren't any doctors. They were all away too.

What was worst

The worst thing was when you had children. I had two small children and a girl to help in the household – she was one of the girls who had to take on this sort of work. Whoever left school at 14 had to work for a year as household help. I can't remember when that began. Later older girls had to serve the army. All the women who lived nearby had small children as well. We were quite well off for food because the Nazis were very pro-children, they wanted us to have children so they gave food portions to children that were just about as big as for the adults. So imagine a man and then a child. So women who had more children always had plenty of food while the women who were working were always hungry. My parents for example. I was really shocked when I saw them again because they had lost so much weight. The adult food quota was not enough to feed them properly. In addition to the children I had several miscarriages, two or three, and each time I got extra food for three months, or until the miscarriage, then I didn't get anything extra. You made sure you got it straight away as soon as you were pregnant. My husband also provided some food. I would get a package with from my husband with some sausage or something. He was always passing by on the way somewhere. So it was dependant on you family whether you got enough to eat. It wasn't like the first world war when there was nothing to eat and we were always hungry. I remember in about 1917 when I was a girl in Berlin the whole winter there was nothing to eat but swedes. What was a poor housewife to do? In the morning we had them sweet as marmalade; at lunch we ate cooked swede and in the evening we had them fried. Without fat of course. We were so sick of swede. Everybody was so sick of swede. The way we liked them best was raw from the kitchen table, before they had been cooked. We were always so hungry we would eat anything. In the second world war we had enough food until after the war, then we starved. Between 1945 and 1948. During the war we had enough to eat. The worst thing during the war was that the men were all away. Occasionally they came home for holiday, but sometimes there was a whole year between holidays.

Did you have the feeling he became alienated?

No, that didn't happen. More selfish. Imagine you don't have anyone with whom you can have a decent conversation. You've only got toddles and the girl who helped and she was just as hopeless. Of course we had neighbours but we had so much work we had no time. You just had no one to talk to the whole time – just children asking questions.

There were times when I said " I just need a man. It doesn't matter which man, but a man. So I can walk down the street and look into the show windows on the arm of a man."

I couldn't do that alone. Occasionally perhaps in the evenings. He was away for more than a year. That was really long. But then there were the poor women whose husbands never came back. I had good luck in that respect. We had married in 1936 so we knew each other a bit before the war began. But a lot of people married someone they had only known a fortnight, and then it would be over, the husband never came back.

Did you become more independent?

No. Or actually, yes we were more independent. The husbands of the

women in my street were all civil servants and so we got our salaries. I
don't know if the people got paid whose husbands worked as train
conductors or something, but I know a lot of women worked and they
became more independent. But at the time we didn't notice it. We only
noticed later because after the war when the men came back again there
were a lot of suicides among those who returned. Not because they were
separated from their families but because they couldn't adapt to the
conditions we had been used to live under.

The women had children; they had sat with those children under the bombs
and they had either died or not – we didn't care either way., it was
completely irrelevant to us if we survived. The only thing we cared about
was getting the bed clean enough for the children to sleep in, that we got
some sort of food and could cook it so the children had something to eat.
We just wanted to be able to feed the children and do the washing,
everything else was completely unimportant. You could only just exist
with ration cards and you had to queue for hours to exchange them for
food.

Later there were bombs in Stettin although the people living in Rhineland
had many more than we did If you lived in the area of Duesseldorf or
Krefeld you got no sleep the whole war. They spent all their days in the
cellar. They had bomb alarms every night, night after night. We didn't have
as many in Stetting although towards the end it was pretty bad. That's how
it was. The English flew their planes either to Berlin for Stettin. We had the
radio on and listened for the announcement. Actually once it was dark that
was our primary activity even the children., listening for the
announcements. We had to do everything also on the side, the radio was on
constantly. We would know the planes were coming but we wouldn't know
their direction until they were at a certain point on the Holstein coast. From
that point they would fly on to Berlin or to Stettin. Or sometimes to the
coast because they mined the coast in that area. They didn't only attack the
factories, they mined the harbour and actually everything.

There were five neighbouring houses and we all had small children. It was
really difficult when the alarms went off and the bombs landed almost
immediately afterwards.. You had to get the children dressed and ready. We
were well organised and everything was kept ready so you only had to grab
it, but still you had a few moments of real fear yourself. Today you can't
imagine what it was like, night after night with no sleep. Young women are
tired today but they don't have to deal with bombing raids. After the war we
would wake up in a shock thinking the sirens were wailing. It took about

five years until we could sleep again at night. The same when a car alarm went off – immediately you thought it was the sirens. It took a long time to recover from that.

We had a system whereby one of us women would stay awake and listen for the pre-warning. If that came they would wake the others, go from door to door knocking them awake. We didn't always have to wake the children immediately. But that didn't happen every night. Sometime the planes would fly on to Berlin and then the sirens would sound again, but only a short time. If it was a bomb alarm the sirens would wail constantly. We would be so relieved. Every German had a radio and after ten good music would be broadcast and we really enjoyed it.

What did you do in your free time?

Free time? I didn't even have time to read. Once when my husband was home we dared to go out. He was in Stettin at the time and he had had to go to Berlin for four of six weeks for an educational course. When he returned we really wanted to go to a wine bar in the city and have a drink. The city was 20 minutes away by tram, so it wasn't that far away. I had a young girl and we left her with the children but on that evening their was an alarm. It was in June when there were never alarms because the nights were so short. We were in the wine bar in the city, in a cellar that was completely underground so we were safe but the poor girl was in the suburbs with our children. I never went out again in the evenings. Once and never again. You can imagine how I felt.

So you could talk to your neighbours if you had time but we had too much work for that. We had to sew everything for our children and you can't imagine how bad the materials were. I sewed coats for the children out of old trousers or out of old coats that other older children had grown out of.

Did you have to spend a long time getting food?

Yes, queuing was one of our main occupation. So first you queued for milk, and then you had to queue for vegetables and then for bread.

Could you get all the things you needed for your recipes?

I can't really remember. There would always have been salt, and what you couldn't get, well you got used to doing without. The quality of the food became ever worse. The milk that I fed my son; well if you took today's milk and tipped it out of the bottle then filled the bottle with water again, that was the sort of milk we raised out children on. But you hardly notice if the change in quality is slow. Just like the newspapers, you don't notice the quality if there is nothing else to read. Do you understand? If changes are just small, bit by bit. And at that time people didn't complain as they would today. But I never read the papers anyway. In the *Sturmer* they used such common language and I just didn't read it. One thing good though about living in a dictatorship is that if the paper said something would be done, then it was. Today you read in the paper that they are thinking about doing something, and in five years you are lucky if they have made a decision. That really was the main advantage.

I had a garden, though how I found time to keep it I don't know. We dug up black currant bushes from elsewhere to make our gardens. And I kept hens in the cellar!. We built a hen house with hen run in the cellar!. Without these eggs I wouldn't have done nearly as well through the war. It really helps when you have an egg. We made most things ourselves and so we didn't starve, that came after the war when we lost kilos.

Did people help each other?

People only helped each other later. Only really once the war ended. Perhaps because I was never really in need I never really needed help. But you know after alarms when the windows are broken and there is no electricity, and when it is cold, well what do you do? Later coal was distributed.

Did the children suffer from the bombing?

Actually it was the adults that suffered more. The children just kept going to school. One of the neighbours had school aged children and they continued in school until it was all in ruins. When everything was kaput in Stettin, at Christmas time 1944, then it was dreadful for everyone. When the Russians were nearing East Prussia then everyone fled. There were so many refugees, people who had been sent into the countryside from Berlin. Our army was in full flight but we didn't hear that from the army news, or on the radio or read it in the newspapers. We heard it from the refugees. In the papers they used a wonderful term – they called it 'absetzen' (set down). In Vietnam they used the same sort of vocabulary.

We were all exhausted. Not me as much because I had my garden and the eggs, but most people.

Were you among those who fled?

Yes but refugees from East Prussia were arriving a month or six weeks before we left. Some of them had been taken by ship. We had large ships like the Wilhelm Gustow and others that had been built for the leisure organisation KDF and were later used to transport troops I think. They took refugees on board but when they were in the Baltic sea they were shot at or hit mines and they sank. Half the refugees were saved by war ships and all sorts of other boats and they were brought to Stettin because that was the nearest harbour. The girls doing their mandatory household help year had to report to the harbour and hep these people. The stories those poor girls told. We had to send them there go even during air raids. Mothers of small children didn't have to go but everyone else available had to go and help. They told harrowing stories. They had pulled these women from the ice cold water. It was January and freezing cold, and they had lost their children or half their family and all the while they were being bombed. And these young girls told us these stories, just imagine. The girls that were of that age, let's see, those born around about 1930, they didn't have any youth at all. They had a dreadful time. Those girls might enjoy some years now, whatever they can, but they had nothing at all then. They had a diabolic time. We ourselves had a lovely youth. I was lucky to be born in the year I was. My children were very small during the war and they had what they needed. They never noticed all the things they never had. But those girls had to help and the stories they told when they got home you wouldn't believe. You see when the air raid sirens went off you grabbed the children you could and made for the cellar. If you had more than you could take you had to go back for the others and sometimes they were no longer there. Lots of stories like that. They lived through the most atrocious things. When I heard that I never took just one child down to the cellar. I took them both; one under each arm and it was really difficult because we would slip in the rush to get down. It was night and everything crashed and banged and shook. Not at all enjoyable although it could be an amazing sight if you dared to stay and watch.

Near the end of the war we had a slit trench really near us at the corner of the settlement and we couldn't get any further. We were caught there in the slit trench with the children. I had never watched the bombing because I had my children and I had to comfort them and keep them busy until they went to sleep. I can't remember what we told them to explain why it was so loud and there were so many bangs. I had never watched but this time I did. My cousin looked after the children and I watched the bombing because she said 'You have to watch, it is so beautiful.' Yes, and it was beautiful, absolutely beautiful. There were planes all over Stettin and they dropped illumination rockets. We called them 'Christmas trees' because that's what they looked like, enormous Christmas trees. The whole city was lit up and these rockets would go off, single rockets that illuminated bit by bit over the whole city. That was an amazing sight. It was as bright as day for hours on end. They couldn't miss their targets. They had to hit them. I only watched for a quick moment, but it was amazing.

So all these refugees arrived, and what happened then?

These refugees naturally didn't want to have to go any further and they certainly didn't want to get on a ship again. They wanted to travel by train. There were more and more to the extent that we started wondering what we should do if the worst came to the worst. Slowly we started to realise that the Russians were getting closer and closer. For example, navy personnel lived across from us and eventually the wife of a navel commander. He had a ship, I have forgotten the name. He was only allowed to leave at the last moment and he was allowed to fill the ship with refugees. Our problem was that our children were too small and we needed prams. My cousin's youngest was six months old and she also had a toddler and they couldn't walk and they needed nappies and such like. Mine were a little bit bigger but not much. You couldn't get paper nappies and baby food in jars as you can today. They didn't exist. So we had a great deal of work. Work, exhausting work, that is what war is. You had to make it all yourself, everything for the children.

So anyway, for that reason we hoped that we would be able to get a transfer to Kiel by ship. Kiel was mined, we knew that and we didn't hold out much hope of arriving alive. We gathered all the children's coats, typed address lists that we sewed inside so that fishermen who found us would know where to deliver us. We knew that when a ship sank everything would be chaos. But the alternative was to go with the prams at night over the countryside. The woman across the road told us that they would be sending boats and that it would work out. We were barricaded. The Stettiner didn't let anyone leave. We always said, what would we do when the enemy marched in, what did they do in the middle ages, blistering bad luck as we always said. Later when it got worse and worse there weren't even any alarms. We couldn't leave the house and we daren't undress the children at night. We were fully dressed in bed, even with our shoes on. There was nothing we could do. The enemy stood on the other side of the Oder River and shot at us in our beds, that's what it felt like. The alarms came only after the first shots were falling around us.

When the authorities realised … they had so many difficulties with the small children that they let women with small children leave. Anyone in the workforce was forbidden to leave.

How long was it until you were allowed to leave.

Well we were in Stettin until 23 February, then we left. When the Russians finally arrived I was no longer there to see it. I left with the children and a backpack. We put as many layers of clothing on the children as we could and stuffed socks and things into their pockets and in the lining. I had sewn small backpacks for the children to so they could carry their own gloves and small things like that. The first time we put on our backpacks I thought I would not be able to stand up at all. We walked for hours. I had my two children and my cousin had a pram and couldn't take as much because she needed nappies.

You know one thing, for the first years after the war, for about 10 years, I couldn't remember all this. The body must protect itself. I had no memory at all of what had happened. Only after about 1955, ten years later, things started coming back when I met other people I had known there. Then I remembered some things, but a lot was gone completely. I can't remember if we needed some sort of approval, we must have because without food ration cards you couldn't survive and you had to have tickets to be able to enter another region. We must have had papers for the children because in those years you had to be exact about who was who because the food cards were named. So there was no doubt and no mix ups. And actually the moment we were leaving on 23 February was also the moment when our house had windows again, from top to bottom. A delivery of glass had got through and they had fixed all the broken windows in the house. Maybe the Russians had moved their troops or maybe we had had a couple of nights without alarms, I no longer remember. In the end most of Stettin was just rubble and most of the raid were just mining the harbour and that didn't rock the city as the bombs did. So much was already kaput there wasn't much left to bomb.

At this time my husband was in middle Germany. He was in the air force and he was in a special command with one person from the NAKK, the driver. I think there were six men and they had to organise the fighter program. That means, they went to the salt mines in the Leipzig area where the factories had been re-established. They should have done that at the beginning of the war. They transferred the machine there that built aircraft and that is where he had to work. There were a lot of foreign workers there as well. My other relations were all in the north and my parents were in Berlin where they had much worse bombing than we did. On the Elbe we stayed with friends at an evacuation station, so we could wash and so forth. You don't believe how much time you need.

Did you walk?

No we went by train but the train couldn't go into the station for example in Wittenberg where we had friends, but stopped five kilometres outside because all the stations were in ruins. My husband was in Leipzig so I travelled with a different train to Leipzig. And then I walked to where I thought he was. But he had not got my letter and he wasn't there. He had been shifted to Dresden, towards the front with his command. As the troops retreated the technical commandos tries to save the materials so the Russians didn't get it. So he was missing and I was alone there. No one was there but me but he came back safely later.

And did the Russians come?

No the Russians didn't come. I didn't fall into the hands of the Russians They went north to Stettin but I had already left. From about 25 February for about a month we stayed in Leipzig area, near the command of my husband. He had a private room and he was able to accommodate us in his landlady's house.

Did you go west from there?

No, at the time three was no east and west. We fled south when we realised the Russians were getting closer. The command had a special radio, I don't know what type, but they heard things that I was not party to. The command fled and we fled too, further to the south. We had a car that we filled with food and even cutlery and plates. We took half the canteen and we drove as far as we could. We landed in Kupfstein near the Austrian border and stayed in a quarry for a fortnight. Then the Americans came. Oh no, beforehand we hid in Ismaning which is north of Munich. The areas we fled to were so beautiful – the men knew where they were going. One of them was from Nuremberg, he was a Bavarian and he knew every track and stone. We travelled on side roads so we wouldn't run into troops. On these roads we realised what poor condition our army was in. We saw planes that were stranded because there was no petrol to fly them. As we fled they bombed the bridges behind us. There were low flying strafer planes, but I can't remember any more whether they were Russian planes. We wanted to go to Prague but in the end we stayed within German borders for some reason, because it was not safe there either.

Under the low flying strafer planes there was the most beautiful valley, a mountain valley with one road so it was impossible to dodge the planes when they flew over. I grabbed one child and leapt out of one door into the ditch and and my husband grabbed the second child and leapt out of the other door. There was no alternative. There were already burning cars along the road.

We got as far as Ismaning without getting hit and took shelter in a barracks there. There were about a dozen people there and everyone had a bed which was wonderful. The men then returned to Munich to get new orders. They didn't come back and didn't come back and then suddenly one of them dived through the window, and then another all without belts or epaulettes. In Munich they'd got mixed up with the revolution. There was an insurgency in Munich, a revolution that was completely local. I don't know what it was called but I saw a program on TV about it recently. It never spread beyond Munich. The revolutionaries took their car way and their uniforms and locked them up but they absconded after a couple of hours.

So now we all became civilians. Most of the men were officers. My husband had a Masters in electromechanical engineering so he had the rank of Major and there were others who were similar. We had our private luggage with us and they had civvies with them as well as their uniforms. The whole group now donned civilian clothing, whatever would fit. Nothing matched anything else, what we call in Germany *Raeuberzivil* (bandit civvies). I'll never forget the men and their hats. Some had shorts, others long pants and boots. Then we fled during the night towards the south right to the border with Tirol. We ended up in a quarry. That was still Germany and because the men still had their identification papers the mayor of the town had to give them accommodation and the accommodation was a forestry workers hut in the quarry. The men made beds or brought them from other huts. We were twelve people and we had six beds, three bunk beds pushed together, and a long table with two benches like they have here in Hessen. That was new for me because we didn't have them at home, our chairs had backs in them. We had a tile stove. There were six men and four females. I was the only woman and there was a young secretary and my two children and together we built a harmonious, happy and completely harmless family. What else could we do with small children. The first night the men dug holes and buried their uniforms.

Then the Americans marched in. We were in the quarry and actually no one was meant to leave as it was a dangerous undertaking. I remember the town mayor coming one day and he insisted on seeing our papers again, the ones he had previously been shown. Everyone had to save their own lives somehow or other because up in the mountains there was still fighting. The SS was still fighting nearby. It was really vicious.

We women had to leave, especially me but the others as well, and the men sat in the hut, played cards with their hats pulled down over their faces and hoped they survived. One of them, an accountant whose name I have forgotten, was not so shy and he left the hut and his watch and fountain pen were taken from him. The black Americans liked that sort of thing. We hid our wedding rings and I couldn't find mine again. The next winter my children had colds and I got out the herb tea and found the rings again. I had hidden them in the herb tea then forgotten where they were.

They say there were a lot of suicides at this time?

That was later, afterwards. For example when the many active officers returned. We had a nasty saying that active officers were just unskilled labourers for the economy or on the land, When they returned home from the war they had to work as unskilled labourers. They had to pick up a shovel, everyone had to pick up shovels, not only officers, but the officers had had a good education and had never had to do such work. The women were different because we had had to live under the bombs and had learned to cook milk on an open fire in the back yard but army personnel had been given their food, given their clothes and their munitions.

During the war my husband said every time he came home that he was pleased to be returning to Russia. In war you can't avoid service but living with children under bombs, that is dreadful. You can't adapt – it's impossible. You don't have the daily grind – I think it is easier in a camp. My brother for example never went to war. He was also an electrical engineer and worked in Berlin building instruments for submarines. They were transferred to the north later in the war and ended up in Schleswig-Holstein. They always had a salary from their company, sometimes only half a salary or very little but regardless of their profession or education they all had to pick up shovels and rebuild the factory. That is how they started again and afterwards when the factory was rebuilt they needed this and that professional. But you know. People.

And then there were cases in Berlin where everything was in ruins. They had grown up with a house and garden and had had a good life and suddenly they had nothing at all. Maybe only a knife, fork and plate.

You know for years afterwards in Nuremberg even when we had our own apartment, that was about 1949-50 when I was working, I stood and washed my bed linen on the stove and rinsed in the bath. I only had one so I could only wash one. In 1945 it was even more difficult.

There were exceptions of course, when men came back to areas that had not been as badly damaged or where there was something left of a house. But almost all of us were beggarly. I mean imagine, everything was gone. You sat on the train with a backpack with just a few things.

Were people glad or sorry when it was all finished.

You didn't have time to think. You were upset and cried when you had a miscarriage. Then of course you were deeply unhappy. But then you had been unhappy the whole war. You never knew if you would see your husband again.

Was it a relief when the war ended?

It wasn't worse, it was a relief that it was all over. But it was awful too because there was nothing to eat. After three months we got a quarter of a pound of sugar per person – but we had 3 months with children and nothing to eat, not a single grain of sugar. The children were so hungry they stole noodles and ate them out of the packet before they were cooked. They ate a whole packet of noodles one day before I got home. We were upset because they had been meant for all of us. Everything was rationed, everything was sliced then sliced ever thinner and there was no way to get more.

Were there rapes in the American sector?

The Russians raped, we didn't need the Americans to do it. The Americans gave the children food but there was a lot of talk about the Americans throwing away food and pouring benzine over it so the Germans couldn't eat it. The plan was that we deserved to be punished, so we were made to starve. When a whole population starves people will take rubbish out of bins to eat. People who were in their own homes and had connections had more to eat. At this time in my family some of the older family members in Berlin starved to death. The younger people had a better chance of survival.

What sort of work did you get after the war?

I was kitchen maid in Nuremberg and my husband worked on an assembly line. I am a librarian by training but everything was in ruins. In Nuremberg everything was rubble and their own librarians were unemployed. They didn't want any more and certainly not one from Prussia. So I helped in a kitchen, peeling potatoes and washing vegetables.

In a factory?

No in a restaurant. I went to the employment bureau and they got the job for me.

Were the children at home.

I got the children into a kindergarten. Of course I had to run around a lot to get a place. It was their first kindergarten. You see we had always had secure circumstances. During the Nazi time Mothers with children at home got holidays – that was all taken care of by the Nazis. They simply sent people to others to take care of. "Oh you are doing well, you can feed another mouth," they would say. That's what they did.

In Nuremberg I went to the Interior Ministry because I always had problems during the school holidays. When mothers work the children are left on the street. In the first winter my husband had difficulty with work. It was terribly cold and he was unemployed half time so he was able to mind the children and see to their homework. I only worked half days too, from 10 to 3pm but beforehand I had to queue and afterwards I had to queue to get food. You queued for hours.

I went to the Interior Ministry and said I was a refugee and had to work and received nothing. Then for a small amount of money, I think 2,50DM per child per day, I got them in a children's home not far from Nuremberg. The children were registered at this home other wise they would have got diphtheria from the cold. Nuremberg was really bad.

You know Nuremberg was the city where the trials were hold after the war. In the beginning all the higher civil servants were arrested. Everyone who was still at liberty had to register – the police came and you had to register. We were so used to hearing that people were arrested and didn't return that my husband packed his army bag with all the food I had, everything he could get in, and went and registered with the police. He did come back, but many people who were taken off in their slippers didn't return. This wasn't happening only in Nuremberg but throughout Germany. We thought it a ridiculous process taking the men away so long – you see everything was in ruins.

In Nuremberg the rubble was two stories high and the Americans had bulldozed two roads through it. That was the Nuremberg inner city. It was impossible to live there so people lived further out wherever they could. We had 22 square meters. I went to the city council who told me they were re-opening a Kindergarten. It was the first one, so it had all the experienced kindergarten teachers and so our children didn't have to grow up on the street. I could never understand the Nuremberg dialect but the children could. In Kindergarten though they spoke good high-German (*Hochdeutsch*) and that counts for something in Bavaria. The Kindergarten teachers in this kindergarten were wonderful. But my poor daughter went to school in autumn of 1945 and there were 65 children and only one teacher, an old man of 65 who had been recalled from retirement. All the teachers who had been educated by the Nazis had been thrown out of course. I suppose it was the same for my son but I was so busy and working that I didn't have time to notice.

A woman where we lived gave the children slate plates and slate pencils. She gave the children what they needed otherwise they would have had nothing. These cold hungry children learned reading and writing with a piece of slate and a slate pencil. They stayed at after school care the whole day. They had keys around their necks and off they went. I realised only when I was leaving Nuremberg in 1954 that they had had to walk for half and hour and cross the Pegnitz bridge and it had no sides for the first years. Other priorities were more important than building sides on the bridge; you can only do one thing at a time. These two small children crossed the river on a side-less bridge for their first school years. Some things just happen, others you don't know about.

Do you think we have learned something from the war?

I don't know, I think I have given up on humankind. Listen, after all our experiences we never gave our children toys that had anything to do with war or shooting or flying. My son made his own guns. I had to destroy so many guns. Today he is Major in the army! My son never had war toys but it made no difference.

We were peaceable people, we were pacifists really. No one wanted war. I remember Hungarian foreign workers telling us we were lucky and had everything. They were right. We didn't want to go into Hungary or anywhere else. None of us wanted to invade anywhere or kill anyone. Our men didn't march off happily, they were frightened. My personal experience was that they were all frightened.

Do you understand war better than your son?

You know everything that my son learned about being a soldier we taught him and we did that in an awful way. Someone once said when our cities were burning that we paid for it dearly, but that good schools are expensive.

Do you watch war reports from other countries on TV

I turn them off. I don't need to see them, I know that already, it is always the same. Of course I am sorry for them but what can you do? You are only human and you can't carry everything. You simply can't. I learned that in 1948 when I collapsed.

I was working in the kitchens and then I got a a very good position as librarian in the American special services. My own profession. But no free days for a whole year, no Saturday, no Sunday. I worked for six hours a day which isn't so long but there was never a day off for housework. No Christmas day off. There came a day when I simply broke down. I just lay there. Finished. I couldn't get up.

Then they gave me holidays and I went to the Bavarian woods and slept for 14 days, just slept. I was at a hotel where the Americans or British had had been quartered. They had just left and it was being renovated for use as a guest house but was not finished. They were happy to bring breakfast to my room so I didn't have to use theirs. I ate then went back to sleep. At lunch

time I would go somewhere for lunch then go back to sleep. After 14 days
my husband joined me and we looked around the area a bit. For fourteen
days all I did was sleep. A person can only take on so much; that's what I
learned at that time. You see, after the war we had so-called refugee-
anaemia. Many of we women had no period for about nine months. Then
suddenly they came. That was the post war period; we were completely
exhausted.

**Someone else told me that she wondered whether not having periods
was the result of being frighted of the Russians.**

Frightened, yes. It was five years until we stopped waking up in the night.
Partly that was to do with having potatoes as your main food. We ate
primarily soup made of potatoes. When my husband got work as an
assembly worker they were allowed to buy the left overs. Then we got
potatoes from others who had enough. I would cook up a pot in the early
morning and that's what we ate. Potatoes with a bit of salt to make them
taste and then potatoes for lunch. In the evening we would cook them with
something else if we had managed to find anything. Then of course you
have to get up in the night because these potatoes were so full of water.
There was never enough and we were exhausted. When I got my period
back I bled so much I thought I was having a miscarriage but the doctor
said no, it was the exhaustion and that it was quite common. We hadn't had
periods for so long, now they came back suddenly.

You see during the flight you thought incessantly about where you might
get your next meal even if you aren't the sort of person who worries about
food. And then you think about how you are going to cook it. My husband
found a ceramic hotplate. When the others slept I would have it on next to
me while I sewed so I didn't freeze. I would patch the clothes that the
others had to put on again in the morning. I remember once being in a
panic because I didn't have any material more for the patches. What was I
to do? Everyone else was as exhausted as I was.

We had to find wood for cooking too. We were allowed to get it from the
woods but for that you had to have a vehicle so you had to borrow one.
There was a car at my workplace but it was ruined by getting wood. We
would have to take the children, drive to the woods, chop off the branches
and load them into the car and drive them home. It was for cooking, not
heating. We could do without heating. You can freeze but you have to eat.
You know how much wood you need for cooking. Then the men got some
beams, I'll never forget them. They got them from a house across the river,

across that bridge without sides the children had to cross. The beams weren't just lying around or they would have been long gone. The men found this beam that they thought we could dislodge. No one else had seen it. So we went across the bridge in the dark with a push cart and pushed the beam all the way home.

Then of course there was the washing to be done. In Bavaria they have a sort of sloping board that they use to do the wash. Women would stand there and use a brush to scrub the clothes. In Berlin it was considered the greatest sin to use a brush to scrub clothes but in Bavaria it was considered a sin not to use a brush! In Prussia we used a corrugated board and rubbed the clothes on that. Just like women in Portugal who use stones. But in Nuremberg and Bavaria they scrub the clothes and you had to do that because the soap was so bad. It was like the sand soap you buy today. Mostly what you needed to get things clean was strength. No wonder we were exhausted.

It was not only physical exhaustion with was mental exhaustion because you couldn't see a way out. As refugees we didn't get any money. Anyone with a savings book had it barred. We didn't get anything so we had to exist on what we were able to earn. We could hardly buy our food cards with what we earned because we didn't earn much. Things only got better after the currency reform when things suddenly had a value. We thought we had reached the bottom. We worked for the people who had been born there and who had things. We helped as cleaning women and sometimes we were given an old bed or a broken mattress. We didn't care it was broken, at least it was something usable. In those years you noticed what it is like when the women are exhausted. You had so much to do in the house that it was difficult. Women needed four weeks rest then they could deal with all the problems. When they had reached a certain level of exhaustion they couldn't cope with anything. Things would fall out of your hands, you'd cut yourself, hit your head, break things. All that doesn't happen if you are rested. On top of it all we got colds and flu and there was only aspirin to help, no other medicines. Then the children got sick. My children got yellow fever.

The worst thing was the hopelessness. I worked as a kitchen help and my husband as assembly worker. The first weeks he worked as a technical helper in the rubble, looking for gas or electrical fittings that could be removed for reuse. So first he had to shovel rubble, and then he was a technical helper and then he went to the work department and said he had to work to be able to eat and they said do you want to join us, and he did.

He was an engineer not an assembly worker. In the meantime I was in the special services and earned more. You see I can't spend the whole day just thinking of food; that makes me sick. But I had books again. The Amerikahouse even had German literature and I could stay until 10pm as guest. But the first winter, 45/46, that was dreadful. It was so bitterly cold, really it was the very worst.

CLARA H. 1907: WAR, FLIGHT AND DEPORTATION

Clara H. born 1907, lived in Stettin (now Szczecin, Poland) during the war

Did women help each other when the men were away?

Not more than normal, but they did when they had to because the men were away. Whoever could work had to do so.

My sister died in 1941. She had to work with the Postal services. I was working with the Postal Services sorting mail but she had to deliver mail. She was 24 years old and had a four year old son. We lived together in one house and I took care of the boy during the day. Of course we helped each other out. That was my youngest sister.

She got a red pimple on her back and it was so sore she went to the doctor. He gave her ointment but didn't want to give her a sickness certificate. At the time you were not allowed to take your postal satchel, the ones with the thick straps, off your back. The satchel chaffed her so badly I went to the doctor and asked him to write a sick certificate because she was too sick to work. He did that and she stayed in bed for the next couple of days. Then she developed a rash and I said to the neighbour not to let the children near her because it looked like scarlet fever. I got the doctor and her gave her a prescription for ointment and went away again.

That evening her mother-in-law came and we made a bed for her. She had really swollen legs. I asked myself what it could possibly be and thought that it can't have come from the pimple. I went downstairs and took her boy with me. Next morning I went up to give her a drink and some breakfast.

She looked at me with big eyes, and when I wanted to give her something to drink she shut her mouth and died.

She was only twenty four. My mother died at forty nine. But I couldn't bear the way my sister died. I asked the doctor who told me that she had had blood poisoning and that we are defenseless against it. I said to him that he must have seen that the day before and should have put her in hospital. Her husband was fighting on the Russian front and I couldn't let him know. He came back six months later. We don't know what happened to the boy. Her parents in law took him from me. They gave me a letter from her husband saying they should have him.

I was working for the postal service too. We were all mobilised. The Block Leader had arranged all that, you didn't have any say yourself at all.. If he said you had to do something, then you had to do it. I had children but no one asked about that, you were simply mobilised and had to work. I did a lot of night shifts. From eight at night until six in the morning despite the children who were still small.

Stettin was very badly bombed. Once I had left both the children downstairs with an old woman and my sister-in-law and I set off for her house but it had been completely destroyed by bombs. ... when we got there there was nothing. That was the house of my husband. So we had to go back and pick up the children. We found an apartment, everything was gone, windows, doors and ceiling, but there was a roof over our heads. That was in Stettin. Stettin had been completely bombed.

Once on an afternoon in 1944 we had 250 bombers flying over us.

The bombers came at night. We were near a large hill. We had to work and put beams in the bunker. Always the women, the men were away fighting or else had their own work. So we built ourselves a bunker within the hill and used wooden supports to hold it up, so that we had a place to shelter. Everyone was terrified of fire bombs. We built a porch at the front as extra protection. So when the high-explosive bombs rained down we sat in our shelter with the children. I had the keys of our landlady and the businessman, who lived in the house. The landlady said she wanted to see what it looked like outside during the bombing. By the way, I was also air-raid shelter supervisor. So I went out to have a look and saw our area all burning. I went up one flight of stairs, but at such a moment you can't think what one should do, somehow you can't believe it. I hadn't taken any of our papers nor any valuables. I went back down into the bunker and the landlady asked how things were. I said all was in order. You couldn't tell the people in the bunker. There were fifty or sixty people in there. The businessman and his family had been evacuated to be near their parents, and now all was destroyed.

You bury your head and don't want to see and don't want to know. One thinks, it is impossible that our house is still standing. I ran hours to get home and our house was still standing thank god.

The bunker we had in our building had trestles and an oven. There was a butchery in the building. My brother lived two doors away from us at number 12. We lived at number 13. The door between the cellars was blocked. My brother brought a child out of their cellar and wanted to go back for a pregnant woman. There were two navy personnel in the cellar and the son of the butcher. They must have thought it wouldn't be so bad. Just as my brother came to us with this child a bomb came down next door. The pregnant woman and her young child were still in the bunker and my brother couldn't get them out. He almost went wild trying. I had to calm him down. His family had been evacuated and he was all alone. If you are in such a situation and can't get out, all around buildings are burning, then three is a fire-storm. You can't imagine such a thing.

Yes and two years before, that was weird, the story about our Block Warden. Each apartment block had a Block Warden [member of the Nazi Party] and they reigned supreme, they were the boss and gave the orders and you had to do what they said or you would be sent to a concentrations camp. The concentrations camps where the women were sent, you could only leave at certain times. They could exit in the mornings but then not for the rest of the day, it was very difficult. And anyone who who set themselves against anything, or was against something, they would be sent to the concentrations camp.

This Block Warden told me I had to go to the employment office and I had to work. I liked the work, it was clean work and I could do night duty and I had a day free between when I had worked my hours. Now when this big bombing raid happened the Block Leader and his wife and two children were in the bunker. You wouldn't believe it but he and many other people who lived in the house were suffocated by the smoke. Afterwards we looked around to see if he had had any belongings with him and we found a big bag, we used to call them midwives bags because women had their babies at home and the midwives carried these bags of supplies. Today the young people like to carry them. Anyway, we found his bag and inside was salami sausage and also the work books of several women that he hustled. They didn't need to work but for that they had to give him food. We said to each other, that is the punishment for his deeds. Our neighbours believed that as well.

Then our bunker started to burn. We couldn't get out. One woman died, then the Block Leader, but then a soldier who was in the neighbouring bunker came through and said 'Everyone after me!' I had my cousin's child with me, she was two years old and I put a cover over her head and we had to run through the fire. My own children were there too but they were a bit older. We came out in the house across the street. The next day I sat on the street curb and thought to myself, what now? The older part of the city was completely destroyed. We didn't have any clothes, we had no water and nothing to eat. We had nothing. Luckily we lived directly on the River Oder and we climbed into a boat for the night. Then the English came again and they bombed the side they had missed the night before.

The next day my sister-in-law arrived and she took us to my mother-in-law. She was a cold-hearted women. She gave us cold coffee to drink. But I had friends where I went every Saturday and we took the train to them. We got there to find the woman had gone. She had left with her children to go to her parents and she had left me a letter on the table and told me I should treat the house as my own. So we had a good place to stay. My youngest was ready to be confirmed and the Pastor said that we should carry out an emergency confirmation because we don't know if we will be here tomorrow. In the evening we went to the building and he confirmed all the children.

The Russians were on the other side of the River Oder and used artillery to shoot over the River Oder into our street. You heard the whistling of the bullets and you cowered in corners or hid in recesses. My big boy was away and I just had the two younger children. I took the children to Rügen Island where my cousin was but I had to go back because I was working at the postal services and we had been mobilised and daren't leave our posts for fear of being shot.

Were you frightened of your own soldiers?

No, it was the Party. The soldiers helped us leave. So I brought the children away, we got blankets. My brother worked for the railways and he looked after us a bit. We had a suitcase and a relations took us to Strahsund. I took the children on to the Rügen Island and then I had to leave to go back.

We had to stay because we worked for the post, that was in January and the war ended in May. We had to stay and shovel graves, together with the foreigners. Four women had to do that and they said if we left our posts we would be shot, our own Germans. That was the Party; the soldiers had nothing to do with it.

Were the soldiers afraid of the Party.

Yes, they even hung soldiers. When the war ended the Party hung soldiers they met without weapons directly in the city. Their own soldiers.

Why did the Party hang their own soldiers?

Because they assumed they had left their posts as soldiers. At first there was such chaos, no order.

The Russians came over the Oder and we were the last ones to leave, together with the soldiers. At least I didn't have the children with me, just my sister-in-law and mother-in-law. I had a wounded hand, I had got blood poisoning and when the soldiers stopped at the next hospital post I went to to paramedic and showed him my hand. He told me the doctor wasn't there but that he would give me some tablets and come again very early next morning. You have to imagine a little village just with a paramedic and soldiers. My hand was frightfully painful and I told them they should cut it open. He did it without any painkillers or anaesthetic. He made me a sling and I went back and lay in a room until midday. And then my sister-in-law and mother-in-law said that they had to carry on and that I would have to see how I could follow them. I was alone on a country road and I wanted to get to my children. But they were several hundred kilometers away.

I travelled on an open troop-carrier as far as Strahlsund and then in the train station I fell asleep. When I woke up, and I will never forget this, a few coins lay in my lap. I will never forget that. I'd had nothing to eat or drink. I imagine it was a passing soldier because at the time everything was in chaos. My hand was so very painful and it had to be dressed again. I took the train to the main city on Rügen Island, that was Bergen, and went to a doctor so he could take off the splint. He took off the splint and ranted about the refugees. Because he took the splint off too early it took much longer to heal. Where we were there was no doctor and no possibility because the war was coming to an end. Rügen capitulated, the whole island capitulated.

I tried to get further with the children by hitch-hiking. Then the Russians came. We took pieces of sheets that we hung out the window so they saw we wanted to surrender. But now we had nothing to eat. I still had ration cards, 50 grams of fat, 50 grams of meat.

The Russians came into the houses and asked how many people there were. They took radios or cameras if people had them. They didn't take anything from us, there was nothing to take. I was fearful for the children and thought they might be taken. That was what we feared most. But the Russians, the Russians I saw, never did a single thing against children, they were very child friendly. They were quite different to what we thought. But the Poles, they were the opposite. They took the suckling babies and children away in the mornings and made the mothers go out to work and then completely neglected the children. There were a great many children who had no parents and who ran around looking in garbage cans for food. It was gruesome.

The people where I lived went fishing then gave us some herrings. In the meantime my daughter was 14 or 15 years old and we made stones so we could smoke the fish. But we had no salt and you cant live forever without salt so we wanted to go to Stettin. One day it was said that a coal barge was going down to Stettin so I started out with both my children. When we were on our way they started shooting again, even though the war was over. I was terribly sick, the stress went immediately to my stomach. We lay there on the coal and that's how we got to Stettin. When we docked an old Jew greeted us. They had come over from Russia, they were in an appalling condition. Gruesome. I knew Jews before and during the war and they had been very good to us. My father died in the first world war and we were five siblings, I was the oldest and I went every Wednesday to eat with this Jewish couple. A neighbour of ours was a cleaning lady with people who were big businessmen. When these business people went to England they left their business to the nephew of the cleaning lady.

Anyway, we had nothing to eat, you can't believe how long you can keep gong without food. We were now in Stettin where the Russians were and everyone who was capable and wanting to work was told to gather in a certain town square. The Russians would come with big trucks and count out how many people they needed. They were dismantling everything from the factories for miles around Stettin. They took pianos and good cutlery from the great houses and we had to do that for them. They sent it all back home. I was sent with the children as part of a company that occupied a row of houses and an apartment block. There was a corporal and team and we had to dismantle a factory in the suburbs. We women were really frightened and dressed in men's clothes and we neither washed nor combed our hair so we looked like gypsies. My daughter was fifteen and I was really frightened for her. The children had to work with me and after four weeks they got more money than I did, nearly double. We couldn't use the money. If we worked for three weeks we got black bean soup every day at three o'clock. It was cooked in the courtyard in a big copper. On the fourth week we got flour and we got salt from the houses. We could go into the empty houses and take what was there. Only a few houses had people living in them.

On the 5th of May the war ended. I was working with the children and I came back afterwards to these houses where the Russians were stationed and I had to wash their uniforms and also cook for them. They ate their first breakfast at nine in the morning, usually stew and black bread. They took things they needed from the gardens round about. They had plenty to eat but it was all locked away. If we found anything then of course we took it and the black market grew. Anyone who had any clothes sold them, only for money. When I worked for the Russians I had food to eat. There was a Russian women there who was terribly mean to us. There was also a superintendent, in civilian clothes but the soldiers called him commissioner. He watched and he noticed that we weren't getting enough food because this Russian women was diverting it. She had to leave later.

I also attended a funeral of a Russian Major. He wanted to travel from Stettin to Berlin and from there take a holiday. He had an accident in his vehicle and was brought back to his unit in Stettin and was buried there. I had to make certain foods. They take their dead in open wagons. They don't shut the coffin. A young woman who was Sargent sat at the head of the coffin. They cut open a doona then sewed up the covering and used that. He was buried in the middle of the city. When they came back they drank Vodka and ate black bread. The girl got typhoid fever. I offered to help her but she said she wanted someone else because she didn't want to put me in danger. You get such dreadful diarrhea because your intestines are full of ulcers. I visited her in the evenings and we were vaccinated by the Poles. The Russians were really frightened of getting sick. If they got typhoid their hair would be shorn off. They were so frightened of contagion. But I must say I have no complaints about the Russians.

When the girl Sargent was still there and I had to bring a tea into the Major in the evening, then I knew what was ahead of me because I was still a young women, only thirty nine. So I asked this girl if she wouldn't mind taking it in for me and she said, yes she would. I found her very decent. She often brought me something to eat for the boys. You become a completely different person, it is hard to describe. I am actually a very sensitive person and like helping others, but I became very different during that time. That is the instinct for self preservation. You have no alternative.

Then typhoid fever arrived. In the group we had a Russian and she had the rank of Sargent. She was very good to us and often gave us a bit more food. This Russian was called Anvivia and she was so good to us.

Then later soldiers arrived from Kurland in eastern Prussia. They were dreadful to see. They had no shoes and had walked five hundred kilometres on foot. They were put in a camp, not in the city.

My youngest son got typhoid fever. There were no doctors and no chemists and we had no idea what we should do. My sister-in-law was also working for he Russians and she got lots of black tea. I gave him black tea for three months, no food, just black tea. In the end he was just a skeleton. My mother-in-law would say, just let him die. But he continued to live but his feet went blue and were later crippled. He couldn't walk. Then the Poles came.

Then Frau Braunsfehle came, the woman who had left me her apartment. She had two small children and she came to us too. We lived together, two women with the children. She had two girls. We lived there together in one apartment.

A Pole came and wanted the sewing machine. He noticed that something was missing and said I should give it to him, but I couldn't. He threatened us with his sub-machine gun. He said, think about it and I will come again this evening. We were terrified. But he didn't come back. Then this women left to live in another apartment with her children.

It poured with rain and we had to put buckets around to catch the leaks and my son had typhoid fever which was contagious. I caught it from him. I didn't get it as badly as he had it.

In May when the Russians came, I stopped having my period. I don't know why, but I know it happened to a lot of women. We were so afraid of he Russians and the Poles. I would get a very swollen stomach by the end of the day but in the morning it would be normal again.

Later when my husband came back he … you're a woman, you'll understand, he wouldn't touch me. How can I describe it. All tenderness was gone. And I was touched to the quick. I wanted to hold him in my arms but he wouldn't come near me. Perhaps he noticed my swollen stomach, or perhaps my mother-in=law said something to him. Anyway, in two weeks he slowly got back to normal. I suddenly had another period and bled as if I was having three babies. To this day, in my old age, I have never asked him about that time and why he was so withdrawn.

My husband arrived back from the American prisoner of war camp in October. He was released due to malnutrition and he came to Stettin but we were gone. No wait, somewhere on a noticeboard he found the name of our oldest son, that's how it was. Our son had also served in the war, not as a soldier but in the support services. That's why he hadn't been able to stay and I didn't know where he was. My husband had had holidays once a year and on his last holiday he had said that if I saw the end of the war was imminent, he would advise me to go to his colleague in Hamburg, that they had a room ready for us. That was his war time buddy. He told that to our eldest son as well.

Our eldest son was in a Russian prisoner-of-war camp and had contracted yellow fever. The Russians were so frightened of sickness and especially of contagious diseases. But my son made his way to Hamburg and to these people. They were anxious, you couldn't always trust people in those days. He said that he was an honest and dignified man and the woman gave him socks and a hat and he made his way to Zelle where he worked on a farm.

My husband went to Hamburg but our son was no longer there and then he made his way to Rügen Island and asked after us there. They couldn't tell him anything and that is when he came on to Stettin. He found us there. We were living in the house that belonged to his parents. I was at work but he sent one of the girls to find me. She came and said he was there and I said, no that is impossible, that must be Heinz. No, she said, that is uncle Hannemann. I asked the Russian if I could take an hour off to go home. He said, Du (we all used the Du form of you) where has he been? I said, with the Amis. Then he said, well you can go then.

So my husband had to find somewhere to work. The Russians sent men off to Siberia but he was lucky in that he had a friend who was a tug boat operator. They maneuvered large ships about and he got a job with them. He immediately got rations of oil and black bread and also salt and he was able to give us a little bit. We also collected potatoes. We went by foot for two hours. We would open the heaps for them but we had to remove the worms from the middle. For the whole family we would grate one and a half potatoes, that was always counted, into a pot of boiling water with a little oil and salt and you can't imagine how good that tasted. Really fantastic!

How long did you just eat potatoes?

Oh a long time. Nine months. And in between the black beans, we got only black beans. I really can't understand how one can survive so long like that, how we survived. It is a wonder.

Then it was 1946 and I had a cousin at my place who had had a baby on Rügen Island and then later she came to Stettin. She was lucky because she was a seamstress and she could immediately start sewing for a Polish woman and help a little in the house. The child was three years old and she could take her with her and then they had food for the whole day.

Then she had bad luck because the Poles came to this house and into the room in which she was living. She said something to them, this small dainty woman, and they threw her down the stairs. She smashed her knee open on the stair. But then it was a Pole who looked after her and made sure she had it bandaged. Then I looked after her small daughter, little Renate.

My cousin had a small Meissen vase, a very pretty one, and I took it to the black market and she looked after the children. You had to show your wares and say 'five Zloty for this pretty vase, five zloty for this beautiful vase'. I sold it very quickly and then I went to the grocer very quickly and bought a piece of fruit. You can't criticise that, it had to do with hunger.

Then suddenly we heard we had to leave. Germans must leave. But my husband would not leave. My cousin managed to arrange that the Pole for whom she worked signed a bank note and she gave that to us. I gave it to my husband and he took it with him and brought back a large piece of black bread. Then we had to leave and were taken to a camp on the edge of the city and then we were shipped off in the dark in a goods train. I had sewed for each of us a jacket or shirt and a knapsack out of towels but the Poles took them away from us and again we had nothing.

The Germans had to walk in two long lines with Poles walking either side of us. They had rubber truncheons and they used them. We had to gallop to the camp. When we got there we found the camp were pretty one-family houses but all the windows and doors had been smashed out of them. They had destroyed it all. We had another family with us, a grandmother, a mother and two children. The boy wanted to go outside in the morning and see if he could find some water. He came back clutching his stomach. The Poles had laid hand grenades and the boy had picked one up and it had ripped out his stomach.

We were transported from the camp at night and when we arrived in the west we had no idea where we were. We'd arrived in a camp in Segeberg and there of course we were well looked after. We got a warm meal and also bread. Then we were divided into groups. I was so thankful that I had my husband with me, that I had been able to bring him. If that hadn't all happened so quickly and if the Russians had got him he would have been in for it because he had worked for the Russians. He hadn't worked for the Poles, but for the Russians. In the end we'd had to work for the Poles.

So there we were in a small place in Segeberg. We were sent to a farm and for the four of us we were offered a small bathroom. There was nothing in it, no chair, no table, nothing. They didn't offer us coffee or even water. Nothing. He was a German with a big farm. He had a big chest with Maggi cubes and everything from the army that he fed the pigs and we just had to look on. Later he died in a bad way and his wife as well and the farm fell into disrepair. That was his punishment.

My husband went out and found straw for us to sleep on. Later we got paper sacks and we stuffed those with straw. Then my husband worked in the forests so we could get wood. Every month we got a certain amount of wood. We could cut it small and swap it for food. We made beds from the wood, so we had somewhere to lie, but we had a single room and we had to go to the next village to eat. We got ration cards and could swap them for turnips and so forth.

Nearby was an old building with an elderly couple living downstairs. My husband suggested we try to make a home for ourselves upstairs. There was a large room upstairs with a niche which was very dark but we could sleep there. The room was large and there was big iron old stove in it, the type they used to have in the past. So we moved in there and made it habitable. But I was anxious about my youngest son who was still so sick. He could not really walk and he sat outside in the sun most of the time. He got better over time but if I ever sent him shopping he fell over. He slowly improved and with time he was able to help the farmer a little bit. They were digging turf and he was helping and over time that strengthened him.

Later my husband found a job in Neumünster through relations in Kiel, and my daughter also looked for work. They had to walk twenty five minutes to the station, then travel 20 minutes then walk again because Neumünster was an industrial city at that time. Our youngest son also started work there eventually.

Then we heard where our eldest son was. He was in Zelle on a farm. We heard about him from my brother who had once worked for the railways. My brother had been wounded several times in the war and straight after the war he had gone to Hamburg where there was a large home for railway staff and he was in a position support us. He brought us some bed linen and he had coats made for us out of blankets. My cousin's husband was in Schoenberg. The firm had been moved there from Stettin before the end of the war. His father worked there so he started there as well. Then he said to my husband that he could learn clamping there and it would be better than working on a farm. My husband want there on Mondays and came back to us on Saturdays but he could live at my cousins during the week. Six months later this firm moved to Kiel and it was easier for my husband to reach us.

We heard through our relations who knew a concierge living in central district of Kiel that there was an apartment available there. My husband went to see this concierge immediately. The apartment had two bedrooms and a kitchen and we were able to have it. We were so happy. There was no glass in the upper windows, just cardboard, and ivy had grown half way up. My daughter had met a young man and he helped us a great deal. He is now her husband. So we went to Kiel and over time we worked ourselves up. I started work in 1954.

Our eldest son had really bad luck. After the war my husband had picked him up from the farm where he was living because he said we should all be together. But there was little work in the village we were living so he started work at a lumber yard. Then they said they only wanted locals so he could no longer continue, so he went to Bavaria to a lumber yard there. Then a friend said to him that they could earn more if they worked in a mine and he signed up. But we got word that he had joined the legionaries. For six months we didn't know where he was and I almost went crazy. He had to stay with the legionaries for five years. Finally we had a letter from him and he was fighting in Indonesia. Finally in 1954 my brother brought him back to us. He had become a very heavy smoker, and how could I afford that?

He was very lucky because he found work within ten days. He is still at the same workplace. Our youngest so came back from Neumünster where he had worked in an electroplating shop and tried to find an electroplating place in Kiel. He found work at Zeiss-Ikon and he is still there 24 years later. .

Our daughter found work in Neumünster in a lingerie factory and traveled every day from Kiel to Neumünster .Then she had some luck and found a one bedroom apartment in Neumünster. He married such a nice man and he worked at AEG. So in the end everything turned out well.

I can imagine there were difficulties when the men came back

Yes. For example, an acquaintance whom I had brought her with me from Poland, she and her little one who was three years old. They lived with the woman who was the teacher.

We found out that her husband was in Schoenberg with his father. My husband wrote to him but he heard nothing back. Anyone would be happy, wouldn't they, to have found their wife and small daughter? Then one day my husband said he would drive she and her daughter to see him. They arrived and he asked someone to call him. 'Hello Ernst,' he said. 'I have Lotte with me."

But he wouldn't look at his wife. It had been a good marriage but he was living with a couple with a 28 year old daughter and she had got her claws into him. They had had a child and she wouldn't let him go. My cousin wrote to him too and tried to see him but there was nothing to be done. This woman managed to get a furnished room in the town where these people lived and then he went to her. But this girl came on Sunday and said 'Come Walter, we are going walking together.'

Then my cousin went to the parents. She was working in the same firm. We felt so very sorry for her. In 1949 she had another child with her husband but the trust had been broken. She had suffered so much with the Poles, with her knee. I took her in when she had her child because she had to lie down a lot. Her child was full of lice, my cousin had not realised She was an only child and very spoiled but then her mother died young and that is especially difficult. I was the oldest and had to look after the rest because my father died in the first world war.

If there was another war?

When one has lived through a war, you view war differently. If there was another war, I would not leave. I would not flee. I would simply stay where I was.

World War two was different from the first war and I can imagine the next war that comes will be different again. Whoever pushes the button first will be the victor and the others will be gone. Do you think anyone will live? Or are they frightened and is that why they fight using regular forces. I hope it never happens.

Do you know what I find odd? Every women who lived through the war says she would never again want war. Especially if she was alone and had to protect children. But the men, men the same generation who went through the war, why do they play with fire? The men had a tough time as soldiers, but at least they had an enemy. We didn't see our enemy. If you have to fight while you have children, then you are always frightened.

I also think that the scientists who create these atoms bombs should be punished. That should be unacceptable. There does not need to be hunger in the world. Once when I was working at the postal services and we were having lunch. The post building was well camouflaged. We watched the planes fly over, they were like silver birds in the sky, very beautiful. But then they dropped their bombs on the city and it was dreadful. I stuck my nose in the earth. Seeing a city, a whole city annihilated is dreadful. In the morning it was black with ten thousand dead in one night.

Today we saw a news item showing how the Poles are rebuilding Stettin but there are a lot of empty grassed over areas in the old city. At the time we couldn't cope with the dead and they were just covered in chlorine.

FRAU SCHW. 1902. EAST PRUSSIA -

Frau Schw. born in 1902, Lived in Braunsberg Bezirk Koenigsberg (now Poland) during the war.

"If there is every another war I don't want to live."

When the war started, what did the people think? Were they frightened.

Everyone was frightened. Actually we didn't notice much difference when the war started but then they all started shouting for Hitler. My brother-in-law was one of them. Hitler's people daubed all the Jewish shops and threw the goods out onto the pavement. The men from the home-guard stood on the corners and shot people.

The families of the men who were with Hitler were looked after. The others didn't get anything. My brother in law was a member and when I asked him for anything he asked if I was a member. I said 'no' so he said I should leave. Anyone could join the party but the communists were shot.

When Hitler came to our town in Eastern Prussia I was in the potato fields and I didn't bother to go and see him. But everyone else went and cheered. I just kept picking up potatoes. He shouldn't have come.

We were at the town hall once and the mayor was there. When they sang 'Raise the Flags' and he didn't respond, the Germans beat him up. And think what they did in the prisons. If a woman said 'That Hitler and his war,' she would be marched off to the prison. A lot of us went to prison.

They gassed and shot a lot of Jews there. It was barbarous. People were frightened of Jews but they weren't so bad. The Jews in our area were very correct. I didn't have anything against the Jews. Everyone has their own beliefs.

A neighbour once told me I should listen to the radio and then I would really know what was going on. We were not allowed to listen to the radio and I didn't answer her.

My husband was never a member of any party, but still he suffered. My husband had fallen from the roof and was unable to walk and my son was only 15 so he was too young to fight. Because my husband couldn't work due to his injury we only had sixty Marks a month. You can't feed a family on that, so I went out to work and my husband stayed at home.

My husband couldn't work but he had to become a block-attendant and wake people when there were air-raids. My husband couldn't do it alone and so we went together. We saw how Konigsberg was bombed to ruins, saw the women and children and the phosphorus. They all jumped into the lake but they all died. We didn't have an air-raid shelter. We went to the woman in the bottom flat and lay on the floor.

The bombs flew onto the hospitals and the children couldn't go to school any longer. When the bombs fell they killed everyone. Killed the men and the horses. There were so many dead you couldn't walk over them. It was dreadful. If there is every another war I don't want to live.

We didn't want to leave, but we had to otherwise our own soldiers would have had to shoot us. They sent soldiers and said, 'If you don't go we will shoot.'

The Russians were only four km away.

One man said that Hitler was not going to win and he was shot, right there in the city.

I complained that we had to leave everything that we scrounged and saved to acquire.

When they heard me someone yelled 'We'll shoot you if you say that again.'

I said, 'I am not afraid, shoot me if you want.'

Then they said they would shoot my children.

So I had to leave, what else could I do?

The refugee camp was filthy, really filthy – life was dreadful there. Our husbands weren't there. Soldiers brought meat and cooked for us. Actually in Eastern Prussia we didn't go hungry, only later when we went west. I took whatever I had and shared it with the children, then later none of us had anything.

We women had to do everything. We had to turn the soil, something that horses had done previously. And women were not as strong as they had been. They had a really hard time.

Many people fled from my home town but it was freezing cold, 40C below and most of them died. Bombs were dropping onto the hospitals.

We escaped on a ship, traveling overnight to Pilau. On the way a Russian ship saw us and fired at us with canons. The sailors fired back and the ship sank. From Pilau we immediately continued on foot, the whole family, until we were near Danzig and then we walked as we wanted to get to Wittenberg. Then the Russians came again. They raped the women, even the 12 year old girls. Then the Poles came and they took everything away that we had. All we had was the shirts on our backs, nothing else. We were transported further by train but the train stopped on the way and they took all the young girls out. That was the Russians - they used whips. They said the girls would be brought back, but they never came back.

The children had to stay in the train and the married women and we were taken to Warsaw and then on to Berlin.

All my children were sick with typhoid fever. They had sores from head to foot because of the filth in the wagon. We didn't have anything to eat, just water to drink. Then a man came from the rail-road establishment and took them to hospital. They were bathed and their sores were dressed and in three days they were released.

We got to Wittenberg near Berlin. My husband was never a member of any party, but still he suffered. No one believed him. The Russians threw some tobacco on the ground and my husband bent to pick it up. They kicked him so hard he landed on the twenty feet away. They hit him so hard. That was a Friday. On Saturday they took him to hospital and on Tuesday he died.

When I had to state on my pension documents what he died of, I wrote that the Russians beat him to death, my husband was taken to a military hospital and he died there. The Russians wrote on his documentation that he died of a stomach ailment. There had been a witness to the beating but he was never found. They looked for a couple of years but unsuccessfully. So the Russians said my husband died of a stomach ailment when he had never had one in his life and I got no pension. I really suffered from that.

Then my fifteen year old son arrived. I had given him to a farmer because I had nothing to eat. The farmers wife really wanted to keep him, but he had to go to school. I didn't want to tell him his father had died because I didn't want to frighten him, but he told me himself that his father had died.

I asked him who had told him that and he said, 'Mummy he was with me last night, he said he was going to come and get me.'

I buried that son on Christmas Eve. That was 1945. So I lost both my husband and my eldest son.

My other son couldn't come to the funeral because I had given him to another farmer. He didn't know his brother had died. I traveled to where he was and I worked there for five years.

How did you feed your children during the war?

I fed them all by myself. I had to. I had to work in Wittenberg and I was such a good worker they made me supervisor. I worked mornings, afternoons and evening and night shifts. I worked for my children and that's how I fed them.

Then a woman came to me and asked if she could leave for an hour to get her pension. I said of course she could and I asked her where she got her pension from and why. She told me that she got it because her husband had died there. So then I went to the same place and asked about a pension. The administrator was aghast that I didn't get anything and immediately applied for a pension for me. So then I got a pension for two years until I moved to the west zone.

I went to the secretary and said I had to go to the west for a holiday. Two of my children were in apprenticeships there. I went over on a Monday. There were a lot of camps and I was in a camp, but it respectable and the barracks were covered. Every day we had to go for appraisals. When I went for my appraisal they asked me why I came to the west and I said I was alone with two children and the others were in the west and wanted me with them. We had to get approval to move, then we could stay. I was approved so I could go back and I got a pension. My son was already 18 but my daughter was only 16 and I got a pension for her for two years. When I applied for a pension they asked me if I could prove my husband fought in the 1914-18 war and I found someone who had been in the army with him so I got 1800 Marks back pay. But later they took away 1200 Marks because we had had help getting household goods. They shouldn't have done that, but they did.

Was it worse for the women or did he children suffer just as much?

Oh yes the children still think about it. I had six children. My daughter was eight when she fled. The second eldest was 17 and the Russians kept taking her. She is still sick because of that. The children all suffered but she suffered most of all. She couldn't hear any more. Her deafness was caused by fear of the Russians. Then she couldn't see or stand and she was taken to hospital. She got better, but it is still there inside her. Today she is 49 years old but she still suffers.

The Russians took my daughter although I fought for her. Then the Poles came and wanted to take the children. One Pole wanted to shoot me because I protected my children. They ripped everything off me and took me with them. We stood in rows, one row was taken and when they came back it was the next row's turn. I smuggled myself to the other side and went home. The next day I wanted to register for an identification card and they snapped me up again. We had to clean out all the toilets for the Russians and they came after us with whips.

We didn't suffer during the war nearly as much as we suffered after it. What the Russians and Poles did to us was terrible. They took small girls of twelve years old. My youngest was sick and weak at the time and they didn't take her. She protected the others. My eldest daughter was married. She'd married a man in the navy in 1944. She married then he had to leave and she didn't see him again until after the war. She got a letter from Braunschweig that he was alive and had returned home.

Did the men have to suffer as much as the women?

No. The men who were marched back from the Island were commanded by the Russians to sing as they walked. They had bleeding feet but still they had to sing. But they said that in the war they had not suffered as the women and children had to suffer. The Russians took my son away and he was away for two hours. I was so worried. When he came back he said the Russians had shat on the carpets and he had had to clean it up. The Poles were even more dangerous than the Russians. They took my son and another boy and made them watch out the windows in case the Russians came while they did their business.

Was it better in the Western areas with no Russians?

Yes, it was much better, but there they had had worse bombing. But the bombings weren't nearly as bad as the rapes. My daughter came back once with her trousers all torn and streaming blood. She cried so much I wrapped her up in a blanket and took her on my knee. I had her on my knee for five minutes then 15 Russians burst in and grabbed my daughter and they all raped her. You can't punish a person worse than that. The old women took the children and the young ones hid. The Russians searched high and low.

When I was working in Wittenberg I had night shift and came back at 10pm. The Russians passed us in a car then they stopped a woman ahead and all fifteen raped her. It was dreadful. If there is a war at least they should leave the women and children in peace. They are not hurting anyone.

Were people happy when war ended or did they have too much suffering.

No one could be happy. We had no home, no money. We had nothing We had to work for everything anew. In Wittenberg I accumulated things again but then I had to leave it all behind. I have lost everything two or three times.

My son moved to the west and my daughter as well. Two other children were already there and they arranged for me to join them. They lived in Holstein. I have been here twenty five years now.

One son became a locksmith, and another worked in the iron works. The youngest son joined the military. He was there three years then he married.

HERTA S. 1900: A BUSINESSWOMAN'S VIEWPOINT

Herta S. born about 1900, lived in Jena/Sirirle (DDR) during the war.

I had very different feelings about war to my siblings. When I was a child I used to ask myself, why are you so different to the others. That is not a blessing for a child, to be so different and so serious and thoughtful. That was why I kept myself to myself later and for me that was very fortunate. As a girl I was employed as cook and housekeeper. I did an apprenticeship as housekeeper. That was useful for me later as well because my husband and I had businesses and ran a wine bar.

When my husband joined the party they said to me that I should also become involved, but I said I didn't want to join anything. When a woman takes over anything she is very conscientious and thorough. If she is a businesswoman she can't join another organisation because she is so conscientious and thorough and we had an extensive business.

My husband was a member so all the fractions from top to bottom came to us. We had a bar where they all gathered. My husband was popular, but he was a businessman and he knew how to get on with people. In the bar I saw and heard a lot.

One day they didn't want to go home. They wanted to stay and drink and drink. I said to my husband, you go into your office – you are not here – I will deal with them. They had realised that I was very reserved and didn't react when they got political. They didn't want to leave and they didn't want to pay. I said to them, this is a wine bar not a party-political bar. People want to relax here so if you want to talk politics then go to your political-pub, not here, we are a good well-behaved wine bar and everyone is allowed to drink their glass of wine here. I said I can't make any exceptions, and I will stick with that. If that doesn't suit you, then you can leave … there's the door!

It was the first of May. It was early in the morning and soon dawn. My husband had to stay in his office and couldn't take part. That was a fight. Do you know what I did? I threw everything, all the uniforms, out the door. We had a revolving door that lead to some steps I took everything and lay it outside. One of them pretended to sleep and I said 'I don't need your money! Out!' Their things were already outside. I physically threw one of them out. I was strong, had the strength of a man. The one who was sleeping, I grabbed him by the scruff of the neck and spun him around. Door open, out with him!

I could do that because I wasn't a member of anything.

But then they closed the bar. Pretty soon I got notification that the wine-bar would be closed because they wanted to make a sewing room there! That was the result. But I didn't care, I couldn't have cared less. We didn't need to carry on in business. We had no children and we only had the wine bar for the people. We had a holiday house and we could have retired if we'd wanted to.

What did you think when war was declared?

That was logical, he had written a book and his whole program was there to read. When I was still young they weren't really important. I had a good friend who was a socialist. He was really clever. He knew *Mein Kampf* by heart! We used to discuss it and we'd say to each other, 'What if they get into power? None of them have a clean record!'

My friend was a typical socialist. He was high minded but he was also a merchant and he traded with Russia. He supported a cottage industry of instrument makers. He'd have instruments made and then export them to Russia. He did a good trade. His business was in the Erz Mountains. When this war broke out he was really mad. All his people were unemployed. Those people were really poor and he identified with them and now they had no income. So he started a new job-creation business. He wanted music to be compulsory in schools and then the instruments would stay in the country.

Ever since '37 they said if you don't join, you'll get no more deliveries. I was really sorry about that and I pitied him because he had to fight with himself. He said that was the most difficult decision of his life. I said he should close his business He was a general manager and could have worked anywhere. He could have worked in the Finance department because he was a financial genius.

I said, 'Close the business! I don't want to hear any more about it! You can work anywhere!'

But it was against his business ethics.

'I'm an independent business-man he said, I am a free man and if I work for someone else I am a dependent! I wouldn't swap with a general because as a businessman I am king! I'm a free man and I wouldn't swap with anybody.

I said, 'You're right! I wouldn't want to be in your skin.' We were in agreement.

So war wasn't a surprise?

Well it varied a lot, a great deal. People didn't believe it was so critical. It was clear to me because I had had these discussions with this friend of mine. I realised it was all provoked.

What was a cause of the war?

Hitler took the unemployed from the street. They had to do voluntary work. An army of workers with spade. That was great. There was work again and that made people happy That's logical. Everything was fine for a while. That was all written in his program so I knew, but most people didn't read his book. After the first war Germany had been occupied by the French.

The contract they made with the Germans was not fair. We were left so poor after the first war that there were civil uprisings. They really made a mistake and pressure creates more pressure. That's the law of nature.

Did people believe that war was the only way?

They had to! They had said 'A" now they had to say 'B'. Anyone who resisted was shot. That will always be the way. The communists are the same. Now in the west you can be a conscientious objector. Like the Jehovah's Witness who would rather go to prison than fight. They refuse to hold a gun and would rather be sent to an asylum with the murderers and mentally ill. They are the only ones. That is all ideological. You really have to admire them.

What changes did war bring?

We had enough to eat in the beginning because they imported food from the places they had occupied like Czechoslovakia. In our area there was a Duchess whose husband was in the army. He was a Lieutenant Colonel or something like that. She came to me and hugged me and said 'What do you think of our Leader now? Not a single drop of blood!' She was very enthusiastic but I was frightened.

Hitler wanted to crush Communism. He helped Franco , sent the Luftwaffe to Spain, and that was what defeated the communists. But Franco didn't side with Hitler – he didn't help him but stayed neutral. I though to myself, what a rascal! He helped Franco get rid of the communists but then Franco didn't help his fried Hitler! What do you think of that! If my friend helped me out of trouble then I am morally duty bound to help my friend when he is in trouble. I thought Franco was very unethical. He wanted to bring the King back the throne. That was his wish and he achieved it. Hitler wanted the same thing for a time, to get rid of the communists and install the Monarchy. The Hohenzollern rejected him, but that was his real purpose. The Hohenzollern didn't think much of him, they were too proud. They didn't want their crown to be given them from the hands of a private.

Hitler's net got ever wider, he entangled himself more. He should have stopped at the right time. He should have stopped after Poland. Nowadays I think Hitler was the instrument of a higher power. You know what I mean. Communism was hated throughout the world.

War is cruel and difficult regardless of your social standing. There are winners though, people do very well out of the war, creaming off their own bit.

Did you have anything to do with the underground movement?

No, they kept that very secret. Listening to foreign radio was forbidden. You could hear it at night, but it was forbidden. We were always frightened. We knew that it would not end well. The fanatics believed right to the end. Our leader had a gun and he used it in the end.

 The hundred percenters, they were for Hitler and they were convinced he would win the war. He had a weapon but he would only use it at the last minute. They were very secretive and didn't say what sort of weapon it was. One didn't hear that. I remember that well. It was at the end of the war.

There were underground movements that wanted to deal with him. There was a strike and they wanted to kill him but they were unsuccessful. They had the party all under control. They decided everything without consultation. Jena has been a revolutionary city throughout its history because of the students. In the Napoleonic wars they shot people. Jena was always revolutionary and they daubed a Hitler monument, or pushed it over, and they were all shot.

We were all frightened. We were at the mercy of the state. It was a radical state, as was communism. I said sometimes, when we had guests, when all the others were gone, when we had private guests, then we had discussions. When we business people were alone by ourselves, friends of my husbands whom we knew intimately. Then I used to say 'Why do they have to fight each other? They could shake hands, after all what is national-socialism, it is like communism, radical and despotic. Battles belong on the dung heap, I said. If you are up to mischief, how can you put that in writing beforehand? He belongs on the dung heap, I said.

You think that communism and national-socialism are similar?

Unfortunately! They are both so radical, so despotic. Coercion, like it was in Hitler's time. They said that only communism can deliver us from Hitler, just let the Russians come. Then later the die-hard communists said, that's not what we fought for, we thought communism would be different. That's not what we fought for! The elderly were convinced, the youngsters want to get over here to the west. They only see the good side, the freedoms they have here. A die hard communist told me that they are very worried about their youth. I asked, why? You brought them up to be the way they are. You beat your chest but I am sorry for your youth. I didn't do him any harm, but I did speak my mind.

Did you live in a big city?

It is a big city today but not then.

Both of our businesses got direct hits in 1945. My husband and I survived. We had a house in the woods as well, newly built with 8000 square meters of land. We built it for retirement after the war.

Then the Russians killed my husband. The communists were behind that; they influenced the Russians. They broke in in the night, there were shots and they knocked me down as well. Well anyway, I lost my husband in December 1945. A shot through the head and one through the chest. The communists wanted this lovely property. If my husband had done something politically inappropriate then they wouldn't have shot him in December 1945. People like that were sent straight back to Russia.

I went to the Kommandant, into the mouth of the lion as it were, and asked him "Herr Commander, why was my husband killed? Did he break the law? Did he do anything bad? I am a witness to the fact that my husband was a good man, the best sort of human. A socialist and friendly to everyone. He could have been a millionaire, bit by bit, because he had good sense and was intelligent. But instead he stayed a socialist and humane. He never wanted favours. Why was his killed?"

'Yes, well you know how it is. The marauding bandits.'

I said, 'But Herr Commander they weren't bandits! They had the best fur hats I had ever seen. And new uniforms. They shut the relations upstairs in a room. I went onto the veranda and cried for help. Three large Russians came out and hit me about then threw me through a balcony door. I still have the scars. I was bleeding and then I fainted.

My husband got two shots and I can still hear him screaming. But I didn't think they would kill him. He was screaming so loudly I thought they were hitting him. I screamed too, then they threw me in the bathroom, and there was my husband lying in a pool of blood. They threw me in with him. My relations said there were 16 or 20 of them and they chiselled out all the locks.'

The Commander was very polite. He said he would follow it up. They are bandits and they will be tried publicly.

I said "I don't think they were bandits. Where would they get their new uniforms??'

He didn't want to say anything. They had been influenced by the communists you see, they wanted the property. The lovely woodland property.

Then the refugees came from Czechoslovakia. Four families and we had to accommodate them. They just wanted the house. They could have charged my husband, or locked him up they way they locked others up.

I said to the Commander, Herr Commander, did my husband break a law? I am a citizen. Then lock me up!I want some clarity. I want a trial. I am standing here for my husband, the innocent man you killed.

He said 'Calm down ma'am, when we find the perpetrators we will bring them to court.'

When someone has courage, they value that. Do you know why? I once met an officer in Russia, a really intelligent man, and I asked him how it was in Russian families and where the power lay. I wanted to know that. With us the man comes first. I told him that in Germany it was first the man, then the wife and then the children, grandma, and so forth. He told me that in Russia it was grandmother first, then mother, then children then the man. That was confirmed to me by a well traveled woman who told me that the mothers and grandmothers are strong and they say what has to be done. That's why they respect women who are energetic and fight for their rights. They respect them for that.

In Berlin the Russians built a large Russian war monument. *A Mother.* I don't know how tall she is, but tall! With us it is always the men. No they have a mother as monument. She had a large coat and within this coat a child is hiding. That's their war memorial. The mother, not the soldier, they are in first place.

Were women more self sufficient because of the war?

They had to be!

I got material from the rubble and I built houses with my own hands. They said, you wont get any help from us, but I got people and materials from the rubble. I got the sand, the cement, the posts and stones … all from the rubble. I had two foster children too. Two boys. One had become lost and the other was from a children's home.

Did the children suffer from the war.

I don't know if the younger boy suffered but the older boy was about 10 and had lived 10 years in a home. In a children's home during the war and then run by the communists. During the holidays his friends came to my place as well. They just wanted to live in a private home. Then I went begging for the children. They had never had a bratwurst, never had a sausage at all. They didn't know what a sausage was! You know, when children never see or hear anything good, how can they be different? It is a logical progression and we shouldn't be surprised.

What was the reaction when the refugees arrived from the east?

Well, not very good, you know how it is. That makes me sorry even today. You have to experience it to know. Because I was a refugee, I know what it is like to be a refugee and to have to start right from the beginning again. But you know, you can't really judge people for their bad behaviour. That was a real burden for them. They lost so much during the war, so much was in ruins, and then they had the refugees. You can understand why they weren't welcomed with open arms. You see we were bombed out and now the refugees needed food and drink. I got refugees from Poland, a couple who were teachers were resettled in our apartment. In fact, once my door was even broken into for a couple from the west. She had to work and he was always thin. I said they could have one room but they wanted kitchen and bathroom as well. I didn't let them in but they enforced their rights. That was about 1950.

Were there problems when the men returned?

Sometimes. That's logical. The women became self sufficient. They had to exert themselves. You know, the women had their boyfriends during the war. They said, we have to work and who knows what our men are up to. They enjoyed life in their own way. I can judge because I worked in the wine bar. I never spoke about it though. Never!

I had a hairdresser who was a very hard working woman and she had a boyfriend. He died, then she had another one. Then her husband came back home. They all came to me because I could hold my tongue. You have to be able to if you are a businesswoman. I learned how to keep quiet. I just listened and said nothing. Then her husband came back and drank and drank. He was all moralistic. And I said , Edwin, you weren't choir boys during the war either! And during the bombing the women didn't know if they would survive the night. Your wife was young and at least she kept your business going. I had seen how she had employed tradesmen and kept the place up.

I said, Erwin be happy that you are back home again ad try to have a normal life with your Lieschen. What has been must be forgotten. Be glad.

Others didn't come back. Now forget it. I never told his wife that he had spoken to me about it.

German women are hard workers and they'll stand by their man when they have to. In general that is. There are always some floozies, just as there are everywhere, but by and large the women stood by their men.

Was there a problem with women not wanting to be subservient any more?

That happened after the first world war, when it was lost. It was all askew after the first world war and women had to work. We were left so poor after the first war that there were civil uprisings.

Did the women suffer more than the men?

Yes of course. Just as they do today. Maybe then it was even worse. Women have to cope with everything.

ELISABETH B. 1899: POLITICAL AWARE WOMAN LIVING IN A FASCIST STATE

Elisabeth B. b. 1899, lived in Halle an der Saal during the war.

Were you interested in politics before the war?

Yes I was. I was interested in what would be called the FDP today, the Free Democratic Party. I was in the Democratic Party, that was what it was called at the time, in a women's group and we had lectures. I myself had to give a lecture on peace and how we could avoid war.

What was the reaction in 1933?

My husband was in the Democratic Party too, and because he was a member of the Democratic Party he had difficulties in 1933. He was going to be fired from his job as a teacher by the Nazis. We had small children, my daughter was seven and my son was four years old and of course he wanted to stay in his profession. So my husband tried to clarify his political standing and so forth. He was a high school teacher and they didn't want people teaching who were not in the party. He tried to resist but finally when the pressure from the school became overwhelming in 1937 he joined the Party, that is the NSDAP. There was a final push to get people to join, and that is when he joined. But he had the disadvantage of having once been a member of the Democratic party (that was a real disadvantage in those days!) and he was never allowed to hold any office in the NSDAP, not even Blockwart, which was the lowest level of responsibility in the party. He was a member, but nothing else.

And you yourself?

Yes, I was always a big opponent. My membership of the Democratic Women's Group ended immediately because all democratic parties were banned, so I did not take an active political role from that time. I was not a member of anything and mentally, and I don't say this just because of what happened, I was always an opponent of Hitler.

Were there problems between you and your husband because he was a member and you weren't?

No, not for me personally. Towards the end I did join a NASDP women's group but I went so seldom. I went once to a Christmas party and got very dubious looks.

I had always said *Guten Tag* (Good morning) and *Auf Wiedersehen* (Good bye) in shops or, in the catholic south of Germany I used *Gruss Gott* (Greet God) like everyone else. But when I said 'Gruss Gott' the leader of this NSDAP women's group looked at me and said "Frau B., please, Heil Hitler!" So I was reprimanded. That was what it was like. Lots of small things. So I went once to a Christmas Party and was stared at and they said I should come more often, but I was never active.

Did people expect Hitler to declare war?

It was always clear to me that Hitler would corrupt us. In the beginning everything got better. Hitler dealt with the huge unemployment, and then we waited. But when the war began my hopes were all dashed. I said to myself, that is madness to start such a war. Just look at Germany's geography and the countries around her. And then in 1941 Hitler marched into Russia. Madness upon madness!

Did other women distrust events?

You could only talk to very good friend about what you really thought. I was once with a group of women some of whom I didn't know very well, and I said something about the Jews, about the persecution of one race, and someone immediately spoke against me 'Oh no. Frau B.', and so on. . In actual fact you could say every little, even within your own family. You see my son was born in 1929 and in 1933 Hitler came of power and at first that was all very seductive for a boy, dressing in uniforms, snappy, that was something kids loved. So we had to be very careful what we said, careful that we didn't say anything negative.

My son is over 30 now but at the end of the war he was 14 or 15. I remember at the end of the war when Koenigsberg surrendered and the wife of the Commander had to pay through *Sippenhaft*, or clan responsibility, which was where other members of a family are held responsible for the actions of one. When that happened I said to my son, 'Hitler, that criminal!', but I immediately took it back because at the time you had to be worried that your children might denounce you. That happened!

That must have been dreadful!

Oh I had a very good relationship with my son and this incident was quickly forgotten. I continue to have a good relationship with him today.

What did you think yourself when the children were enthusiastic about Hitler?

You had to travel on a double track when you spoke. We had to be so careful. It was really difficult for parents, because you had to hold back for fear of doing yourself and your family harm.

Did you think they might prefer to try democracy when they were adults?

No, I can't say I did. My son was called up right at the end of the war, to be part of the Hitler youth, to 'protect the fatherland with iron fists!' Madness beyond compare!

Was your son enthusiastic to be called up.

No, neither of my children were really enthusiastic about the Hitler youth because they saw for themselves how much pressure was put on its members. But my son was a money manager, so he had a cushy job in the organisation. There were children who really strived to be leader of such a group but neither of my children were interested although they were pressured to be. But then in the end they forced my son to join when he was sixteen. In the end he left his group which was in Czechoslovakia and came home – it was quite an odyssey. If they had caught him he would have been stood against the nearest tree and shot, but he made it home.

He arrived home on 19th April, 1945. Hitler had his birthday on 20th April and the evening before we were sitting together feeling very depressed listening to Goebbels giving this speech 'Vienna will become German again, Berlin will stay German' and so forth and my son said 'You had better believe it because if he says it will be so, then it will.' So even in April 1945 the children believed that all would be well; there would be a 'wonder weapon' – everyone spoke about it. But we adults knew that all was lost long ago.

Were women in general enthusiastic about Hitler? Did he have a special way of talking to them?

I was perhaps an exception because many women were fascinated by Hitler.

Fascinated by Hitler or the whole NSDAP?

No, Hitler embodied the ideas of the NSDAP. So women were enthusiastic about him and then accepted his ideas and I was in fact a real exception. I was always very quiet when people spoke about him. I hated hearing him speak. Of course everyone heard his speeches.

Did that have to do with the idea that women should be housewives?

The reaction against the communists was forced on us. I really don't know how to explain women's reaction to Hitler. I can't put myself in their shoes because I myself never liked the man.

Could you have a different political opinion to your husband in those

days?

Yes and that was very noticeable with us. But my husband had a career and he was told what he had to do. He said sometimes, when I objected, that I didn't know what it was like and he had to do what he was told. So I kept my own counsel.

You understood him?

Yes, I didn't hold it against my husband. He never promoted these ideas himself, but he was more sympathetic to them than I was.

You were alone, especially afterwards. Did that make you more independent?

Yes, I became responsible for the whole family myself. I was over fifty when the war ended but I went back to work. I had to get food somehow.

Under Hitler my husband could not progress in his career because he had been a Democrat, but at least he was allowed to stay in his job and we were grateful for that. But then when the Russians came he was taken away. We never really knew why, although we suspected that it was because of a colleague who had been a committed Nazi and that he had denounced my husband.

So now you were alone.

Yes that was when the most difficult time started for us because during the war my husband had been too old for the army, although he had to take part in exercises on Sundays, and my son too young and only called up at the very end. But after the war I was alone, and how did I cope? It was a daily struggle for survival. We starved. For years I weighed our portion of bread and divided it up between us every morning. We each had a small tin, the type that had once held coffee, and we each kept our bread there. If we had eaten as much as we wanted we would have consumed our ration immediately and it would have been gone. I must confess I weighed exactly the same amount for us all,. I didn't say 'let the children have it all' as I once would have done, because I knew the children still needed me. Then there was the question how was one to find any other food at all.

Now I had a sister who was responsible for the education of those young people who wanted to do an apprenticeship on a farm, so she had lots of contacts amongst the local farmers. She started spinning wool after the war, getting the wool from the farmers and washing it, then spun it using a very old spinning wheel which had previously just been used as decoration in our living room. It had belonged to our great grandmother. She repaired it and sat there spinning just as our predecessors had in their time. She developed a real gift for spinning and she took the spun wool back to the farmers and was given food in return. She and my mother moved in with me because my husband was no longer there and I had room. When she went with the wool to the farmers I said to her 'Don't just bring butter, bring wheat or oats or something that will really fill our stomachs. We were always so happy to see her again and to top up our meagre rations. I'll never forget, a cousin came with oats one day. We cooked it up and then as I was taking it out of the kitchen I slipped and fell. We scraped it off the floor and ate it anyway.

Something my son said really characterised this time. When he was seventeen my son said that what he wished for as an adult was to have a complete sack of oats and one of sugar and enough bread. He didn't wish for butter or cheese or sausage, but just something to take away the hunger. But we survived those years, thanks mostly to my sister. We also collected tiny potatoes that had been left behind during harvest. We did anything just to survive. In those years we learned what starvation was.

After the war, the men were gone. Did you feel sorry for your daughter having no partner?

Yes, well my daughter was a beautiful young girl and always had boys who liked her. She was pretty and had a nice personality so she always had boyfriends. My daughter's husband is disabled. He lost an arm in Russia. He was a driver in a tank and took a direct hit. She became engaged in 1946. At the time I didn't think much about it because my daughter had an education as a teacher so she had her profession. But the whole responsibility for the family of five (with my sister and mother who had broken her hip and needed care) sat on my shoulders. I had to make sure we had enough to eat and had something to wear.

How old were you are the time?

I was born in 1899 so I was 47 years old. Now I am 77 years old. I would never have guessed that life would turn out so well for me as it is now.

Do you think it could happen again?

It depends on the government and if people are influenced by a demagogue like Hitler to go to war. But I don't think it will happen again.

Do you think people should become more active and political.

People should take more of an interest in politics, especially women. There are still women today who are completely apolitical. My son suggested to me that before the next election people should fill out a questionnaire with very simple political questions. And when someone doesn't know where to put their own cross on the election sheet, and someone else tells them how to vote, that is not the way it should be. But that happens in every democracy. People my age who have lived thorough a war have learned to see the complete picture and not be swayed by small things.

I said to someone recently that I have developed a sense of thankfulness. He asked who I am thankful to and I said fate – I am just thankful that I have been able to live on to a better life.

Did you have a feeling of comradeship with other women?

You mean a sense of togetherness? Yes. At the time we lived in Halle an der Saale where the Russians came, in a small street with single-family houses where everyone knew each other and this street developed a real feeling of belonging together during the hard years. I still have good contact with many of those women these many years later. I must say though that when I came to west Germany I did not develop such close bonds. People here were not interested in what had happened to us in the DDR. They just don't understand it. But when I meet someone who lived through the post war period in the DDR, then I have an instant bond. We understand each other.

Were there refugees in Halle?

I didn't have them in my house because I had my mother and sister living with me. You couldn't do what you liked with your own home. If you had space, then people were put there. There was someone with us, but you couldn't really call her refugee. That was an older sister of my husband from Frankfurt an der Oder who suddenly appeared on our doorstep with her suitcase. She later left and we didn't have anyone else.

Do people understand why the Germans were treated so badly by the Russians after the war?

Well, during the Hitler years there was constant anti-Russian propaganda. Russians were depicted as 'Untermenschen' , sub-humans. The Russians suffered a great deal because of us, so I imagine it was partly retribution. The person who carries all the blame is Hitler, that is what I believe. But what I still don't understand is how a single person can control and influence great crowds of people so that they cheer him, and you can't deny it, crowds of people cheered him on.

Were people sorry Germany could not reach its goals?

Yes, certainly. It is really true but many don't want to believe it, that we didn't know about the dreadful things that were happening in the concentration camps. Certainly what is true for my family and for my close friends. I personally only knew about Dachau, which is in Bavaria. We thought it was a place where people with wrong ideas were sent to be re-educated. We had no idea about the extermination of the Jews.

Were you under pressure not to do things in case you were sent there?

Oh yes, certainly. For example, listening to foreign radio. I heard English radio quite by accident the morning that Hess flew to England. I was alone at home and I said to myself, my God, what will happen now? But I couldn't tell anyone. I did talk to my husband about it and he wondered if I had misheard. You didn't dare tell anyone because you could be hauled away to the concentration camp.

Dictatorships don't want you listening to other propaganda. It is a bit like that in the DDR now.

Do you think the war has had after-affects for you and your children?

For me certainly. My son is completely sure that a war cannot happen again but I have to say, I think it is born into people unfortunately, perhaps particularly the Germans.

Are people more politically aware now?

No I don't think so. I'm afraid political things just don't interest most people. I know people who complain that there is much too much politics on the television. They like singing and dancing, but not political shows. You have to have a bit of intelligence to understand politics.

ADDENDUM: WAR LOSSES: 1939-1945

In 1954 the German Ministry for Displaced Persons reported that eight years after the end of the war they were still uncertain as to the the fate of many hundreds of thousands of army personnel, particularly in the East and that they also had no knowledge of the fate of the 750,000 civilians who had been abducted from the east. The report that the population was hoping to work with the Red Cross to help people find their loved ones[98].

It has been estimated that the second world war caused thirty-six million deaths, seven million missing presumably dead and thirty-five million wounded[99]. In addition to the 6 million Jews and countless gypsies that died as a result of persecution, the German Press and Information Office estimated that nine and a half million Germans died as immediate victims of the war and the post war period (Table 7). Some fifteen to twenty million Soviet soldiers and civilians were killed and many millions more were maimed, wounded or weakened by malnutrition."[100]

In Britain "when the conflict ended on 2 September, 1945, civilian casualties numbered about 60,000. Of the Armed Forces of the United

---

98 Anon. 1954. Bundesministerium für Vertriebene. *Fluchtlinge, Vertriebene, Kriegsgefangene.*

99 Ernst-Gunther Schenk 1965 "Das menschliche Elend im 20 Jahrhundert" Nicolaische Verlagsbuchhandlung, Herford. p15.

100Encyclopedia Britannica (1974) vol. 16 p80.

Kingdom, 300,000 lost their lives."[101]

Table 7. War losses among German ethnic groups compiled by the German Press and Information Office[102]

Deaths	
Members of the Armed Forces from the Reich who fell plus the supposedly dead among the missing and prisoners of war	3,760,000
Members of the German ethnic group from abroad in the Armed Forces	432,000
Civilian population losses from the area divided later into the four occupied zones	430,000
Civilian losses from the Eastern provinces incl. deportees and expellees	1,230,000
Losses among the civilian German ethnic peoples	886,000
German losses from racial, religious and political persecution	300,000
Total Dead	**7,038,000**
Missing	
Missing among the Armed Forces	1,175,000
Missing prisoners of War	104,000
Missing civilians	258,000
Missing deportees	831,000
Total missing	**2,368,000**

101ibid Vol. 3 p279.

102Ernst-Gunther Schenk. 1965 "Das menschliche Elend im 20 Jahrhundert" Nicolaische Verlagsbuchhandlung, Herford.

Table 8 lists losses among civilian populations caused by bombing attacks.

Table 8. Losses Among Civilian Populations caused by Bombing Attacks[103]

Attack by the German Air Force on Coventry (England) on 14-15.11.1940	380 dead
Attack by the German Air Forces on Rotterdam (Holland) on 14.5.1940	980 dead
Attack of the British Air Forces on Hamburg (Germany) on 24-29.7.1943	42,800 dead 37,000 wounded
Attack of Anglo-American Air Forces on Dresden (Germany) on 13/14.2.1945	135,000 dead
Attack of American forces on Tokyo (Japan) on 9/10.3.1945	83,800 dead
Attack by American Atom Bomb on Hiroshima (Japan) on 6.8.1945	78,150 dead 13,983 missing 9,428 badly wounded 27,669 lightly wounded
Attack by American Atom Bomber on Nagasaki (Japan)	23,752 dead, 23,345 wounded 1,942 missing
Total victims of Bombing attacks in England:	60,595 dead, 86,182 badly wounded
Total victims of bombing attacks in Germany:	450,000 dead among civilians 75,000 dead among police and members of the armed forces.

---

103 ibid p5.